Volume I

Dinosaurs Past and Present

An exhibition and symposium
organized by the
Natural History Museum of Los Angeles County

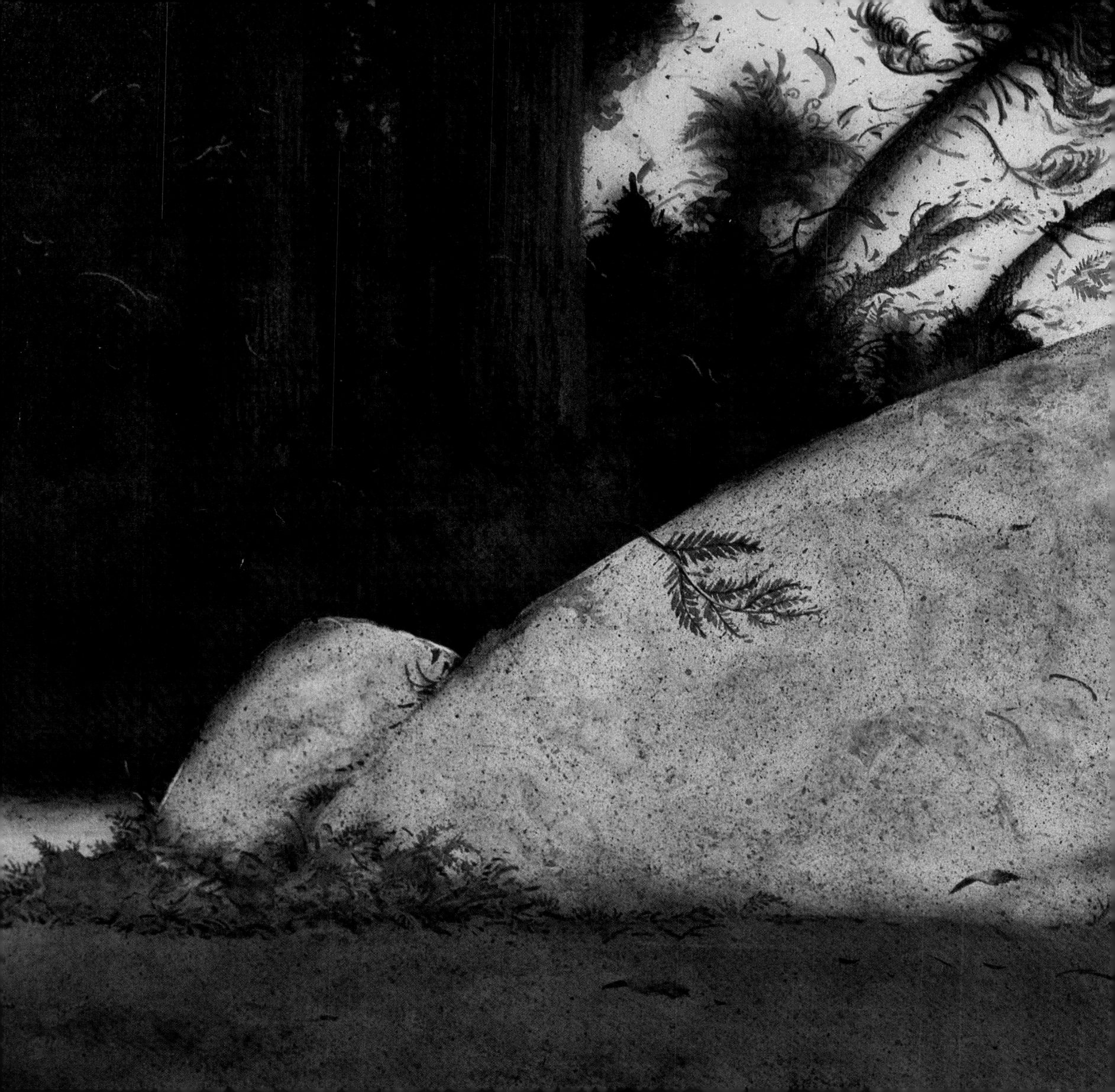

Volume I

Dinosaurs
Past and Present

Edited by

Sylvia J. Czerkas *and* Everett C. Olson

Introduction by

John M. Harris

NATURAL HISTORY MUSEUM OF LOS ANGELES COUNTY
in association with
UNIVERSITY OF WASHINGTON PRESS
Seattle and London

Natural History Museum of Los Angeles County
Los Angeles, California 90007

LC 87–060944

ISBN 0–938644–24–6 (softcover)
ISBN 0– 295–96541–X (hardcover)

Distributed by
The University of Washington Press
P.O. Box C50096
Seattle, WA 98145-5096

COVER: "Crossing the Flats" by Mark Hallett.
© 1986 Mark Hallett
Checklist 140.

PAGES i-iii: "Cool Weather" by William Stout.
Checklist 116.

PAGES vi-viii: "Jurassic Life of Europe" by Benjamin
Waterhouse Hawkins.
Checklist 1.

PAGES x-xi: "*Archaeopteryx* with sauropod" by John Gurche.
Checklist 40.

CONTENTS

Detail of Waterhouse Hawkins's diagram;
see page xv.

ACKNOWLEDGMENTS

The editors wish to thank the following for their generous contributions to the Dinosaurs Past and Present exhibition and this book:

Craig C. Black, Director of the Natural History Museum of Los Angeles County for the original initiation of this project; his continual involvement, guidance, and support assured its success.

The Natural History Museum Foundation for its sponsorship of the exhibit.

The authors of the symposium contributions and each of the artists in the exhibit, both past and present, for their unique and valuable insights.

The staff of the Natural History Museum of Los Angeles County who worked on the exhibit and the publications relating to it: Public Programs, Peter Keller. Foundation, Sandy Brady and staff. Earth Sciences, John Harris and the paleontological staff. Exhibits, Jim Olson, Jerry Campbell, Brian Weber, Cathy Debs, Ron Sabados, Robert Spangenberg, Mary Butler, Chiyoko Onoda, Jane Herwegh, Dan Howell, Charles Fischer, and Robert Reid. Publicity, John Charney, Laura Boucher, Mary Ann Dunn and staff. Photography, Dick Meier, Don Meyer and staff. Education, Joan Grasty and staff. Publications, Robin Simpson and Kathy Talley-Jones. Registrar's Office, Dorothy Galbraith, Jennifer Kilman, and Katy Flynn. Membership, Becky Chapman and staff. Special Events, Kate Sibley and staff. Library, Kathy Donahue and staff. Museum Shops, Shelley Stephens, Elaine Fuess and staff. Printshop, Chuck Orrico. General Services, Ted Bolden and staff. Security, Hugh Crooks and staff. The Scientific Publications Committee.

Our sincere thanks to the following institutions and individuals for the loan of art works and photography:

American Museum of Natural History: Thomas Nicholson, Director, Barbara Conklin, Michael Novacek, Barbara Werscheck, Martin Cassidy, George Gardner, Steven Quinn, and the Photography Department.

National Museum of Natural History, Smithsonian Institution: Nicholas Hotton III, Ian McIntyre, Raymond Rye, Michael Brett-Surman, Robert Purdy, Laurence O'Reilly, Chip Clark, and Photographic Services.

Peabody Museum of Natural History, Yale University: Leo J. Hickey, Director, Copeland MacClintock, Mary Ann Turner, Robert Allen, and Miriam Swartz.

Princeton Museum of Natural History: Donald Baird.

National Museum of Natural Sciences, National Museums of Canada: Ridgeley Williams, Barbara McIntosh, Bonnie Livingstone, and the Photography Department.

Carnegie Museum of Natural History: Mary Dawson.

Vernal Field House: Peter Laraba.

Philadelphia Academy of Sciences: Samuel Gubins, Hollister Knowlton, Kathy Forester, Larry Hutchinson.

Tyrrell Museum of Palaeontology: Philip Currie and Jane Danis.

New Mexico Museum of Natural History: Jon Callendar, Director.

British Museum (Natural History): Allan Charig.

Museum of the Rockies: Michael Hager, Director; Judith Weaver, and the Photography Department.

Field Museum of Natural History: Photography Department.

We also thank Donald Glut, George Olshevsky, and James Jensen for the loan of art works, restoration experts Constantine Cherkas, Nancy Purinton, Abraham Joel, and Richard Gallerani, and framers Harvey and Ruth Ann Winters.

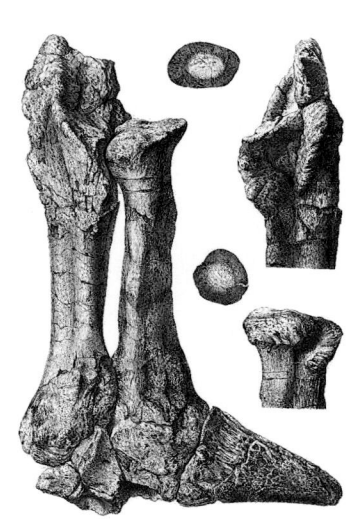

NEAR RIGHT:
Iguanodon mantelli manus by C. L Greisbach. Plate I from Richard Owen's supplement to his monograph on the Reptilia of the Wealdon Formation. Checklist 4.

FAR RIGHT:
Iguanodon by Benjamin Waterhouse Hawkins. Checklist 2.

In working with Benjamin Waterhouse Hawkins on the restoration of *Iguanodon*, Richard Owen had placed a prominent horn on the nose of the creature (far right). Owen later realized that the horn was actually a digit or "thumb spike" of the hand and presented this new conclusion in an 1872 paper that included an illustration of the hand bones by C. L. Greisbach (near right). Recent restorations of iguanodonts (pages 2 and 3, 9) reflect current knowledge about the shape of the skull, skin texture, limb proportions, and general body posture.

Iguanodon and *Hylaeosaurus*, Wealden Formation, by Benjamin Waterhouse Hawkins. Sheet 3 of Waterhouse Hawkins's Diagrams of the Extinct Animals: Vertebrate Animals. Prepared for the Department of Science and Art, British Museum (Day & Son, London). Courtesy British Museum (Natural History).

Megalosaurus and *Pterodactyle*, Oolite and Wealden Formations, by Benjamin Waterhouse Hawkins. Sheet 2 of Waterhouse Hawkins's Diagrams of the Extinct Animals: Vertebrate Animals. Prepared for the Department of Science and Art, British Museum (Day & Son, London). Courtesy British Museum (Natural History).

Waterhouse Hawkins's American studio, showing the skeleton of the first dinosaur discovered in America, *Hadrosaurus foulkii* (center), which was reconstructed by Waterhouse Hawkins, and his life-size reclining model of the animal (left). From *Harper's Weekly* 1869, 13:525.

INTRODUCTION

JOHN M. HARRIS

Dinosaurs have vividly captured our imagination for more than a century. During the considerable time that these "terrible lizards" have been known to science, our concept of the dinosaur has constantly changed in response to advances in paleontological research. In the mid-nineteenth cen-

tury, when paleontology was still in its infancy, scientists and artists had to cope with the available fragmentary evidence to interpret the appearance of these exciting but sometimes bizarre-looking animals. Since then new pieces of the scientific puzzle have continually become available to aid in the reconstructive process. These have been interpreted according to prevailing ideas of reptilian physiology and anatomy with varying degrees of success. With one or two notable exceptions, only during the second half of the present century has the desirability of contrasting dinosaur remains with functionally similar representatives of birds and mammals become widely appreciated and standard practice.

Today a new generation of artists, working within the framework of rigorous analyses provided by their scientific colleagues, has helped redefine our understanding of these fascinating animals. The lumbering giants envisaged by the artists of yesteryear have ceded place to dynamic creatures, both large and small, that are now shown posed naturally in realistic settings.

Perhaps the most striking change to occur in the restorations is in the depiction of body posture. The emerging new look is one of anatomically correct, sleeker, and more varied animals that successfully adapted to almost every ecologic niche now occupied by modern mammals and birds. New information about dinosaur anatomy and physiology has indicated that some dinosaurs were capable of rapid locomotion and may have been warm-

1

Iguanodon bernissartensis and *Iguanodon mantelli* by Gregory Paul. Checklist 73.

HARRIS

blooded. New evidence about dinosaur skin and armor has added to the realism with which these creatures may now be portrayed. Careful study of the paleobotanic record, and of the geologic context in which the fossils were found, has aided accurate reconstruction of the scenes in which the dinosaurs have been depicted.

Recent dramatic advances in our understanding of the behavior and interaction of modern animals have been invoked to interpret the life habits of the long-extinct dinosaurs. Circumstantial evidence indicates that at least some dinosaurs were gregarious and lived in herds. The quantity of fossils from bone beds in western North America suggests that entire herds may have met catastrophic endings through flash floods or volcanic ashfalls. Evidence from fossil trackways preserved in Brazil, the United States, and Canada points to the possibility of predatory dinosaurs hunting their prey in packs. Most intriguing are the indications for parental care that have been found at a dinosaur nesting site in Choteau, Montana.

On February 15, 1986, the Natural History Museum of Los Angeles County opened a traveling exhibition entitled *Dinosaurs Past and Present*, which illustrated how drastically our ideas about the appearance of dinosaurs have changed during the past few decades. Sponsored by the Natural History Museum Foundation, the exhibition featured the work of many artists whose restorations had been selected by Guest Curator Sylvia J. Czerkas. Following its debut in Los Angeles, the exhibition is scheduled to be presented in the United States at the Denver Museum of Natural History (Colorado), the Philadelphia Academy of Sciences (Pennsylvania), the National Museum of Natural History, Smithsonian Institution (Washington, D.C.), the American Museum of Natural History (New York), and the New Mexico Museum of Natural History (Albuquerque), and in Canada at the Tyrrell Museum of Palaeontology (Drumheller, Alberta) and the Royal Ontario Museum (Toronto). In conjunction with the opening of the exhibition in Los Angeles the Natural History Museum convened a symposium at which invited speakers, both artists and scientists, discussed important new dinosaur restorations and paleoenvironmental interpretations that collaborative effort had made possible. The realization that the exhibition and symposium would be of interest to a larger audience than that fortunate enough to attend prompted the publication of this book.

The symposium contributions, most of which are represented here,* fall into four discrete, but related sections. The first, with papers by Robert T. Bakker, George Callison, and Martin G. Lockley, explores the different lines of evidence that enable scientists to attempt accurate reconstructions of dinosaurs. The second, with contributions by Mark Hallett, Dale A. Russell, and David D. Gillette, dwells on the interaction that is desirable between artists and scientists to achieve accurate restorations of dinosaurs and their environment. (The reader should be aware of a distinction in terminology; throughout the book the term *reconstruction* is used in the sense of piecing together the original but often fragmentary fossilized parts of extinct animals, whereas *restoration* is used to describe the depiction of their original appearance—muscles, flesh, skin, and all.)

The third section (Volume II), with papers by Gregory S. Paul, John R. Horner, Kevin Padian, Stephen A. Czerkas, and Philip J. Currie, provides examples of how the physical evidence can be interpreted, correctly or incorrectly, in the restoration of extinct animals. The book concludes, appropriately, with a contribution by J. Keith Rigby, Jr., that sheds additional light on the end of the age of dinosaurs.

In the first contribution Bakker explores the premise that even the largest dinosaurs were energetic and active animals, basing his case on careful investigation of comparative and functional anatomy, interpretation of footprints, and physiological and ecological studies. He presents persuasive evidence that *Triceratops* could gallop and that other large dinosaurian quadrupeds were less constrained in their locomotory activity than the largest of the living terrestrial vertebrates. Curiously

*Two contributions—Super-dreadnaughts of the dinosaurian world, by Kenneth Carpenter, and A reassessment of reptilian diversity across the Cretaceous-Tertiary boundary, by Robert M. Sullivan—are scheduled for publication elsewhere.

enough this concept of the "dancing dinosaur" was shared by early workers but fell into disrepute during the first half of the present century when dinosaurs were construed as giant, slow-moving, cold-blooded reptiles.

It is the sheer bulk of many of the dinosaurs that leaves a lasting first impression. There were, however, also dinosaurs that only achieved the size of small chickens. Callison explores the morphological and physiological restraints that would have affected such tiny dinosaurs and comments on their locomotory capacities, reproductive strategies, and other aspects of behavior.

Lockley draws attention to information available from careful study of dinosaur tracks, an area of investigation that has long been ignored. Such trackways may provide compelling evidence of gait and posture of the animals that left the tracks. They may also contribute to a census of ancient communities and afford potential insight into behavior. Caution must, however, be exercised in exploring behavioral ramifications because the presence of tracks of several different individuals in one rock unit does not necessarily imply that they passed through the area simultaneously.

Hallett stresses the desirability for effective interaction of artists with paleontologists to produce accurate, realistic, and artistic interpretations of extinct animals and the world in which they lived. He relates incidents from his own experience to exemplify this interrelationship from an artist's point of view. Russell emphasizes the same theme but from a paleontologist's standpoint, noting that artists are the eyes of paleontologists and that paintings are the windows through which nonspecialists can see the world of the dinosaur.

The best-known early dinosaurs from North America have been excavated from the *Coelophysis* quarry in New Mexico. Gillette explains how our understanding of this late-Triassic biota has slowly improved over the past century as a result of continued collecting, and how artists' restorations of the late Triassic age of transition have been modified accordingly.

Paul, who has worked closely with Bakker, surveys the wealth of information documented from the fossil record to assist an artist in achieving a meticulously accurate product. Some dinosaurs, the duck-billed hadrosaurs, for example, have left articulated skeletons, trackways, and even mummified remains to aid in the restorative process, but most are represented by far more fragmentary material. Paul guides the reader through the dinosaurian spectrum, providing insights into the questions that must be resolved in attempting an accurate restoration and stressing the need to consider many different areas of evidence to refine intuitive interpretations.

Horner gives a fascinating account of the ecological and behavioral implications that may be derived from two dinosaur nesting sites in Choteau, Montana. Here, two species of dinosaurs appear to have nested repeatedly over a number of years, each manipulating their egg clutches into a different arrangement. Horner describes the egg clutches, immature dinosaurs, and associated fossils that he and his team have found, explores the behavioral implications that these convey, interprets the paleogeography of the sites, and provides a vivid restoration of the scene when the area was used for a nesting ground.

In the one contribution not devoted to dinosaurs, Padian relates a case history of the paintbrush being mightier than the pen. When pterosaurs, the flying reptiles of the Mesozoic era, were first discovered, their strange anatomy provoked controversy among the scientists that studied them. After it became generally agreed that they were reptiles, their image as clumsy, bat-winged gliders persisted for much of the ensuing two centuries. Padian shows how the bat-winged interpretation stemmed from the erroneous identification of a juvenile pterosaur as a bat and why, despite conclusive evidence from well-preserved specimens that were found subsequently, pterosaur wing membranes continued to be depicted like those of bats.

To many of us the armored *Stegosaurus*—with flat plates above its spine and spikes on its tail—is one of the most familiar dinosaurs. Artists have portrayed the arrangement of this armor in different ways; in some restorations the plates are shown rampant or nearly so, in others they droop nearly parallel to the flanks of the animal. Moreover, the number and arrangement of plates and

"Pleasures of Science" by Arthur Lakes.
Checklist 5.

spikes possessed by different species have sparked controversy. Czerkas focuses on the debate as to whether stegosaur plates were arranged in matched pairs or a single row. He traces the history of these alternative concepts and justifies a compromise solution.

Dinosaur Provincial Park in Alberta, Canada, is famous for the diversity of dinosaurs that have been recovered within its confines. Initially it was the completeness of preservation of articulated dinosaur skeletons that attracted collectors to the area, and some five hundred major specimens have found their way into more than thirty-five institutions around the world. More recently attention has been focused on all the fossil remains from this locality—plants, insects, and clams as well as immature and adult dinosaurs, both large and small—permitting more accurate reconstruction of the ecology and habitats in which the dinosaurs flourished. Currie gives an account of recent research projects in the area and how the resulting information has been used in the restoration of ancient habitat displays for the new Tyrrell Museum of Palaeontology.

That dinosaurs became extinct at the end of the Mesozoic era has been common ground in the debate whether this extinction was a gradual phenomenon or catastrophic event. During the past decade the second alternative has been given much support by the recognition of a widely distributed iridium-rich horizon at the Cretaceous-Tertiary boundary. This iridium was apparently of extraterrestrial origin, resulting from the impact of an asteroid on the Earth's surface. One plausible consequence of this impact was a dust cloud that may have blanketed the planet—blocking the sun's radiation, reducing the prevailing temperature, and contributing to mass extinction of a variety of life forms including, some presume, the dinosaurs. The discovery of six sites in McCone County, Montana, that indicate that some dinosaurs may have survived the Cretaceous Armageddon to persist into the Tertiary period, is therefore exciting. Rigby provides an account of these sites, presents arguments to support a Paleocene-age interpretation for the dinosaurian remains, and reconstructs the environment in which these last surviving dinosaurs existed.

THE
EXHIBITION

HOSTS OF THE EXHIBITION

NATURAL HISTORY MUSEUM OF LOS ANGELES COUNTY
Los Angeles, California
February through August 1986

DENVER MUSEUM OF NATURAL HISTORY
Denver, Colorado
October through December 1986

THE ACADEMY OF NATURAL SCIENCES
Philadelphia, Pennsylvania
February through April 1987

NATIONAL MUSEUM OF NATURAL HISTORY, SMITHSONIAN INSTITUTION
Washington, D.C.
June through August 1987

AMERICAN MUSEUM OF NATURAL HISTORY
New York, New York
October through December 1987

NEW MEXICO MUSEUM OF NATURAL HISTORY
Albuquerque, New Mexico
February through April 1988

TYRRELL MUSEUM OF PALAEONTOLOGY
Drumheller, Alberta
June through August 1988

ROYAL ONTARIO MUSEUM
Toronto, Ontario
October through December 1988

Iguanodons by Douglas Henderson.
Checklist 99.

Allosaurus by Charles Knight. Checklist 15.

Diplodocus by Charles Knight. Checklist 17.

Triceratops by Charles Knight. Checklist 18.

DINOSAURS PAST AND PRESENT

DINOSAURS PAST AND PRESENT

Deinonychus and *Iguanodon* by John Gurche. Checklist 39.

OPPOSITE:
Daspletosaurus and *Styracosaurus* by John Gurche. From *The Dinosaur Heresies* by Robert T. Bakker (William Morrow and Co., Inc., 1986). Checklist 42.

16

Free-standing *Maiasaura* hatchling by Stephen Czerkas. Checklist 48.

Carnotaurus sastrei by Stephen Czerkas. Checklist 51.

DINOSAURS PAST AND PRESENT

Allosaurus by Stephen Czerkas. Checklist 52.

Proceratops by Sylvia Czerkas. Checklist 55.

20

Edmontonia by Kenneth Carpenter. Checklist 65.

Sauropelta and *Velociraptor* by Kenneth Carpenter. Checklist 59.

OVERLEAF: "*Chasmosaurus* (= *Pentaceratops*) *sternbergii* Herd in Dry Cypress Swamp" by Gregory Paul. Checklist 85.

CHECKLIST OF THE EXHIBITION

In this list dimensions of paintings are given width by height; dimensions of sculpture are given length by width by height.

1. "Jurassic Life of Europe," circa 1870
   Benjamin Waterhouse Hawkins
   Oil on canvas, 86½ x 32 in., 219.7 x 81.3 cm.
   Museum of Natural History, Princeton University
2. *Iguanodon*, circa 1850
   Benjamin Waterhouse Hawkins
   Cast resin, 20 x 14 x 8 in., 50.8 x 35.4 x 20.3 cm.
   Private collection
3. *Megalosaurus*, circa 1850
   Benjamin Waterhouse Hawkins
   Cast resin, 24 x 12 x 10 in., 61 x 30.5 x 25.4 cm.
   Private collection
4. *Iguanodon mantelli* manus, circa 1870
   C.L. Greisbach
   Lithograph, 16½ x 21¾ in., 41.9 x 55.3 cm.
   Plate I from Monograph on the Fossil Reptilia of the Wealdon Formation, Supplement No. IV, Dinosauria (*Iguanodon*), by Richard Owen. London: Palaeontological Society, Monograph 25, 1872.
5. "Pleasures of Science," 1879-1880
   Arthur Lakes
   Six watercolors, each 12 x 9 in., 30.5 x 22.8 cm.
   Peabody Museum of Natural History, Yale University
6. "Drilling Holes for Blasting Powder," circa 1877
   Arthur Lakes
   Three watercolors, each 12 x 9 in., 30.5 x 22.8 cm.
   Peabody Museum of Natural History, Yale University
7. *Diplodocus longus* skull, circa 1880
   F. Berger (E. Crisand, lithographer)
   Two lithographs, each 21⅝ x 11⅝ in., 54.3 x 29.5 cm.
   Plates I and II, Sauropoda, U.S. Geological Survey. From *Marsh's Dinosaurs*, J.H. Ostrum and J.S. McIntosh. New Haven, Conn.: Yale University Press, 1966.
8. *Brontosaurus excelsus* skeleton, circa 1880
   F. Berger (E. Crisand, lithographer)
   Lithograph 29¾ x 11⅝ in., 75.6 x 29.5 cm.
   Plate XC, Sauropoda, U.S. Geological Survey. From *Marsh's Dinosaurs*, J.H. Ostrum and J.S. McIntosh. New Haven, Conn.: Yale University Press, 1966.
9. *Brontosaurus excelsus* femur, circa 1880
   F. Berger (E. Crisand, lithographer)
   Lithograph, 11 x 20⅛ in., 26.7 x 45.7 cm.
   Plate LXXI, Sauropoda, U.S. Geological Survey.
   From *Marsh's Dinosaurs*, J.H. Ostrum and J.S. McIntosh. New Haven, Conn.: Yale University Press, 1966.
10. *Brontosaurus excelsus* vertebra, circa 1880
    F. Berger (E. Crisand, lithographer)
    Lithograph, 29¾ x 45¾ in., 75.6 x 116.2 cm.
    Plate XXXII, Sauropoda, U.S. Geological Survey.
    From *Marsh's Dinosaurs*, J.H. Ostrum and J.S. McIntosh. New Haven, Conn.: Yale University Press, 1966.
11. *Brontosaurus excelsus* humerus, circa 1880
    F. Berger (E. Crisand, lithographer)
    Lithograph, 10½ x 18 in., 26.7 x 45.7 cm.
    Plate XLVIII, Sauropoda, U.S. Geological Survey. From *Marsh's Dinosaurs*, J.H. Ostrum and J.S. McIntosh. New Haven, Conn.: Yale University Press, 1966.
12. *Compsognathus longipes*, circa 1882-1889
    Artist unknown
    Lithograph, 12¾ x 16½ in., 32.4 x 41.9 cm.
    Printed in 1977, School of Art, Yale University
13. *Laelaps aguilunguis* and pliosaur *Cimoliasaurus magnus*, 1897
    Edward Drinker Cope
    Pencil, 8¼ x 5⅛ in., 20.9 x 13 cm.
    Private collection
14. *Dryptosaurus*, 1897
    Charles Knight
    Gouache, 23 x 15⅞ in., 58.4 x 40.3 cm.
    American Museum of Natural History, K:AM 189701
15. *Allosaurus*, 1904
    Charles Knight
    Oil on canvas, 36⅞ x 24 in., 93.7 x 61 cm.
    American Museum of Natural History, K:AM 190401
16. *Stegosaurus*, 1946
    Charles Knight
    Oil on canvas, 18½ x 14¼ in., 47 x 36.2 cm.
    Natural History Museum of Los Angeles County
17. *Diplodocus*, 1906
    Charles Knight
    Oil on canvas, 37 x 27¼ in., 94 x 69.2 cm.
    Section of Vertebrate Fossils,
    Carnegie Museum of Natural History
18. *Triceratops*, 1901
    Charles Knight
    Oil on canvas, 36 x 24 in., 91.5 x 61 cm.
    National Museum of Natural History,
    Smithsonian Institution
19. *Corythosaurus casuarius*, head study, circa 1920
    Charles Whitney Gilmore
    Cast resin, 5¾ x 2¼ x 7½ in., 14.6 x 5.7 x 19 cm.
    Private collection
20. *Kritosaurus notabilis*, head study, circa 1920
    Charles Whitney Gilmore
    Cast resin, 4¾ x 2¼ x 4½ in., 12.1 x 5.7 x 12.9 cm.
    Private collection
21. *Monoclonius crassus*, head study, circa 1907
    Richard Swann Lull
    Cast resin, 8 x 4 x 4½ in., 20.3 x 10.2 x 11.4 cm.
    Private collection
22. *Monoclonius recurvicornis*, head study, circa 1907
    Richard Swann Lull
    Cast resin, 7 x 3¾ x 4½ in., 17.8 x 9.5 x 11.4 cm.
    Private collection
23. Dinosaur landscape, 1933
    Ernest Untermann
    Oil on canvas, 36⅜ x 23⅞ in., 92.4 x 61.2 cm.
    Vernal Field House

24. *Diplodocus*, no date
    Rudolph Zallinger
    Egg tempera, 21¾ x 11⅜ in., 55.3 x 28.9 cm.
    Collection of the artist

25. *Anatosaurus*, no date
    Rudolph Zallinger
    Egg tempera, 9¾ x 8½ in., 24.8 x 21.6 cm.
    Collection of the artist

26. *Protoceratops*, no date
    Rudolph Zallinger
    Egg tempera, 18⅝ x 7⅛ in., 47.3 x 18.1 cm.
    Collection of the artist

27. Study for the Yale mural, "The Age of Reptiles," circa 1940
    Rudolph Zallinger
    Egg tempera on masonite, 82½ x 12⅛ in.,
    209.6 x 30.8 cm.
    Peabody Museum of Natural History, Yale University

28. *Camarasaurus*, 1984
    Jean Day Zallinger
    Colored pencil, 16½ x 7⅛ in., 41.9 x 18.1 cm.
    Collection of the artist

29. *Coelophysis*, 1984
    Jean Day Zallinger
    Colored pencil, 15⅞ x 7⅛ in., 40.4 x 18.1 cm.
    Collection of the artist

30. Baby *Psittacosaurus*, 1984
    Jean Day Zallinger
    Colored pencil, 8⅛ x 10¼ in., 20.7 x 26 cm.
    Collection of the artist

31. *Psittacorus*, 1984
    Jean Day Zallinger
    Colored pencil, 8¼ x 5½ in., 20.9 x 14 cm.
    Collection of the artist

32. *Stegosaurus*, 1984
    Jean Day Zallinger
    Colored pencil, 8¼ x 7½ in., 20.9 x 19.1 cm.
    Collection of the artist

33. *Hesperosuchus* and *Coelophysis*, no date
    Peter Zallinger
    Oil on board, 13 x 8¾ in., 33 x 22.2 cm.
    Collection of the artist

34. *Allosaurus*, no date
    Peter Zallinger
    Oil on board, 8½ x 8½ in., 21.6 x 21.6 cm.
    Collection of the artist

35. *Allosaurus fragilis*, no date
    David Thomas
    Bronze, 14½ x 3 x 8½ in., 36.8 x 7.6 x 21.6 cm.
    Collection of the artist

"What Happens When *Apatosaurus ajax* Seeks Aquatic Refuge from *Allosaurus fragilis*" by Gregory Paul. Checklist 80.

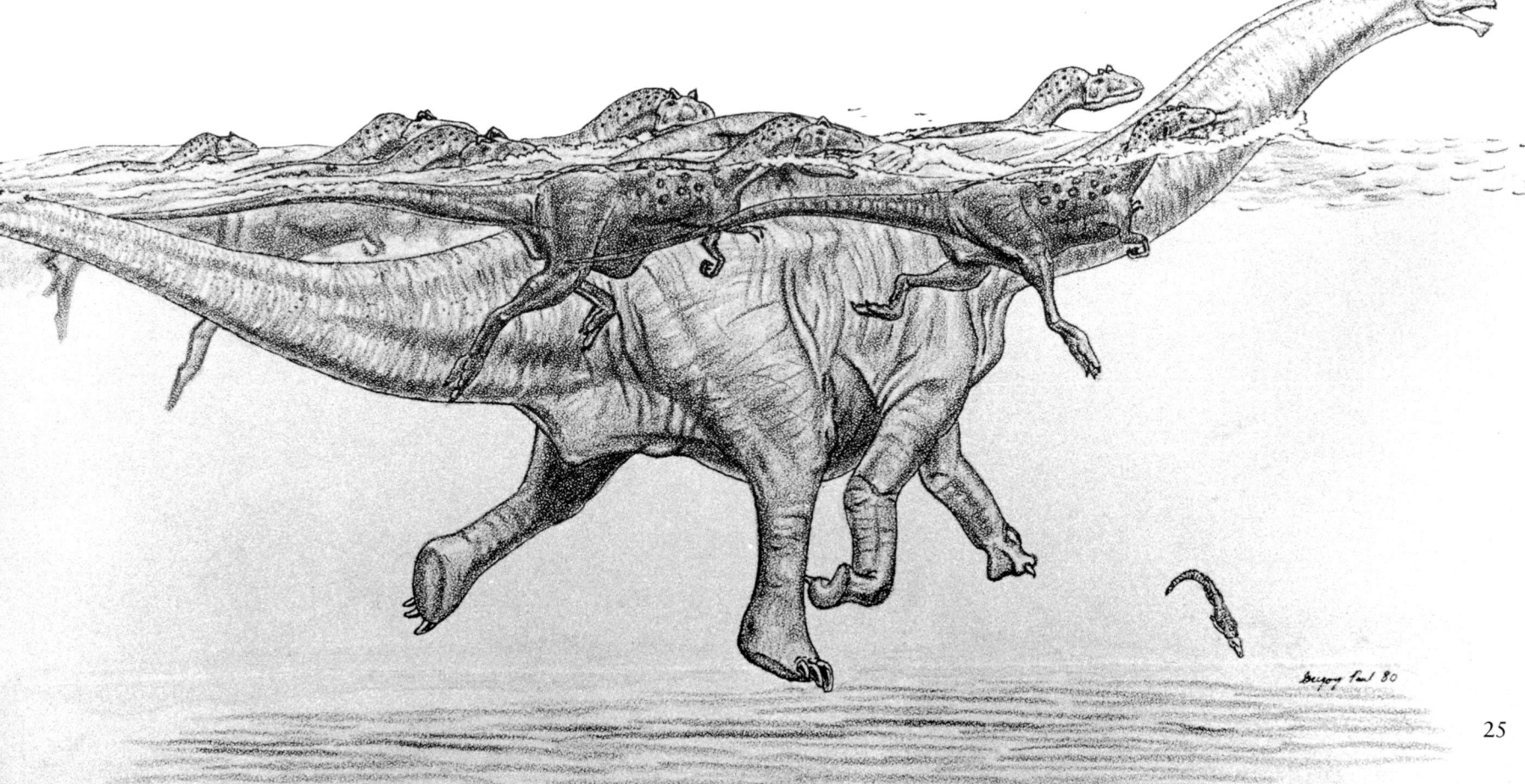

DINOSAURS PAST AND PRESENT

OPPOSITE: *Maiasaura* Herd by Douglas Henderson. Checklist 97.

"*Maiasaura* Herd, Aerial View" by Douglas Henderson. Checklist 102.

"Cretaceous Seaway" by Douglas Henderson. Checklist 103.

Camptosaurus and *Camarasaurus* by
Douglas Henderson. Checklist 109.

36. *Ceratosaurus nasicornis*, no date
David Thomas
Bronze, 14 x 3½ x 6½ in., 35.6 x 8.9 x 16.5 cm.
Collection of the artist

37. *Triceratops* and young, no date
Doris Tischler
Bronze, 7½ x 4 x 4 in., 19 x 10.2 x 10.2 cm.
Collection of the artist

38. Sauropod, no date
Doris Tischler
Bronze, 14 x 5 x 11 in., 35.6 x 12.7 x 27.9 cm.
Collection of the artist

39. *Deinonychus* and iguanodont, 1985
John Gurche
Acrylic, 13¼ x 19¼ in., 33.7 x 48.9 cm.
Collection of the artist

40. *Archaeopteryx* with sauropod, no date
John Gurche
Acrylic, 18½ x 9⅝ in., 47 x 24.4 cm.
Collection of the artist

41. *Archaeopteryx*, 1982
John Gurche
Acrylic, 8½ x 10½ in., 21.6 x 26.7 cm.
Collection of the artist

42. *Daspletosaurus* and *Styracosaurus*, 1985
John Gurche
Acrylic, 11 x 11¾ in., 27.9 x 29.9 cm.
Collection of the artist

43. "Poling in Shallow Water," 1977
Margaret Colbert
India ink on scratchboard, 8¼ x 6½ in.,
20.9 x 16.5 cm.
Collection of the artist

44. "Patience in the Rain," 1977
Margaret Colbert
India ink on scratchboard, 8⅜ x 8⅜ in.,
21.3 x 21.3 cm.
Collection of the artist

45. "Contest for Dominance," 1977
Margaret Colbert
India ink on scratchboard, 8⅜ x 7⅞ in.,
21.3 x 19.7 cm.
Collection of the artist

46. Study for Jurassic Mural, 1985
Eleanor Kish
Acrylic, 69¾ x 41⅝ in., 177.2 x 105.7 cm.
New Mexico Museum of Natural History

47. Hatchling *Maiasaura*, 1984
Stephen Czerkas
Resin, 10½ x 7 x 6½ in., 26.7 x 17.8 x 16.5 cm.
Collection of the artist

48. Free-standing *Maiasaura* hatchling, 1984
Stephen Czerkas
Resin, 14½ x 5¼ x 8¾ in., 36.8 x 13.4 x 22.2 cm.
Collection of the artist

49. *Maiasaura*, 1984
Stephen Czerkas
Resin, 33½ x 9½ x 13½ in., 85.1 x 24.1 x 34.3 cm.
Collection of the artist

50. *Tyrannosaurus*, 1984
Stephen Czerkas
Resin, 33½ x 17¼ x 15¾ in., 85.1 x 43.8 x 40 cm.
Collection of the artist

51. *Carnotaurus sastrei*, 1986
Stephen Czerkas
Resin, 26 x 11 x 17½ in., 66.1 x 27.9 x 44.5 cm.
Collection of the artist

52. *Allosaurus*, 1984-1986
Stephen Czerkas
Resin, 264 x 38 x 73⅛ in., 670.6 x 96.5 x 185.8 cm.
Natural History Museum of Los Angeles County

53. *Stegosaurus*, 1986
Stephen Czerkas
Resin, 26 x 10 x 17 in., 66.1 x 25.4 x 43.2 cm.
Collection of the artist

54. *Stegosaurus*, 1976
Sylvia Czerkas
Resin, 7 x 2¾ x 4½ in., 17.8 x 7 x 11.5 cm.
Collection of the artist

55. *Proceratops*, 1975
Sylvia Czerkas
Resin, 3 x 3 x 3½ in., 7.7 x 7.7 x 8.9 cm.
Collection of the artist

56. *Tyrannosaurus rex*, 1979
Sylvia Czerkas
Resin, 20¾ x 14 x 13½ in., 52.7 x 35.6 x 34.3 cm.
Collection of the artist

57. *Sauropelta*, 1983
Kenneth Carpenter
Pen and ink, 13¾ x 10½ in., 34.9 x 26.7 cm.
Collection of the artist

58. *Sauropelta* skeletal study, no date
Kenneth Carpenter
Pen and ink, 13¾ x 9 in., 34.9 x 24.1 cm.
Collection of the artist

59. "A Fight to the Death," *Sauropelta* and *Velociraptor*, 1985
Kenneth Carpenter
Pen and ink, 13¾ x 11 in., 34.9 x 27.9 cm.
Collection of the artist

60. *Euoplocephalus*, 1984
Kenneth Carpenter
Pen and ink, 11 x 17 in., 27.9 x 43.2 cm.
Collection of the artist

61. *Euoplocephalus* skeletal study, 1981
Kenneth Carpenter
Pen and ink, 11½ x 8 in., 29.2 x 20.3 cm.
Collection of the artist

62. "Sudden Encounter with a Tail Club," *Euoplocephalus* and *Daspletosaurus*, 1985
Kenneth Carpenter
Pen and ink, 11 x 14 in., 27.9 x 35.6 cm.
Collection of the artist

63. "Face Off," *Edmontonia* and *Albertosaurus*, no date
Kenneth Carpenter
Pen and ink, 10¾ x 10½ in., 27.3 x 26.7 cm.
Collection of the artist

64. *Edmontonia*, no date
Kenneth Carpenter
Pen and ink, 17 x 12½ in., 43.2 x 31.7 cm.
Collection of the artist

65. "When Push Comes to Shove," *Edmontonia*, 1985
Kenneth Carpenter
Pen and ink, 14½ x 11½ in., 36.8 x 29.2 cm.
Collection of the artist

66. *Velociraptor (= Deinonychus) antirrhopus*
muscle study, no date
Gregory Paul
Pencil on paper, 26½ x 9½ in., 67.3 x 24.1 cm.
Framed with photograph of pen-and-ink skeletal study
Collection of the artist

67. "*Velociraptor antirrhopus:* Fighting Pair," 1977 and 1985*
Gregory Paul
Pencil on paper, 22 x 16¾ in., 55.9 x 42.5 cm.
Collection of the artist

68. "*Albertosaurus libratus* Pair Invites a *Monoclonius
albertensis* Herd to Dinner, The Latter Firmly Decline,"
1979 and 1985*
Gregory Paul
Pencil on paper, 21⅞ x 16⅝ in., 55.6 x 42.2 cm.
Collection of the artist

69. "*Archaeopteryx lithographica* and Pterosaur Flocks on
Solnhofen Island," 1977 and 1985*
Gregory Paul
Pencil on paper, 22 x 16½ in., 55.9 x 41.9 cm.
Collection of the artist

70. "Charging *Triceratops horridus* Group," 1977 and 1985*
Gregory Paul
Pencil on paper, 21¾ x 16½ in., 55.3 x 41.9 cm.
Collection of the artist

71. *Chasmosaurus belli,* muscle study, 1985
Gregory Paul
Pencil on paper, 16½ x 9 in., 41.9 x 22.9 cm.
Framed with photograph of pen-and-ink skeletal study
Collection of the artist

72. *Edmontosaurus copei* herd, 1981
Gregory Paul
Pencil on paper, 21¼ x 12½ in., 54 x 31.8 cm.
Collection of the artist

73. *Iguanodon bernissartensis* and *Iguanodon mantelli,*
1984 and 1985*
Gregory Paul
Pencil on paper, 20¾ x 12 in., 52.8 x 30.5 cm.
Collection of the artist

74. *Hypacrosaurus casuarius,* or *Corythosaurus,*
life study, 1984
Gregory Paul
Pencil on paper, 19 x 9 in., 48.3 x 22.9 cm.
Collection of the artist

* Two or more dates for a work by Gregory Paul indicate that the artist
has revised the original to incorporate new information about the
subject(s).

Dryptosaurus by Charles Knight. Checklist 14.

Chasmosaurus belli by Robert Bakker.
Checklist 91.

75. *Hypacrosaurus casuarius,* muscle study, 1984
Gregory Paul
Pencil on paper, 20 x 7 in., 50.9 x 17.8 cm.
Framed with photograph of pen-and-ink skeletal study
Collection of the artist

76. "*Parasaurolophus walkeri* among Dawn Redwoods,"
1985
Gregory Paul
Pencil on paper, 15½ x 17½ in., 39.4 x 44.5 cm.
Collection of the artist

77. "*Brachiosaurus brancai* Herd," 1977 and 1985*
Gregory Paul
Pencil on paper, 22¾ x 17⅝ in., 57.8 x 44.8 cm.
Collection of the artist

78. *Ouranosaurus nigeriensis,* 1985
Gregory Paul
Pencil on paper, 10½ x 16½ in., 26.7 x 41.9 cm.
Collection of the artist

79. *Brachiosaurus brancai,* muscle study, 1985
Gregory Paul
Pencil on paper, 15½ x 14½ in., 39.4 x 36.8 cm.
Framed with photograph of pen-and-ink skeletal study
Collection of the artist

80. "What Happens When *Apatosaurus ajax* Seeks Aquatic
Refuge from *Allosaurus fragilis,*" 1980
Gregory Paul
Pencil on paper, 12½ x 8 in., 31.8 x 20.3 cm.
Collection of the artist

81. *Chasmosaurus kaiseni,* skull studies, 1979 and 1985*
Gregory Paul
Oil on canvas, 16½ x 24⅛ in., 41.9 x 61.3 cm.
Collection of the artist

82. "*Monoclonius albertensis* Fending Off *Albertosaurus
libratus,*" 1983
Gregory Paul
Oil on canvas, 32¼ x 22¼ in., 81.9 x 56.5 cm.
Private collection

83. "Resting *Velociraptor antirrhopus* Pair," 1980 and 1982*
Gregory Paul
Oil on canvas, 30 x 28 in., 76.2 x 71.1 cm.
Private collection

84. "*Tyrannosaurus (=Daspletosaurus)torosus* in a Fast Run"
1978 and 1985*
Gregory Paul
Oil on canvas, 40¼ x 24¼ in., 102.3 x 61.6 cm.
Collection of the artist

85. "*Chasmosaurus (=Pentaceratops) sternbergii* Herd in Dry
Cypress Swamp," 1977 and 1985*
Gregory Paul
Oil on canvas, 40¼ x 20¼ in., 102.2 x 51.5 cm.
Collection of the artist

86. *Albertosaurus sarcophagus, Anchiceratops ornatus,* and
Hypacrosaurus altispinus, 1979
Gregory Paul
Oil on canvas, 36¼ x 22¼ in.
Private collection

87. "*Monoclonius apertus* Herd Crossing a Stream," 1981
Gregory Paul
Oil on canvas, 31½ x 22 in., 80 x 55.9 cm.
Tyrrell Museum of Palaeontology

88. *Maiasaura peeblesorum,* 1980 and 1985*
Gregory Paul
Oil on canvas, 27¼ x 22⅛ in., 69.2 x 56.2 cm.
Collection of the artist

89. "Ambush at Como Creek: *Allosaursus atox* Pack Versus
Diplodocus carnegii,"
1978, 1983, and 1985
Gregory Paul
Oil on canvas, 65⅞ x 42⅛ in., 167 x 107 cm.
Collection of the artist

90. *Barosaurus,* 1968
Robert Bakker
Pencil on paper, 11 x 8½ in., 27.9 x 21.6 cm.
Private collection

91. *Chasmosaurus belli,* circa 1971
Robert Bakker
Pencil on paper, 13⅜ x 12 in., 34 x 30.5 cm.
Private collection

92. *Deinonychus antirrhopus,* 1969
Robert Bakker
Pencil on paper, 18 x 11½ in., 45.7 x 29.2 cm.
Peabody Museum of Natural History, Yale University

93. *Kritosaurus incurvimanus,* 1985
Vladimir Krb
Oil on canvas, 35⅜ x 25¼ in., 89.9 x 64.2 cm.
Collection of the artist

94. *Styracosaurus albertensis,* 1985
Vladimir Krb
Oil on canvas, 35⅜ x 27¼ in., 88.9 x 69.2 cm.
Collection of the artist

* Two or more dates for a work by Gregory Paul indicate that the artist
has revised the original to incorporate new information about the
subject(s).

95. *Opisthocoelicaudia skanzynskii*, 1985
Vladimir Krb
Oil on canvas, 25¼ x 35¾ in., 64.2 x 90.9 cm.
Collection of the artist

96. "Lunch on Warning," *Tyrannosaurus rex*
and *Triceratops*, 1985
Douglas Henderson
Tinted lithograph, 18 x 13 in., 45.7 x 33 cm.
Collection of the artist

97. *Maiasaura* herd, 1985
Douglas Henderson
Pastel, 28⅜ x 17¾ in., 72.1 x 45.1 cm.
Natural History Museum of Los Angeles County

98. "Iguanodons in the Dead Fall," 1985
Douglas Henderson
Tinted lithograph, 15½ x 11 in., 39.4 x 27.9 cm.
Collection of the artist

99. Iguanodons, 1985
Douglas Henderson
Tinted lithograph, 15½ x 11 in., 39.4 x 27.9 cm.
Collection of the artist

100. "Candide and Conegonda," *Coelophysis*, 1985
Douglas Henderson
Tinted lithograph, 14 x 20 in., 35.6 x 50.8 cm.
Collection of the artist

101. "Gathering Herd," 1983
Douglas Henderson
Pastel, 24¼ x 13½ in., 61.6 x 34.3 cm.
Museum of the Rockies

102. "*Maiasaura* Herd, Aerial View," 1983
Douglas Henderson
Pastel, 15⅜ x 18¼ in., 39.1 x 46.4 cm.
Museum of the Rockies

103. "Cretaceous Seaway," 1983
Douglas Henderson
Pastel, 20 x 19 in., 50.8 x 48.9 cm.
Museum of the Rockies

104. "Miller's Chickens," *Velociraptor* and
Protoceratops, 1985
Douglas Henderson
Tinted lithograph, 20 x 14½ in., 50.8 x 36.8 cm.
Collection of the artist

105. "Loose in the Nursery," *Maiasaura* and
Albertosaurus, 1985
Douglas Henderson
Tinted lithograph, 22 x 15 in., 55.9 x 38.1 cm.
Collection of the artist

106. "Theme of the Fast Carriers," *Diplodocus*, 1985
Douglas Henderson
Tinted lithograph, 22½ x 15¾ in., 57.2 x 40 cm.
Collection of the artist

107. "The Green Crew," *Maiasaura*, 1983
Douglas Henderson
Tinted lithograph, 18 x 15 in., 45.7 x 38.1 cm.
Collection of the artist

108. *Camarasaurus* trackway, 1985
Douglas Henderson
Pencil on paper, 12½ x 15½ in., 31.8 x 39.4 cm.
Collection of the artist

109. *Camptosaurus* and *Camarasaurus*, 1985
Douglas Henderson
Pencil on paper, 21¼ x 15½ in., 54 x 39.4 cm.
Collection of the artist

110. Three hysilophodants and a *Nicrosaurus*, 1985
Douglas Henderson
Pencil on paper, 20¾ x 14¾ in., 52.7 x 37.5 cm.
Collection of the artist

111. "Baby," 1981
William Stout
Watercolor, 9¾ x 15¾ in., 24.8 x 40 cm.
Collection of the artist

112. "The Shadow," 1980
William Stout
Watercolor, 19 x 16½ in., 48.3 x 41.9 cm.
Collection of the artist

113. "Nesting," 1981
William Stout
Watercolor, 25½ x 9¼ in., 64.8 x 23.5 cm.
Collection of the artist

114. "The Marsh," 1980
William Stout
Watercolor, 25 x 16½ in., 63.5 x 41.9 cm.
Collection of the artist

115. *Mamenchisaurus*, 1981
William Stout
Watercolor, 24 x 14½ in., 61 x 36.9 cm.
Collection of the artist

116. "Cool Weather," 1981
William Stout
Watercolor, 22¾ x 13⅜ in., 57.8 x 34 cm.
Collection of the artist

117. "High Fashion," 1980
William Stout
Watercolor, 11 x 14 in., 27.9 x 35.9 cm.
Collection of the artist

118. "Lunch," 1980
William Stout
Watercolor, 12 x 11 in., 30.5 x 27.9 cm.
Collection of the artist

119. "Claws," 1981
William Stout
Watercolor, 13½ x 17½ in., 34.3 x 44.5 cm.
Collection of the artist

120. "Under the Stars," 1980
William Stout
Watercolor, 20 x 16 in., 50.8 x 40.7 cm.
Collection of the artist

121. *Archaeopteryx*, 1980
William Stout
Watercolor, 20¾ x 5 in., 52.7 x 12.7 cm.
Collection of the artist

122. "The River," 1975
Mark Hallett
Gouache, 54½ x 19½ in., 138.4 x 49.5 cm.
Collection of the artist

123. "Dawn of a New Day," 1984
Mark Hallett
Gouache, 11¾ x 14¾ in., 29.8 x 37.5 cm.
Collection of the artist

124. "A Clash of Bone," 1984
Mark Hallett
Gouache, 22¾ x 12 in., 57.8 x 30.5 cm.
Collection of the artist

125. "Leader of the Herd," 1979
Mark Hallett
Gouache, 18¼ x 21 in., 46.4 x 53.4 cm.
Collection of the artist

126. *Iguanodon* studies, 1984
Mark Hallett
Pencil on paper, 11⅛ x 18 in., 28.2 x 45.7 cm.
Collection of the artist

127. *Saltasaurus*, 1981
Mark Hallett
Gouache, 8½ x 10½ in., 21.6 x 26.7 cm.
Collection of the artist

128. "A Fight to the Death," 1984
Mark Hallett
Gouache, 13¼ x 15 in., 33.7 x 38.1 cm.
Collection of the artist

129. "Red Huntress," 1984
Mark Hallett
Gouache, 11¾ x 15 in., 29.9 x 38.1 cm.
Collection of the artist

130. Sauropods, 1985
Mark Hallett
Gouache, 27 x 18½ in., 68.6 x 47 cm.
Collection of the artist

131. Ornithopods, 1985
Mark Hallett
Gouache, 22 x 12 in., 55.9 x 30.5 cm.
Collection of the artist

132. Theropods, 1985
Mark Hallett
Gouache, 17 x 13½ in., 43.2 x 34.3 cm.
Collection of the artist

133. Stegosaurs, 1985
Mark Hallett
Gouache, 13 x 7½ in., 33 x 19 cm.
Collection of the artist

134. Prosauropods, 1985
Mark Hallett
Gouache, 11 x 7 in., 27.9 x 17.8 cm.
Collection of the artist

135. Ceratopsians, 1985
Mark Hallett
Gouache, 18 x 8 in., 45.7 x 20.3 cm.
Collection of the artist

136. Ankylosaurs, 1985
Mark Hallett
Gouache, 17¼ x 7 in., 43.8 x 17.8 cm.
Collection of the artist

137. *Triceratops* herd and *Tyrannosaurus*, 1984
Mark Hallett
Gouache, 22¼ x 14 in., 56.5 x 35.6 cm.
Collection of the artist

138. "The Ferns Await the Outcome," 1984
Mark Hallett
Gouache, 22 x 14¼ in., 55.9 x 36.2 cm.
Collection of the artist

139. "Awakenings of Hunger," 1985
Mark Hallett
Gouache, 23½ x 16 in., 59.7 x 40.7 cm.
Private collection

140. "Crossing the Flats," Mamenchisaurus, 1986
Mark Hallett
Gouache, 48 x 18 in., 122 x 45.7 cm.
Natural History Museum of Los Angeles County

141. *Stenonychosaurus*, 1981
Ron Seguin and Dale A. Russell
Resin, 108 x 21 x 48 in., 274.4 x 53.3 x 121.9 cm.
National Museum of Natural Sciences,
National Museums of Canada

142. Dinosauroid, 1981
Ron Seguin and Dale A. Russell
Resin, 33 x 20 x 56 in., 83.9 x 50.7 x 142.2 cm.
National Museum of Natural Sciences,
National Museums of Canada

143. *Stegosaurus*, 1901
Charles Knight
Cast resin, 30 x 17½ x 9¼ in., 76.2 x 44.5 x 23.5 cm.
Private collection

144. *Stegosaurus stenops*, 1986
Stephen Czerkas
Resin, 20 x 11 x 13 in., 50.8 x 27.9 x 33 cm.
Collection of the artist

THE SYMPOSIUM

Natural History Museum of Los Angeles County
February 15, 1986

THE CONTRIBUTORS

Robert T. Bakker, Ph.D. (VOLUME I), holds the Jacob Wortman Curatorship of Fossil Mammals and an Adjunct Curatorship at the University Museum, University of Colorado at Boulder. He began his studies of dinosaurs as an undergraduate at Yale University in the 1960s and continued at Harvard Graduate School where he was elected to the elite Society of Fellows. Dr. Bakker is a skilled artist as well as a dynamic speaker and writer; his recent book, *The Dinosaur Heresies* (William Morrow and Company, Inc., 1986), tells the story of dinosaur evolution in a lively style.

George Callison, Ph.D. (VOLUME I), is especially interested in how fossil reptiles and mammals work. He has led many expeditions to mid-Mesozoic fossil localities of the Rocky Mountains, where his parties have found the smallest adult dinosaurs as well as numerous new and unusual species of other small vertebrates that shared living space with dinosaurian behemoths. Dr. Callison is Professor of Biology at California State University, Long Beach, and Research Associate in Vertebrate Paleontology at the Natural History Museum of Los Angeles County.

Philip J. Currie, Ph.D. (VOLUME II), is Assistant Director, Collections and Research Programmes, of the Tyrrell Museum of Palaeontology in Drumheller, Alberta; he was a major figure behind the development of this new museum and the associated field station, which are together the largest exhibition and research center for dinosaurs in North America. Dr. Currie studied at McGill University, receiving his M.Sc. in 1975 and his Ph.D. in 1982. His major finds have been an *Albertosaurus* skeleton and the earliest known bird footprints. His current research focuses on small theropods, the origin of birds, and ceratopsian behavior. He is Alberta Coordinator of Canada-China Dinosaur Project and Adjunct Professor at the University of Calgary.

Stephen A. Czerkas (VOLUME II) is a professional paleontologist and artist who produces miniature and life-sized models of Mesozoic reptiles that are scientifically accurate and beautifully realistic. His series of life-sized *Maiasaura* babies are on display in the new dinosaur hall of the Philadelphia Academy of Natural Sciences, and his 22-foot (6.7-meter) *Allosaurus* will be on permanent display at the Natural History Museum of Los Angeles County when it returns from its tour with the exhibit Dinosaurs Past and Present. He is currently completing three life-sized *Deinonychus* individuals for the California Academy of Sciences in San Francisco.

Sylvia J. Czerkas, Guest Curator of Dinosaurs Past and Present and coeditor of this book, is a professional artist whose work has been shown in galleries and museums throughout America. She was guest curator and exhibits coordinator for Death of the Dinosaurs at the Griffith Park Observatory planetarium and a continuing series of museum exhibits presented in conjunction with the book *Dinosaurs, mammoths and cavemen: The art of Charles R. Knight* (Dutton, New York, 1982), which she coauthored with Donald F. Glut; she was also Guest Curator for Chevron of a section of the California Academy of Sciences 1985 Dino Fest. With her husband, Stephen, she spends part of each summer digging for dinosaurs.

David D. Gillette, Ph.D. (VOLUME I), has been Curator of Paleontology at the newly opened New Mexico Museum of Natural History in Albuquerque for the past four years. Since moving to New Mexico, his research has turned entirely to Mesozoic studies of the American Southwest, including work at the Ghost Ranch *Coelophysis* quarry in New Mexico, the Petrified Forest National Park in Arizona, and many sites elsewhere in New Mexico. In 1986 he organized the First International Symposium on Dinosaur Tracks and Traces in Albuquerque; with his wife Lynett, he has been coordinating the development of the Ruth Hall Museum of Paleontology at Ghost Ranch, Abiquin, New Mexico.

Mark Hallett (VOLUME I) is an artist, writer, and naturalist based in Pasadena, California. He teaches classes in zoological illustration at the Natural History Museum of Los Angeles County and biomedical illustration and anatomy at Otis Art Institute in Los Angeles. He has created numerous habitat murals for museums and zoos in California, including the San Diego Zoo, the San Diego Natural History Museum, and the Natural History Museum of Los Angeles County. He is illustrator and codesigner of *Zoobooks* (Wildlife Education, Ltd., San Diego), a series on living animals and extinct and endangered species; he created all the illustrations for the June 1985 issue on dinosaurs.

John R. Horner, Ph.D. (VOLUME II), who is Curator of Paleontology at the Museum of the Rockies, Montana State University, Bozeman, has led fossil collecting expeditions that have resulted in discoveries giving indication of communal nesting grounds and parental care of hatchlings in some species of dinosaurs. With James Gorman, he has written a popular book on *Maiasaura* or "good mother lizard" (*Maia: A Dinosaur Grows Up,* Museum of the Rockies, 1986), a species that he discovered and described. He was a 1986 recipient of the prestigious MacArthur Foundation Award and has also been awarded an honorary doctoral degree from the University of Montana.

Martin G. Lockley, Ph.D. (VOLUME I), Associate Professor of Geology at the University of Colorado in Denver, is conducting pioneering research on trackways of dinosaurs in the western United States. He is attempting to revive the lost art of animal tracking, to apply its techniques to the fossilized evidence of the movements of dinosaurs in all ancient habitats where they are preserved, and to devise methods of documenting the information contained in the tracks. He is finding that the tracks yield a census of life in dinosaur communities, including information about assemblages of dinosaurs, the behavior of individuals, and the ecosystems through which the animals moved.

Everett C. Olson, Ph.D., coeditor of this book, is Professor Emeritus of Zoology at the University of California at Los Angeles and member of the faculty of the Center for the Study of Evolution and The Origin of Life at UCLA. A specialist in vertebrate paleontology, he has authored numerous influential books and papers on the evolution of reptiles, vertebrate paleoecology, and the origins of mammals. He is a member of the National Academy of Sciences and Past President of the Society of Vertebrate Paleontology and the Society of Systematic Zoology. In 1980, the Paleontology Society honored Dr. Olson with their most prestigious award, the Paleontological Medal.

Kevin Padian, Ph.D. (VOLUME II), is Associate Professor of Paleontology and Biology at the University of California at Berkeley. His major interests include dinosaurs, pterosaurs, macroevolution, the systematics of reptiles, and the origins of major evolutionary features.

He was editor of *The Beginning of the Age of Dinosaurs* (Cambridge University Press, 1986). His current research projects include the taxonomic revision of the early pterosaurs and (with Paul E. Olsen) studies on the relationship between fossil footprints and the stance and gait of the trackmakers.

Gregory S. Paul (VOLUME II), is a Baltimore paleontologist and artist who has been studying and drawing dinosaurs since early childhood. He worked informally at Johns Hopkins University under Robert T. Bakker from 1977 to 1983, a period that he believes was critical to the development of his technical and aesthetic style. He was responsible for the paleontological design of AeroVironment's fully mobile half-sized model of *Quetzalcoatlus northropi*. Mr. Paul is author of a number of scientific papers on dinosaurs and has recently finished writing and illustrating a book on predatory dinosaurs of the world to be published by Simon and Schuster, New York.

J. Keith Rigby, Jr., Ph.D. (VOLUME II), is Assistant Professor in the Department of Earth Sciences, University of Notre Dame. He received his Ph.D. from Columbia University in 1977; his dissertation concerned Paleocene mammalian biostratigraphy. Since then he has conducted studies of continental stratigraphy and vertebrate paleontology throughout North America and Canada and has been involved in studies of European fossil vertebrates as well. In 1984 he found dinosaurs in deposits of Paleocene age; his paper in this book describes aspects of these and other more recent finds and their implications about the climate and habitat of the last of the dinosaurs.

Dale A. Russell, Ph.D. (VOLUME I), is Curator of Fossil Vertebrates at the National Museum of Natural Sciences, National Museums of Canada, in Ottawa. He received a doctoral degree in 1964 from Columbia University in New York, under the supervision of Edwin H. Colbert. His research interests include dinosaurian anatomy, faunistics and extinction, and the implications of the terrestrial fossil record for the evolution of extraterrestrial life. Dr. Russell is completing a book on the dinosaurs of North America to be published by the National Museum of Natural Sciences.

Figure 26

THE RETURN OF THE DANCING DINOSAURS

Robert T. Bakker

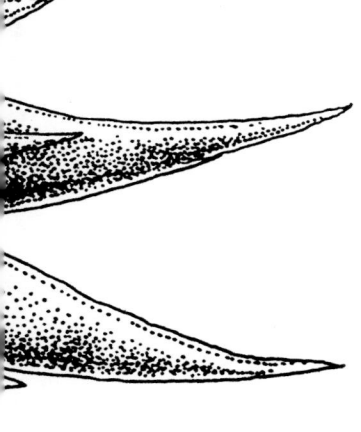

Dinosaurs were evolutionary deadends—lumbering, swamp-bound, cold-blooded behemoths that managed to rule the earth only because the worldwide habitat was a steamy tropical jungle. This is the classical view of dinosaurs, the view preached in nearly all the books and exhibits of the 1950s and early 60s. But the nineteenth-century scholars who first discovered dinosaurs saw clear-cut resemblances to modern warm-blooded birds. The early artistic reconstructions of dinosaurs show lively leaping theropods and brontosaurs that reared up on their hind legs to feed on conifers in a dry-land environment. Since the late 1960s there has been a dinosaur renaissance, and many lines of inquiry lead to the conclusion that the nimble-footed restorations of the last century are correct. Fossil footprints show that dinosaurs cruised at warm-blooded speeds. Marks left by ligaments and muscles show that dinosaurs had great power at shoulder, elbow, hip, and knee. The design of dinosaur vertebrae and back muscles provided many giant herbivorous species with the capacity to rear up high in the foliage. Pound for pound, most giant dinosaurs were stronger, faster, and more maneuverable than the rhinos and elephants of today. The Dinosauria ruled by virtue of their fundamentally superior adaptive plan.

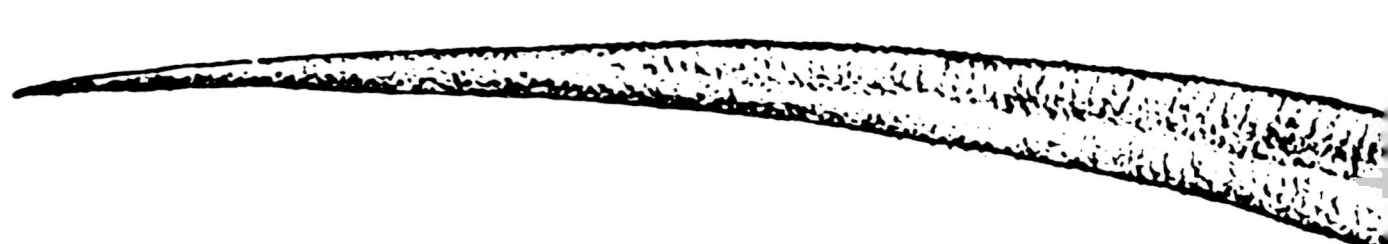

Figure 1. *Dryptosaurus* by Charles Knight, 1897. Courtesy American Museum of Natural History, K:AM 189701. Checklist 14; see also pages 30 and 31.

Charles R. Knight made his *Dryptosaurus* dance. Knight painted the New Jersey theropod dinosaur in 1890 in a scene full of energy and power—two dryptosaurs leaping, twisting, and rolling on the ground in mortal combat like a pair of half-ton fighting cocks (Fig. 1). Knight's composition was not considered controversial because the notion of leaping dinosaurs was accepted at that time as one defensible line of thought about dinosaur behavior. C. B. Beecher (1901) at Yale University mounted the first full skeleton of a duck-billed dinosaur in 1901, and the pose was that of an animal frozen midstride in a high-speed bipedal run, with the right hind leg pushing off the ground and the left leg flexed as it propelled the beast forward. (In my opinion that mount, still proudly displayed in the Great Hall, is unsurpassed by any of the dozens of more recently mounted duckbills.) Beecher's mount was accepted into the mainstream of multiple hypotheses about dinosaurs. The idea that all big dinosaurs were slow and sluggish had not yet gained supremacy within the paleontological community.

Indeed, at the dinosaurs' first entry into the annals of science in the 1820s and 1830s these Mesozoic beasts had impressed English and German

Figure 2. *Deinonychus antirrhopus* by Robert Bakker, 1969. Courtesy Peabody Museum of Natural History, Yale University. Checklist 92.

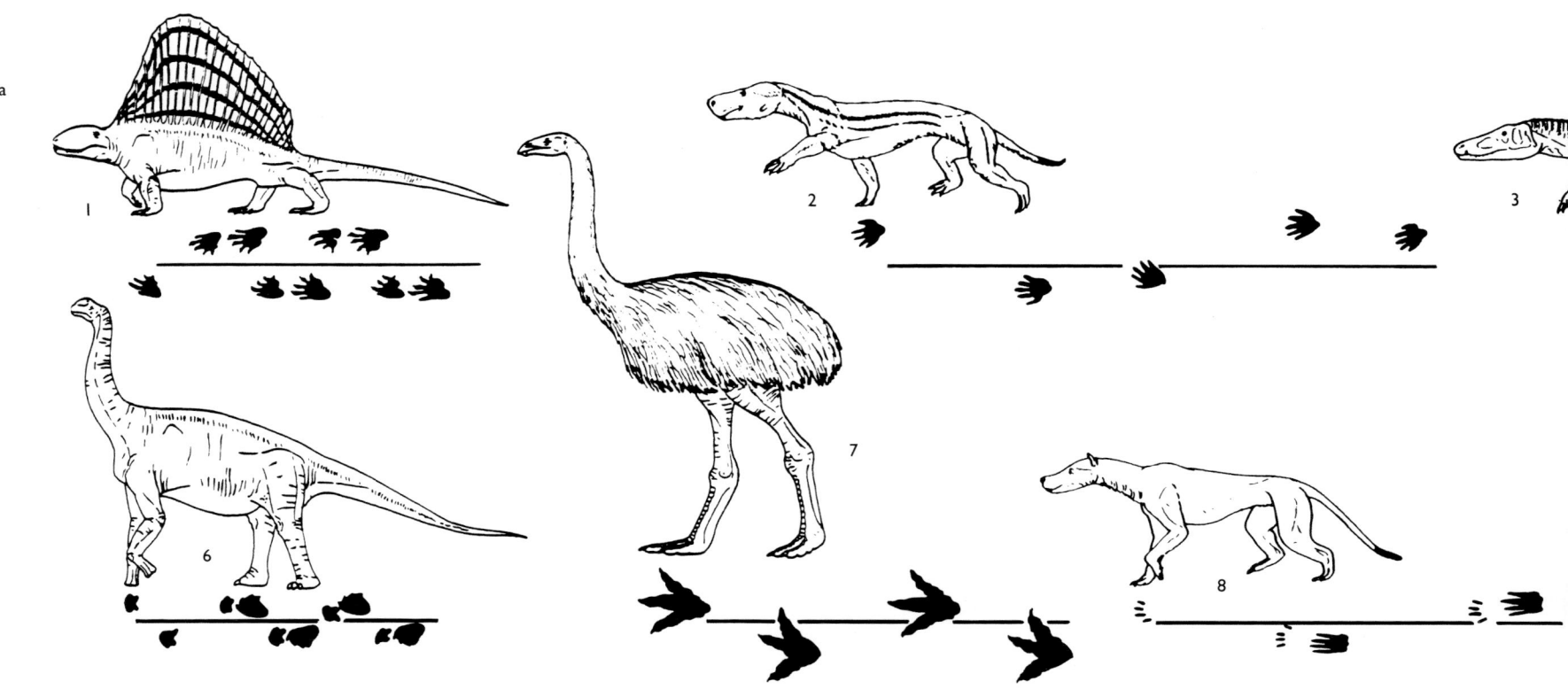

Figure 3. A bestiary of fossil trackmakers, each with a plan view of the trackway drawn to match (a), and other trackway samples (b).

3a.
1. early Permian *Dimetrodon*
2. early Triassic cynodont
3. advanced mid-Triassic thecodont of the cheirothere-type
4. late Cretaceous tyrannosaur
5. late Cretaceous duckbill
6. early Cretaceous sauropod of the astrodon-type
7. New Zealand moa
8. Miocene beardog
9. Pleistocene mammoth

scholars with a peculiar mixture of avian, mammalian, and reptilian features (Buckland 1824; Owen 1841; Riley and Stutchbury 1836). Dinosaurs were not simply large-scale models of lizards or crocodilians. O. von Meyer (in Owen 1849, 1879) was the first to recognize the unique properties of dinosaurs, and he coined the classification Order Pachypoda (stronglimbed) for the first three genera discovered up to that date: *Megalosaurus, Iguanodon,* and *Hylaeosaurus.* He emphasized the very strongly built sacra and mammallike limb construction present in these three dinosaurs, features that found no close counterparts among the extant Reptilia. Gideon Mantell (1844), the peripatetic surgeon and naturalist who discovered *Iguanodon* and *Pelorosaurus,* the first known sauropod, saw a remarkable mechanical sophistication in the way

iguanodont teeth performed their masticatory function, and Mantell concluded that the dinosaur must have matched the modern ox in the efficiency with which tough vegetable food was triturated by jaws and molars. In his masterful book on life through the ages, *The medals of creation,* Mantell (1844) explained at length how, at every joint and osseous process, the dinosaurians approached closely the level of organization of the "viviparous quadrupeds" (a Victorian term for the Mammalia).

The 1860s and 1870s saw the spectacular discoveries of nearly complete dinosaur skeletons in Europe and North America—the *Iguanodon* herd at Bernissart, Belgium, and the brontosaur-stegosaur-allosaur fauna from the Rocky Mountain states—and these new specimens too seemed to confirm that the Dinosauria were more than gi-

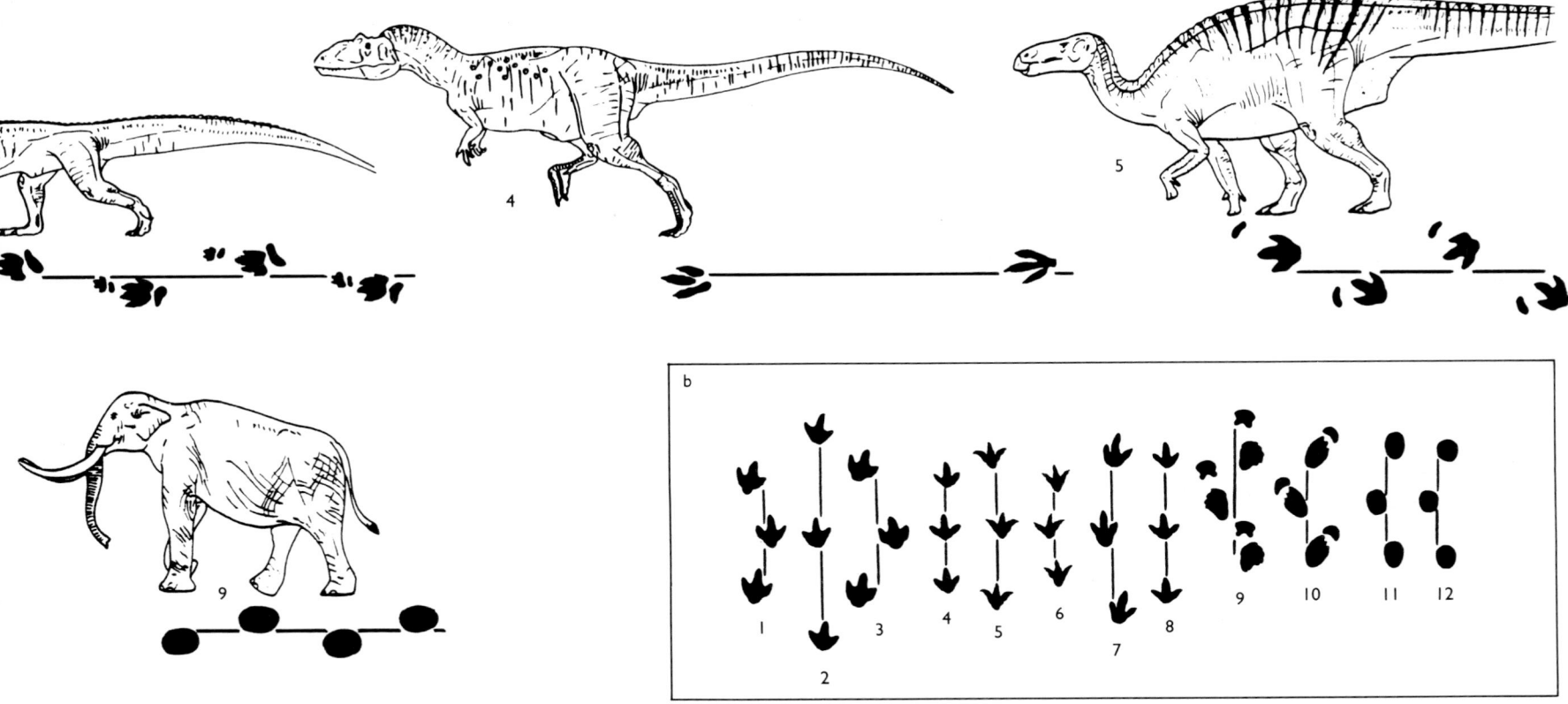

3b. 1–3   duckbilled dinosaurs (Hau-
           bold 1974)
    4–8   moas (Owen 1879; Williams
           1871)
    9–10 sauropod dinosaurs (Bird
           1944)
    11–12 mammoths (Alf 1966; Hark-
           ness 1882)

gantic versions of iguanas, alligators, and monitor lizards. Thomas Henry Huxley (in Ostrom 1976) argued with his usual lucidity that the small dinosaurs, like *Compsognathus,* were the direct ancestors of birds, and in America Yale's O. C. Marsh (1896) agreed. The birdlike adaptations suggested a level of locomotor activity far above that seen in typical modern reptiles. Marsh (1896) restored the quadrupedal *Triceratops* with fully erect forelimbs like those of a modern white rhinoceros, thus giving the five-metric-ton horned dinosaur a markedly light-footed carriage. Marsh, Osborn (1904), and Riggs (1903, 1904), who all had dug skeletons from the Morrison Formation between 1877 and 1901, noted the immense strength at the hips in the huge sauropods *Brontosaurus* and *Diplodocus* and in the stegosaurs and interpreted these multiton di-

nosaurs as tripodalists that reared up on their hind limbs and tail, kangaroo-style. Osborn (1904) described *Diplodocus* as exceptionally light and agile, despite its size, twice that of the largest elephant. All students of the Dinosauria did not place equal weight on the avian, mammalian, and reptilian qualities of dinosaur anatomy, but there was a wide acceptance of the idea that dinosaurs were not necessarily constrained by the metabolic and locomotor limits seen in the extant Reptilia.

This healthy diversity of opinion about dinosaurs contracted quite suddenly in the first two decades of the twentieth century. By 1930 the theory of lively dinosaurs had been driven to the fringe of paleontological viewpoints (Gilmore 1915, 1920; Gregory and Camp 1918). Every freestanding mount of a large quadrupedal dinosaur set up

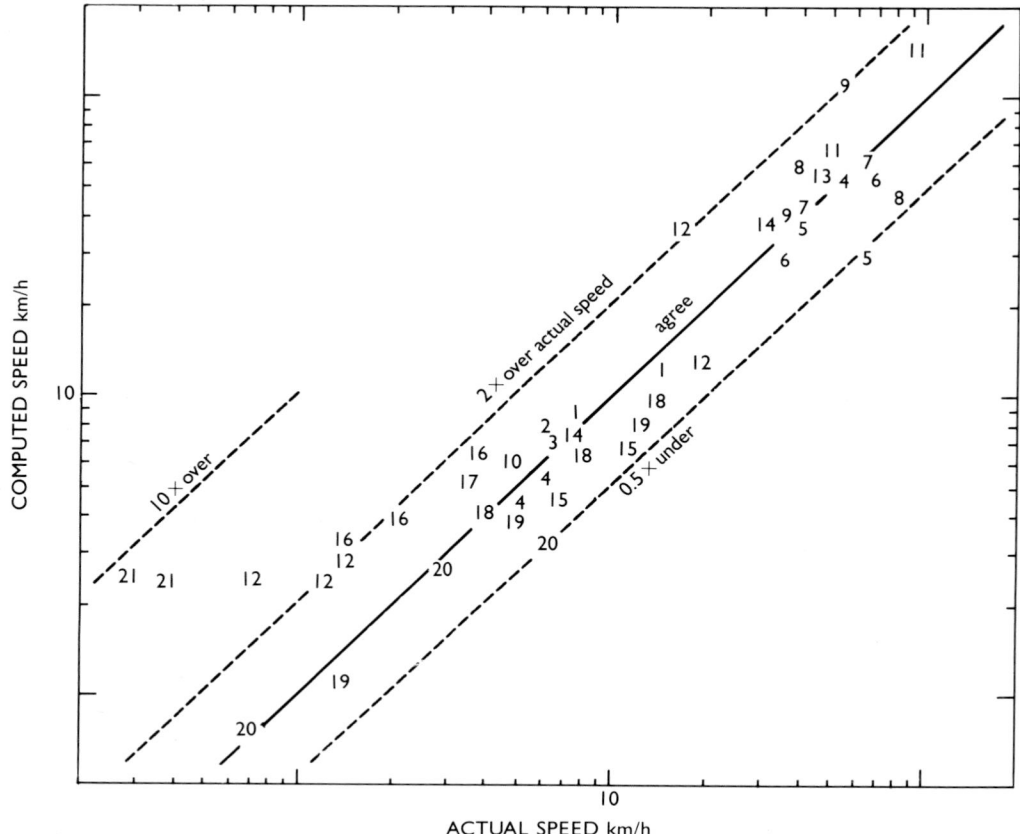

Figure 4. Actual observed speed and the speed calculated from the trackway using Alexander's formula (1976). Sources of observed speeds: 1–4, 6, 10, 13, 15 from Muybridge ([1887] 1957); 7, 8, 9, 11, 12 from Gambayran (1974); 14 from Alexander; 17–20 from Sukhanov (1974); 21, original.

1 Indian elephant
2 bactrian camel
3 ox
4 horse
5 reindeer
6 red deer
7 Mongolian gazelle
8 Saiga antelope
9 roe deer
10 domestic pig
11 cheetah
12 domestic cat
13 domestic dog
14 human
15 ostrich
16 pigeon
17 Komodo dragon
18 *Phrynocephalus* (lizard)
19 *Eremias* (lizard)
20 *Teratoscincus* (lizard)
21 Eastern box turtle

in North American museums had all four paws firmly planted on the ground as if the maximum speed possible were a short-strided shuffle. Nearly all had the elbows skewed out to the sides in an awkward semisprawl. Dinosaurs had lost their position as acceptable ancestors for birds, and most popular and technical books portrayed the larger Dinosauria as species trapped within a fundamentally reptilian design that could not permit anything more lively than a tortoise level of locomotor exuberance. The agile, giant tripodalists of Marsh, Riggs, and Osborn became the slow-footed quadrupedal brontosaurs and diplodocines of countless restorations published between 1915 and 1965.

Why did the paleontological consensus coalesce around the slow-footed paradigm? Why was the fast-and-agile point of view driven from the limits of scientific respectability? These questions deserve a thoughtful and detailed analysis from a historian of science. I suspect that part of the answer is that the best minds in vertebrate paleontology were attracted to other problems and other taxonomic groups, especially to the conceptual richness of the mammal fossil record. Matthew, Osborn, Jepsen, and Simpson—among the best thinkers among American vertebrate paleontologists—were devoted to the Mammalia, and Gregory and Camp (1918) and Romer (1922), the premier morphologists of the lower vertebrates, were far more intrigued by mammallike reptiles, amphibians, and fish than by dinosaurs. By far the best lower-tetrapod paleoecology was carried out by E. C. Case at the University of Michigan and E. C. Olson at the University of Chicago. Neither was attracted to dinosaur studies but instead lavished great intellectual care on the Permo-Carboniferous reptiles and amphibians.

Between 1909 and 1945 Charles W. Gilmore published extensive descriptive memoirs on dinosaurs, and these studies shaped the new, narrow interpretations of dinosaurian biology. Gilmore's work had a plodding adequacy devoid of the depth of biological insight shown by Mantell, von Meyer, Huxley, and Riggs. Gilmore described bones as nearly totally inanimate creations and never displayed any firsthand experience with the muscular anatomy or joint structure of extant species. Unfortunately Gilmore's lead-footed reconstructions became the universal standard for textbooks and museums.

I think that I am historically correct to place the beginning of the dinosaur renaissance at Yale in the early 1960s, where John Ostrom challenged the dogma that the duckbills were swamp-bound vegetarians. When he found the beautiful specimens of the small theropod *Deinonychus*, Ostrom began to see exceptional locomotor agility in these carnivorous dinosaurs and a few years later resurrected the theory of dinosaurs as direct ancestors of birds, a proposition that is now proven as conclusively as it is possible to prove any phylogenetic hypothesis (Ostrom 1976). My first commission to reconstruct a dinosaur was for the frontispiece of Ostrom's monograph on *Deinonychus* (Fig. 2). I drew *Deinonychus* running at high speed, the right hind leg far off the ground and the left about to propel the animal through the air in what the locomotor scientists call the "suspended phase," when the body sails forward with no contact with the ground.

During the 1960s at Yale the leaden-footed consensus about dinosaur appearance and mode of life was challenged. Following Ostrom's lead in bringing the dinosaurs out of the swamps, I wrote my first scientific paper (1968) during my senior year, arguing that the brontosaurs too were terrestrial and no more bound to soggy terrain than are modern Indian and African elephants. A. Romer had successfully worked out the hind-limb musculature of dinosaurs in the 1920s, and I thought that I might have a go at the fore limb. It bothered me that Romer's studies of the hind limb showed a very advanced, fully erect, and quite birdlike organization, and yet Gilmore's reconstructions portrayed a primitive, sprawling forelimb. Yale permitted seniors to spend a full year on a single research project as part of the Scholar of the House Program. I spent a year on dinosaur fore limbs and became convinced that *Triceratops* was as well designed for speed, fore and aft, as are the modern white rhinos (Bakker 1971, 1972a). In the years that followed at Harvard and Johns Hopkins Universities, I published quite a few restorations of dinosaurs trotting, galloping, and dancing. Greg Paul joined me at my lab in Baltimore in 1977 and absorbed many

of the heretical views. In turn, Greg has been very generous in sharing his restorations of dinosaur joint action and muscle anatomy with other artists.

In the 1960s and early 70s my first publications about a fast-paced triceratops (Bakker 1971) stirred up a tsunami of hostile reaction from the old guard. The most influential dinosaur expert of the past generation in North America was quoted in *Time* as saying that dinosaurs could not possibly gallop. It was not a matter of anatomy but of simple engineering constraints: five-ton animals cannot be designed to run fast. At this point I came face to face with the powerful bias of unbridled uniformitarianism. The argument is as follows: (1) The range of present adaptations is the perfect and complete standard of what type of adaptations could have evolved in the past. (2) Evolution is so fast and comprehensive in its action that modern-day species fill out all the possible adaptive roles completely and there are no adaptive limits left unexplored. (3) We cannot accept the idea that any extinct creature exceeded the limits of strength, speed, or agility found in living species. (4) A case in point: because the biggest animal that gallops today is a bull white rhino of about three metric tons body weight the inviolable upper limit to galloping animals is three tons. (5) A big bull *Triceratops* reached five or even ten metric tons, depending on the species. (6) Ergo, *Triceratops* could not possibly gallop because it far exceeded the upper galloping limit.

Everything I have learned about the fossil record persuades me that this extreme uniformitarian position is very wrong and misleading. Take the example of the elephant. The largest land mammal today is the bull African elephant, often reaching five metric tons. Is five metric tons the ultimate limit for an elephant? Certainly not. Several Pleistocene proboscideans—notably the imperial mammoth—exceeded the African elephant in both average and maximum size. The biggest cheetah today averages sixty kilos adult weight (Hanks 1979), but Plio-Pleistocene species grew to at least twice that weight, were taller than lions, and yet retained a cheetah-type of limb and body configuration. The biggest soaring seabird today is the wandering albatross, with a three-meter wingspread.

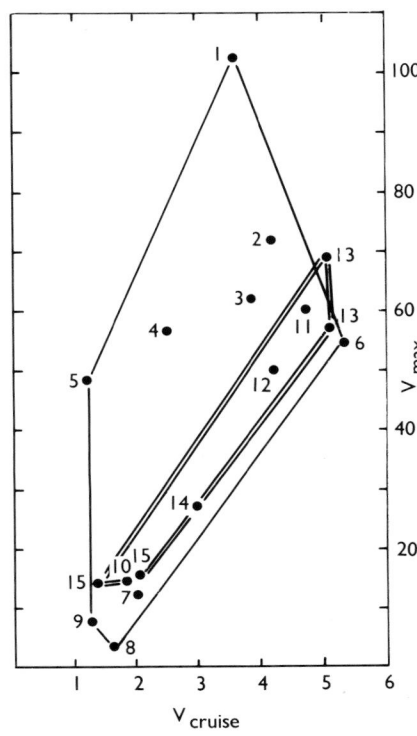

Figure 5. Cruising speed (calculated from trackways in the wild) and top speed. The single-line polygon is based on data for herbivores and omnivores; the double-line polygon, data for predators. Trackway data from Jaeger (1948) and Murie (1964); speed data from Bakker (1983).

Herbivores and omnivores

1 prongbuck
2 American elk
3 mule deer
4 moose
5 American bison
6 giraffe
7 Oregon ground squirrel
8 American porcupine
9 Eastern ground squirrel
10 Virginia opossum

Predators

11 red fox
12 brown hyena
13 coyote
14 badger
15 striped skunk

Figure 6. Footprint breadth, limb length, and speed in fossil species.

- ■ Permo-Carboniferous reptiles and amphibians
- ● cheirothere-type thecodonts
- ○ ornithopod dinosaurs
- t theropod dinosaurs
- d Triassic Therapsids
- r primitive Triassic diapsid reptiles (rotodactylids)
- s salamanders
- S sauropod dinosaurs
- M moas
- E elephants
- ★ other mammals
- A nodosaurid dinosaur

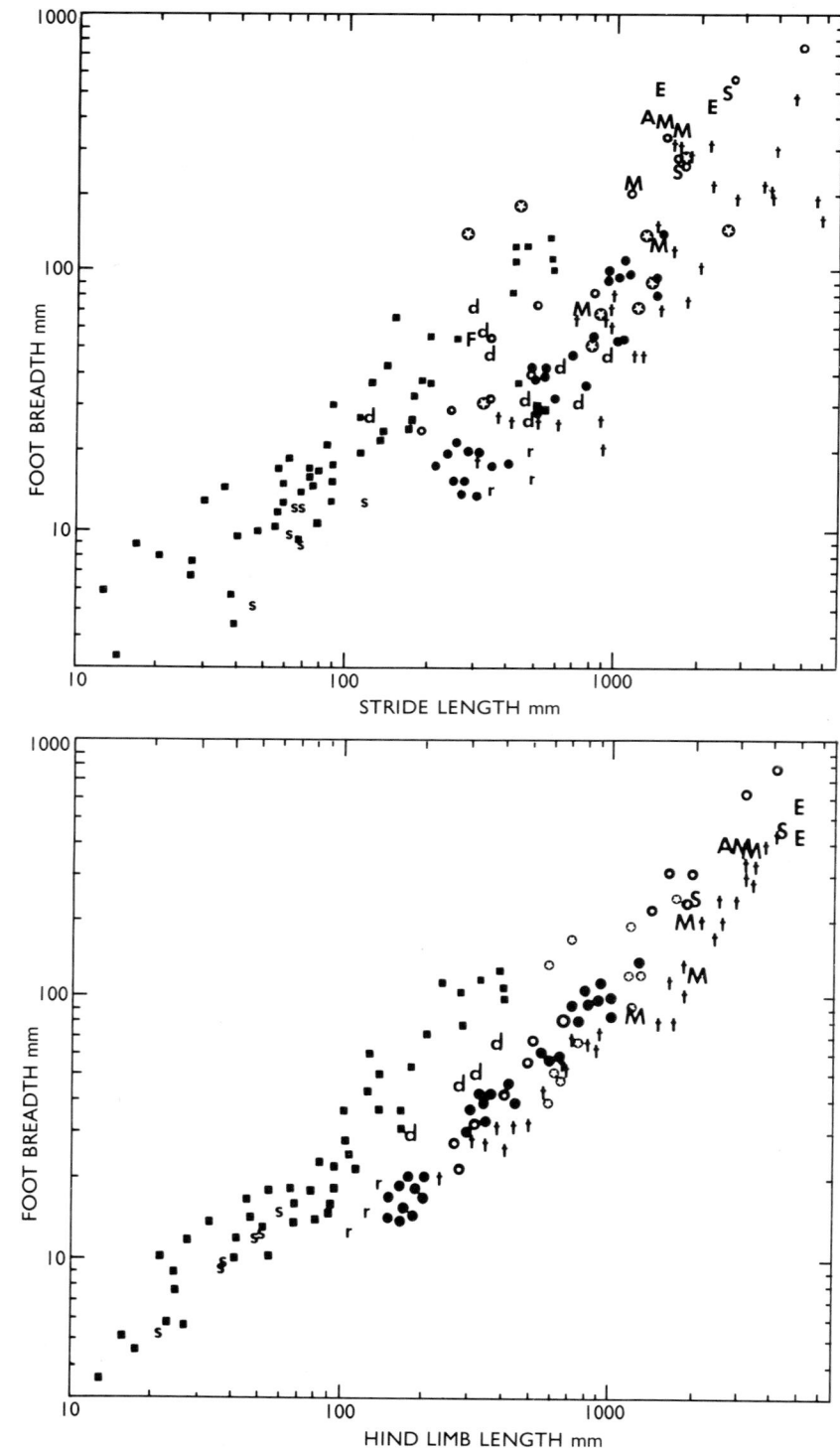

Pterosaurs of several species grew larger by a factor of two or three or even more.

These examples show that in the past the adaptive boundaries of extant species have been breached, sometimes in spectacular fashion. How can we be so sure that the upper weight limit of fast runners was not greater than three metric tons? The only way to interpret the function of extinct creatures, without the bias of the present, is to analyze the strength and speed of each joint with the basic principles of biophysics, muscle physiology, and joint mechanics. The key to accurate interpretation of a fossil species is to be prepared to be surprised; do not assume that all the ancient creatures and ecosystems fit neatly into the ecological typecasting of modern species.

In this article I will discuss how studies of fossil footprints and joint structure can lead to the conclusion that the big quadrupedal dinosaurs did indeed dance. I am under no delusions, however, that there is now a universal consensus about dinosaurs being entirely endothermic and endowed with as high a level of exercise metabolism as are rhinos (Bennett and Dalzell 1973). But at least the idea of hot-running dinosaurs is once again a very important and defensible line of thought, a vocal opposition to the Gilmorean mainstream of the last half century.

Fossil footprints are the only direct evidence left by the locomotor activity of individual dinosaurs (Fig. 3), and Alexander (1976) created quite a stir when he announced that he had an elegantly simple formula for calculating walking speed from tracks, using only hind-limb and stride length. Alexander's first calculations showed that brontosaurs and other big dinosaurs walked very slowly—only a few kilometers per hour—and some writers took these results as proof that all large dinosaurs were strictly limited to shuffling speeds (see Russell and Béland 1976; Currie and Sargeant 1979; Farlow 1981; Kool 1981). But if you go to a South African game park and survey the footprints left along stream beds and shores of water holes, as I did in 1976, you will see that most of the trackways left by lions and zebra were not made during runs at maximum top speed. Instead, most trackways of

extant mammal species seen in the wild record leisurely paces made during the slow, unhurried daily and seasonal routine: herbivores moving quietly as they feed; carnivores moving from one shade tree to another; predators and prey both going to and from watering places; longer walks that are part of seasonal migrations from one local habitat to another. Top-speed runs are very important in the evolution of limb structure, but maximum speed accounts for only a tiny fraction of the total footsteps taken by an individual animal during its lifetime. Fossil footprints should be viewed as the documentation of an average daily cruising speed, not of top speed. Over the last three years I have made a comprehensive survey of tracks made by both extinct and living species, to compare dinosaur speed

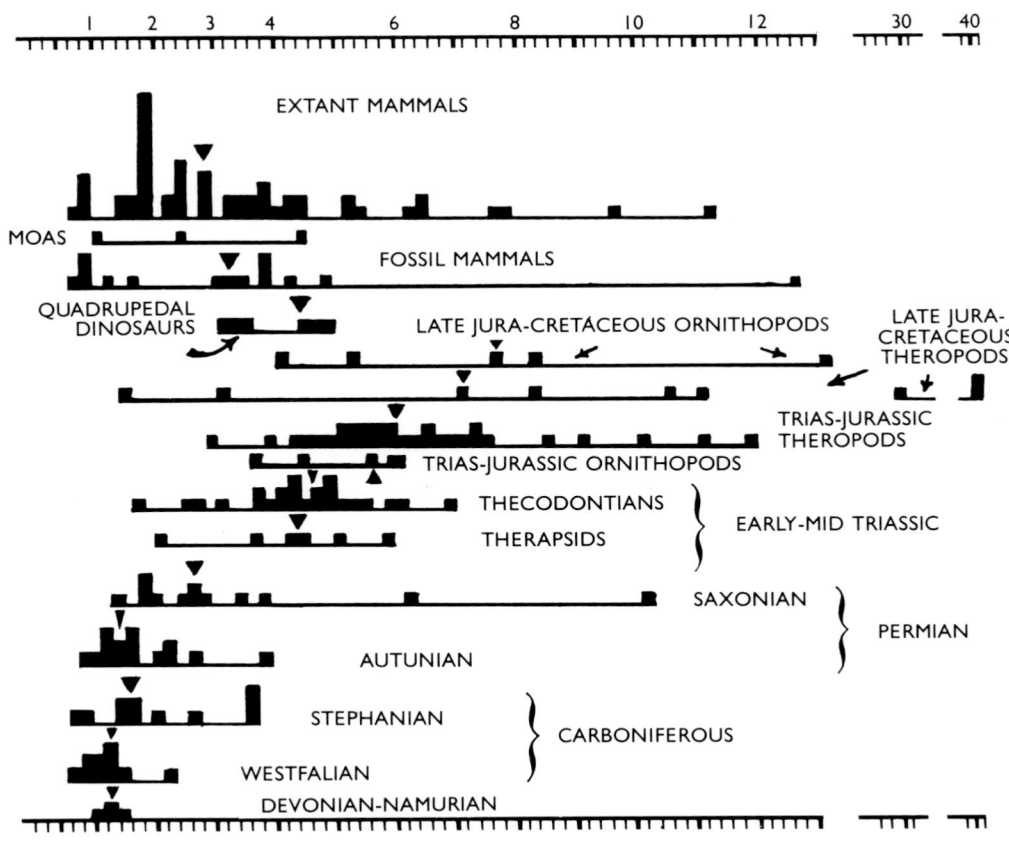

Figure 7. Frequency distribution of footprint-speeds for successive samples, from the Carboniferous to the age of mammals. Fifty percentiles marked by an inverted triangle.

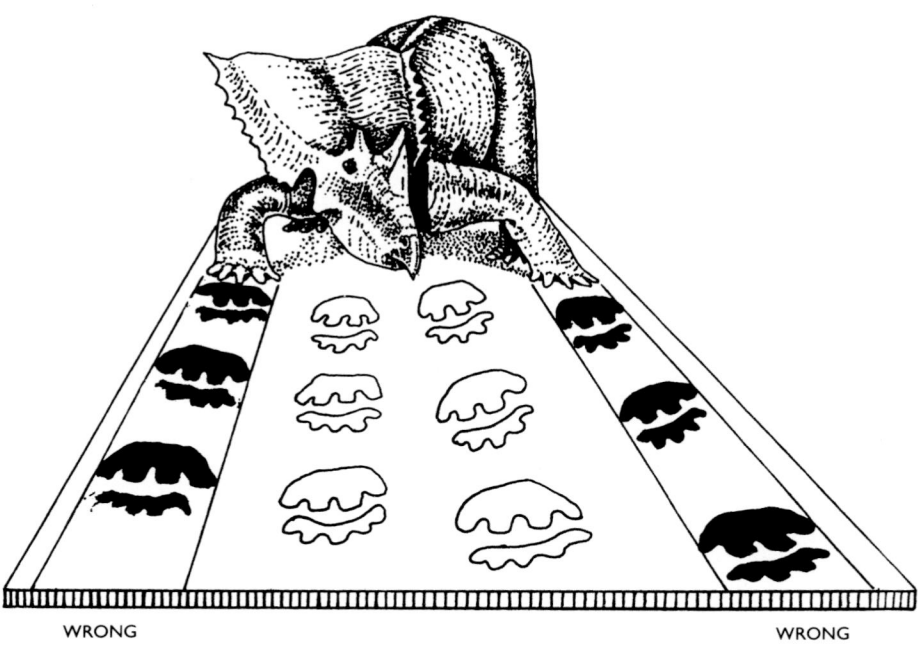

WRONG   WRONG

Figure 8. Some horned dinosaur reconstructions do not match the footprint pattern of quadrupedal dinosaurs. The sprawled-out reconstruction was used in the chasmosaur mount at the National Museum of Natural Sciences, National Museums of Canada.

CORRECT

with that of land vertebrates from the Carboniferous to the present.

I tested Alexander's formula with data from experiments where the actual speed of the animal was known from motion-picture analysis or tape-and-stopwatch recordings (Fig. 4). If the hind-limb length is known, the formula is reliable, as Alexander stated. Ninety-five percent of the predictions fell within 2½ times the actual speed, and the only serious error was the overestimation of the speed of a box turtle. I then used the formula to calculate the speed of extant species from tracks that had been diagrammed by the neoichnologists, especially Jaeger (1948) and Murie (1964). For some species there are data on both trackway speed and maximum speed, the speed measured when mammologists in jeeps chase animals over open terrain. The results of this survey (Fig. 5) showed that trackway speeds, on the average, were much lower than maximum speeds. The fifty percentile mark for the mammal trackway speed is only 3.7 kilometers per hour (see Sukhanov 1974; Bakker 1984).

I then calculated trackway speed for extinct species, using my own estimates of hind-limb length (Fig. 6). I found that short-legged Paleozoic species had limb lengths about 3 times the foot breadth across the metatarsals; longer-limbed Paleozoic types, such as the sphenacodonts, had limbs 4 times the foot breadth; advanced therapsids (mammallike reptiles) and cheirothere-type thecodonts, 5 to 7 times (larger species had relatively wider feet); ornithopod dinosaurs, 5.8 (duckbills) to 8 (fabrosaurs); sauropods, 4.8; nodosaurs, 4.2; Eocene tapirs, 10; bear dogs, 8; moas, 6 to 8; elephants, 7.8.

The completed survey (Fig. 7) shows that dinosaurs had cruising speeds as high or higher than that of mammals with comparable body size and feeding habits. Mammoths cruised at speeds no higher than that of nodosaurid and sauropod dinosaurs. Moa cruising speed was no higher than that of duck-billed dinosaurs. Theropod dinosaurs cruised at higher speeds than that of modern mammals. Therefore we can conclude that the average everyday pace of dinosaurian locomotor activity was as quick as or quicker than that of the present-day Mammalia.

In addition, the footprint survey showed that the primitive reptiles and amphibians of the Paleozoic cruised at speeds far slower than that of dinosaurs and mammals. Life in the Carboniferous and early Permian must have been played out at a toad's pace. A sudden and dramatic increase in average cruising speed coincided with the rise of the advanced mammallike reptiles (therapsids) and thecodonts at the beginning of the Triassic. And the Triassic acceleration of cruising speed coincides precisely with change in bone histology, documented by Ricqlès (1974), indicating much faster ontogenetic growth rates in both mammallike reptiles and thecodonts. One more bioenergetic indicator changes at the same time: predator-prey ratios. In the early Permian (Bakker 1975) big predators—sphenacodont pelycosaurs like *Dimetrodon*—were superabundant, generally no less than thirty-five percent as common as their big prey. But Triassic predators usually are no more than ten percent as common as their big prey, indicating a sharp increase in the average daily food consumption by the flesheaters. Dinosaur and fossil-mammal ratios are on average lower still; most samples are in the one to seven percent range.

All three indicators—trackway speed, bone histology, and predator-prey ratios—converge in showing that the entire energetic style of the land-vertebrate ecosystem accelerated during the Triassic, first as the primitive tetrapod world was replaced by the therapsid-thecodont coalition in the early Triassic and then in the second transition as the thecodont-therapsids gave way before the Dinosauria at the end of the period.

Sometimes paleontological thought processes are perverted by what I call "pretzel logic." Gilmore (1915, 1920) restored horned dinosaur fore limbs with sprawled-out elbows because, he argued, the olecranon was large and projected far beyond the shaft of the ulna, and therefore the elbow had to be bent. A bent elbow does not, however, necessitate an out-bowed elbow. In modern rhinos the olecranon is strong and the elbow is bent, but the flexure is mostly in a fore-to-aft plane; the elbow is everted only enough to clear the ribcage when the limb is swung backward during locomotion. All large galloping mammals today have projecting olecrana and strong elbow flexure in the fore-to-aft plane—horses, pigs, tapirs, giraffes, cape buffalo (Bakker 1971). When Lull (1933) mounted the fine skeleton of the horned dinosaur *Centrosaurus* at Yale, he claimed that he used as a guide the footprints of a large ornithischian from the Peace River Canyon in British Columbia, Canada (Sternberg 1921). Lull's mount has a toadlike front carriage with widely sprawled fore limbs. Did the Peace River footprints agree with Lull's mount? Absolutely not. The Peace River tracks (probably made by a nodosaur, not a horned dinosaur, but the basic limb anatomy is similar) show a very narrow forefoot trackway, like that of a rhino. Lull had accepted the then-current bias about dinosaur fore limbs, and thus the Yale professor forced the centrosaur into a sprawl even though this posture was thoroughly contraindicated by the footprint evidence. The veteran collector Charles M. Sternberg made the same error of fore-limb posture in mounting the chasmosaur horned dinosaur group at the National Museum of Canada (Fig. 8). All quadrupedal dinosaur trackways show that right and left forepaws were placed down under the body very close to the midline during locomotion.

The biomechanics and soft-tissue anatomy at the shoulder presents, I believe, an unambiguous case for rhinolike forequarters in the big dinosaurian quadrupeds. Extant crocodilians have a semi-erect fore limb that moves very much like the classic Gilmorean restoration of the horned dinosaur fore limb. The shoulder socket (glenoid) of a crocodilian (Fig. 9a) is not a socket but rather a joint surface shaped like a riding saddle tipped up on end, concave top to bottom, and convex side to side. The head of the humerus (Fig. 10a) has a bulbous articular surface. The contact between humerus and glenoid, as seen in a section cut through the joint (Fig. 11a), is very limited and poorly braced by bone because the convex humeral head abuts the convex glenoid surface. This loose structure permits the humerus to rotate about its long axis and swing outward as well as fore and aft. The shoulder ligaments of crocodilians are very strong, since they must brace the joint, and the joint capsule is very spacious and extends far beyond the glenoid onto

Figure 9. Crocodilian shoulder-joint surfaces versus those of horned dinosaurs. a. Outer view of the right scapulocoracoid of an adult American crocodile, with a map of the attachment sites of the muscles, joint capsule, and ligaments. The view is directly into the shoulder socket (glenoid). The articular surface of the glenoid is convex fore to aft and so is not really a socket. The joint capsule is very spacious and extends far forward onto the surface of the scapulocoracoid beyond the limits of the glenoid articulation. b. The same view, looking directly into the glenoid of the right scapulocoracoid of *Triceratops* (USNM 4800). The glenoid is a true socket, convex fore to aft and rimmed completely around by a low ridge of bone. There is no depression for the joint capsule in front of the glenoid. Abbreviations: bi, biceps; cap, joint capsule; clav delt, clavicular deltoid; co br, coracobrachialis; cos, costocoracoideus; lev scap, levator scapulae; lig, the two long shoulder ligaments; scap delt, scapular deltoid; scap co lig, scapulocoracoid ligament and coracoid triceps; scap hum post, scapulohumeralis posterior; tri, scapular triceps.

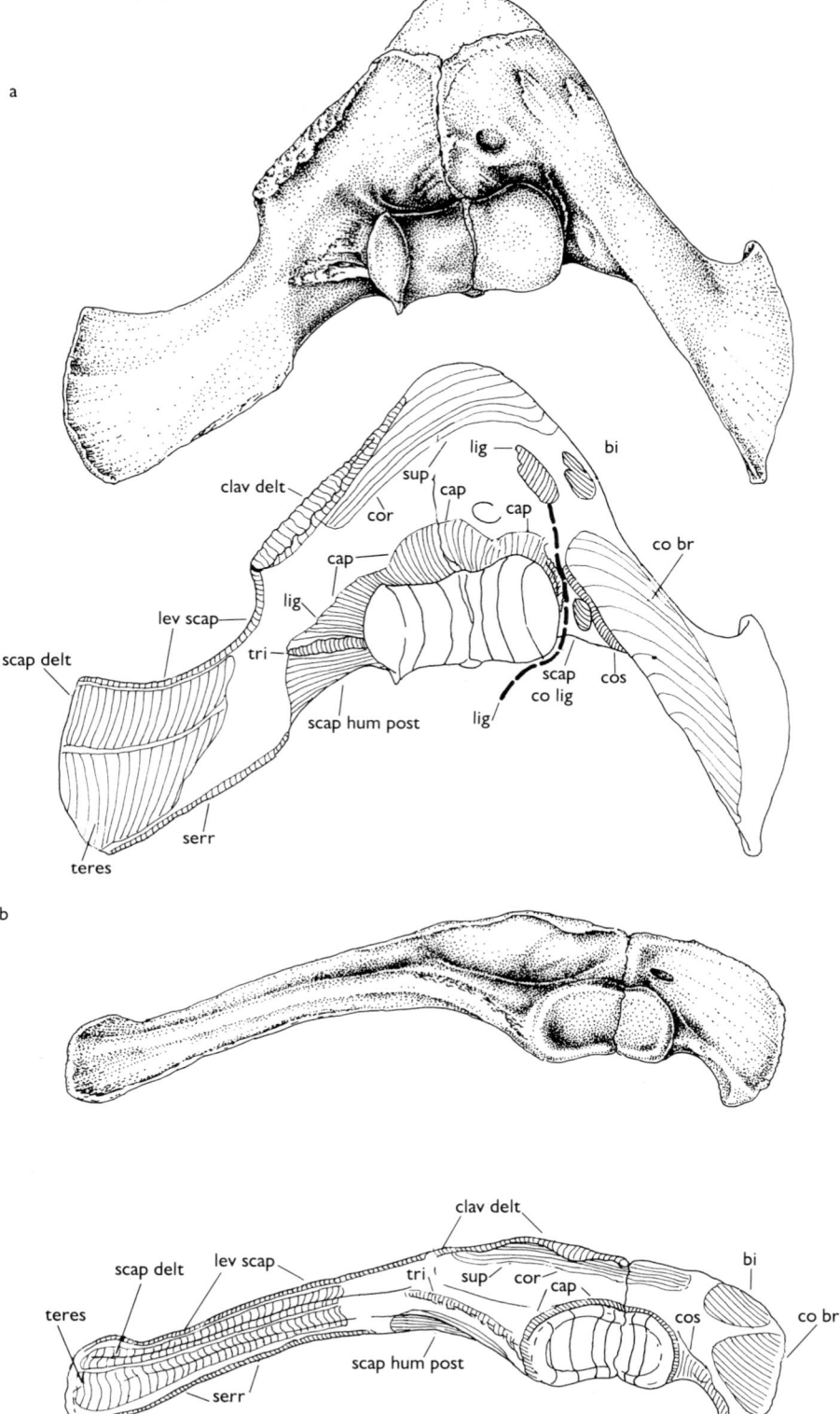

the outer surface of the shoulder blade (scapulo-coracoid). The bony anatomy records faithfully the development of ligaments and capsule; the upper ligament leaves a strong scar on the scapula, and the lower ligament travels through a deep furrow below the glenoid on the coracoid and leaves a raised scar near the anterior border of that bone. Where the joint capsule extends over the scapulo-coracoid plate, the bony surface is depressed and lacks dense periosteal bone; the anterior margin of the capsule is marked clearly by a low, rounded rim of bone.

If horned dinosaurs had elbows bowed out like those of crocodilians, then the shoulder anatomy should agree with the crocodilian condition. It does not. *Triceratops* has a glenoid (Fig. 9b) that is a true socket, a double concavity, concave along its long axis top to bottom and along the short axis side to side. The head of the humerus (Fig. 10b) has less of the subspherical shape seen in crocodilians and is more cylindrical like that of a rhino. Thus the gentle convexity of the humeral head fits snugly into the gentle concavity of the glenoid, as seen in a section though the joint (Fig. 11b). The *Tricera-tops* joint capsule clearly did not extend forward onto the scapulocoracoid plate as it does in crocs because the dinosaur lacks any capsular depression in front of the shoulder socket. Instead of a depression, there is a raised ridge of bone running from the glenoid forward along the scapulocora-coid suture. This ridge would reinforce the glenoid against thrusts of the humerus delivered from directly aft; in crocodilians the thrust is from behind and from the side, so that the ridge is absent, but there is a swelling on the inside surface of the scapulo-coracoid to brace against the thrust component delivered from outside. In horned dinosaurs there is not the slightest hint of scars for big-shoulder ligaments and there is no subglenoid trough for the lower ligament to travel through. The only scarring for the capsule is found along the margins of the glenoid rim, and so the capsule must have been tight fitting as it is in big fully erect mammals today.

All stegosaurs, horned dinosaurs, ankylo-saurs, and sauropods have shoulder-joint anatomy similar to that of *Triceratops*. Fore-limb function

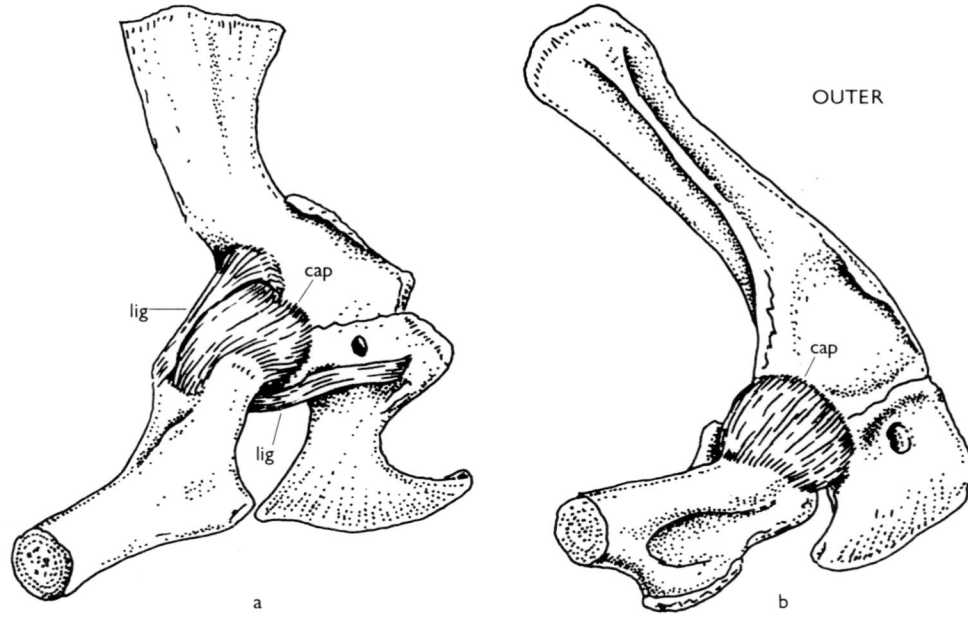

OUTER

Figure 10. The shoulder-joint capsules of an American crocodile (a) and a *Tricera-tops* (b).

in all must have been fully erect, although the degree of backward flexure of the elbow would vary: strong in horned dinosaurs and ankylosaurids, moderate in nodosaurids and stegosaurs, weak in sauropods (Bakker 1975). Ornithopod glenoids retain more primitive characters and so do thero-pods. There is a remnant of the capsular depression in front of the glenoid, and the anterior gle-noid rim has a large gap opposite the capsular depression. More freedom of movement at the shoulder must have been present than was usual in other dinosaurians.

One stumbling block to accepting the idea of a galloping *Triceratops* (Bennett and Dalzell 1973) is that because the fore limb is so much shorter than the hind it would seem that at full speed the rear

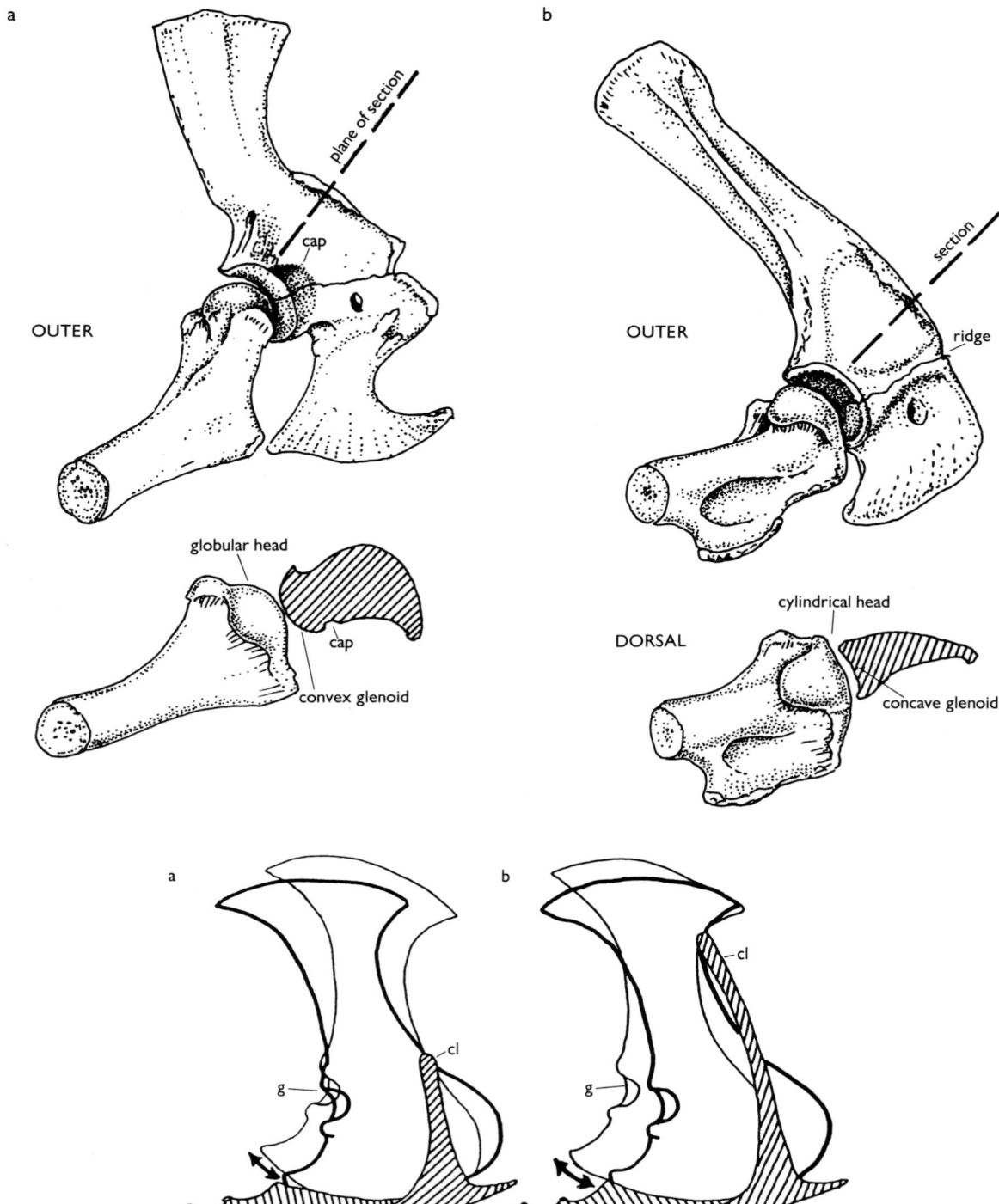

Figure 11. The shoulder-joint geometry of an American crocodile (a) and *Triceratops* (b). Shown are an outer and dorsal view of the shoulder apparatus. The lower two diagrams show a dorsal view of a section cut through the scapula as indicated by the dashed line in the upper two diagrams. In the crocodile, the glenoid is convex in this section and the humeral head is bulbous; but in the *Triceratops* the glenoid is concave and the humeral head is cylindrical.

Figure 12. How modern lizards increase the usefulness of the swinging shoulder blade. a. The primitive reptilian condition, where the clavicle articulates with the scapula at a point only slightly above the level of the glenoid. b. The typical modern lizard condition, where the clavicle-scapula pivot is elevated far up on the anterior scapular edge. Dark outline shows the right scapulocoracoid swung forward; light outline shows the left scapulocoracoid swung aft. Clavicle is diagonally hatched; sternum is vertically hatched. Abbreviations: cl, clavicle; g, glenoid; s, sternum.

BAKKER

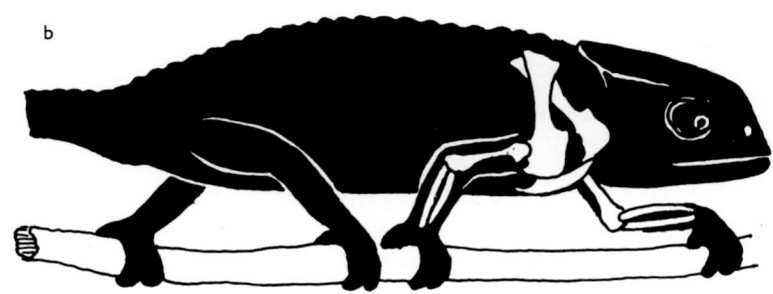

Figure 13. How dinosaurs swung their shoulder blades. a. Modern horse in full gallop, showing the fore and aft swing of the scapula. b. A modern chameleon, drawn from dissection, showing the maximum fore and aft swing of the scapulocoracoid. c. The horned dinosaur *Centrosaurus* showing shoulder swing. d–f. Views of the chest of a centrosaur: d. Ventral view, showing the left scapulocoracoid swung forward, the right scapulocoracoid swung aft. e. Right lateral view. f. Right lateral view of inner surfaces of the left ribs and left scapulocoracoid, showing the sternocoracoideus muscle that powers the backswing of the shoulder blade. Abbreviations: S, cartilaginous anterior sternum; X, bony xiphisternal plates.

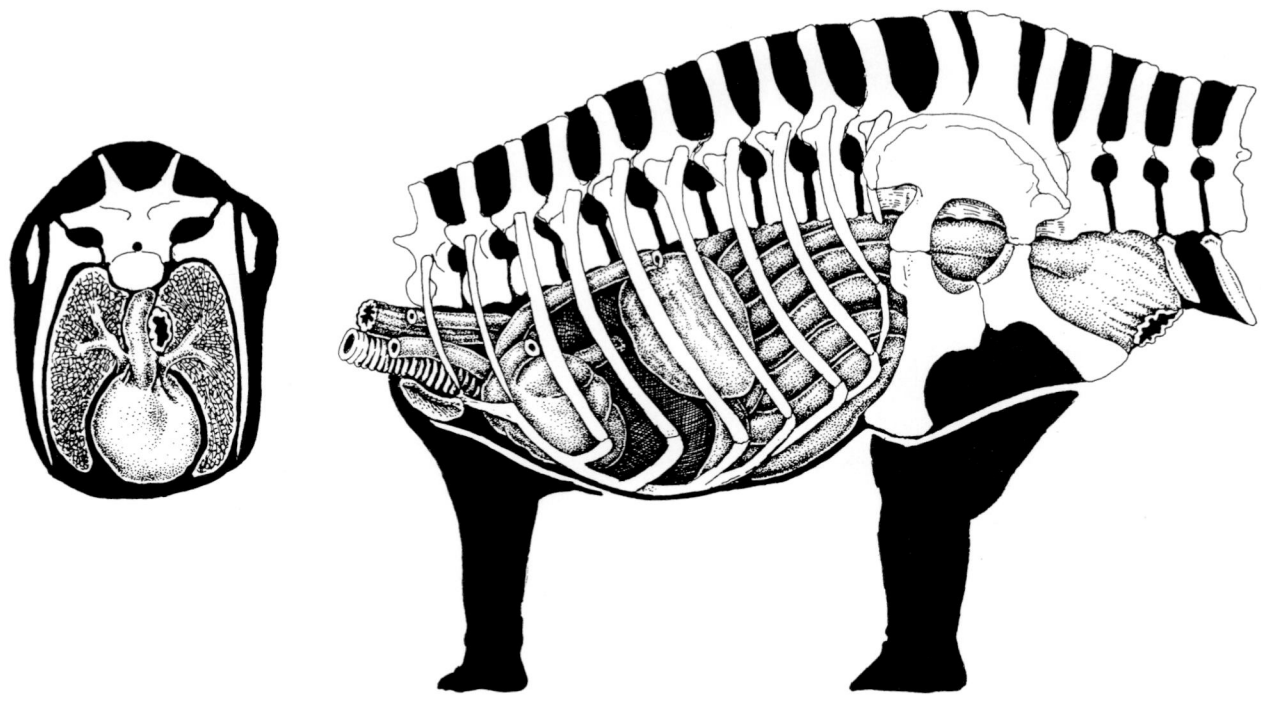

Figure 14. The heart and viscera of *Bron-tosaurus excelsus*. Outer view of viscera (left lung removed to show the heart) and vertical cross-section through the heart and lungs at the third dorsal vertebra. Large oval body aft of the heart is the giz-zard. Ribcage drawn from YPM 1887 and FMNH 7163.

end would travel fifty percent faster than the front end and the beast would either spin in circles or tumble over itself, hips climbing over head. This maladaptive scenario presumes that the fore-limb stroke begins at the shoulder socket and that the shoulder blade remains immovably fixed to the thorax. Extant large ungulate mammals and car-nivores add an extra segment to their fore-limb stroke by swinging the shoulder blade across the flank. Species with relatively long shoulder blades, like rhinos, can thereby increase the functional limb length by twenty to twenty-five percent. When I was working on dinosaur fore limbs at Yale, I ex-perimented with movement cycles that included fore-to-aft swinging of the scapulocoracoid. *Tricer-atops* would have even more to gain from scapular

swing than does a rhino, because all horned dino-saurs have exceptionally long scapular blades ex-tending up and backward from the glenoid, two-thirds the way to the hips. Petersen's work on cha-meleon fore limbs finally convinced me that dino-saurian scapulocoracoids did swing (Bakker 1975). Petersen (1972) showed that chameleon scapular blades swing over wide arcs during locomotion, more so than in more typical lizards.

We can recognize three stages in the evolu-tion of shoulder-blade swing: the primitive tuatara stage, typical lizard stage, and chameleon-dinosaur stage. In very primitive land reptiles the clavicle is a stout brace running up from the chest midline to the front edge of the scapula opposite the glenoid (this condition is retained today by the tuatara). In

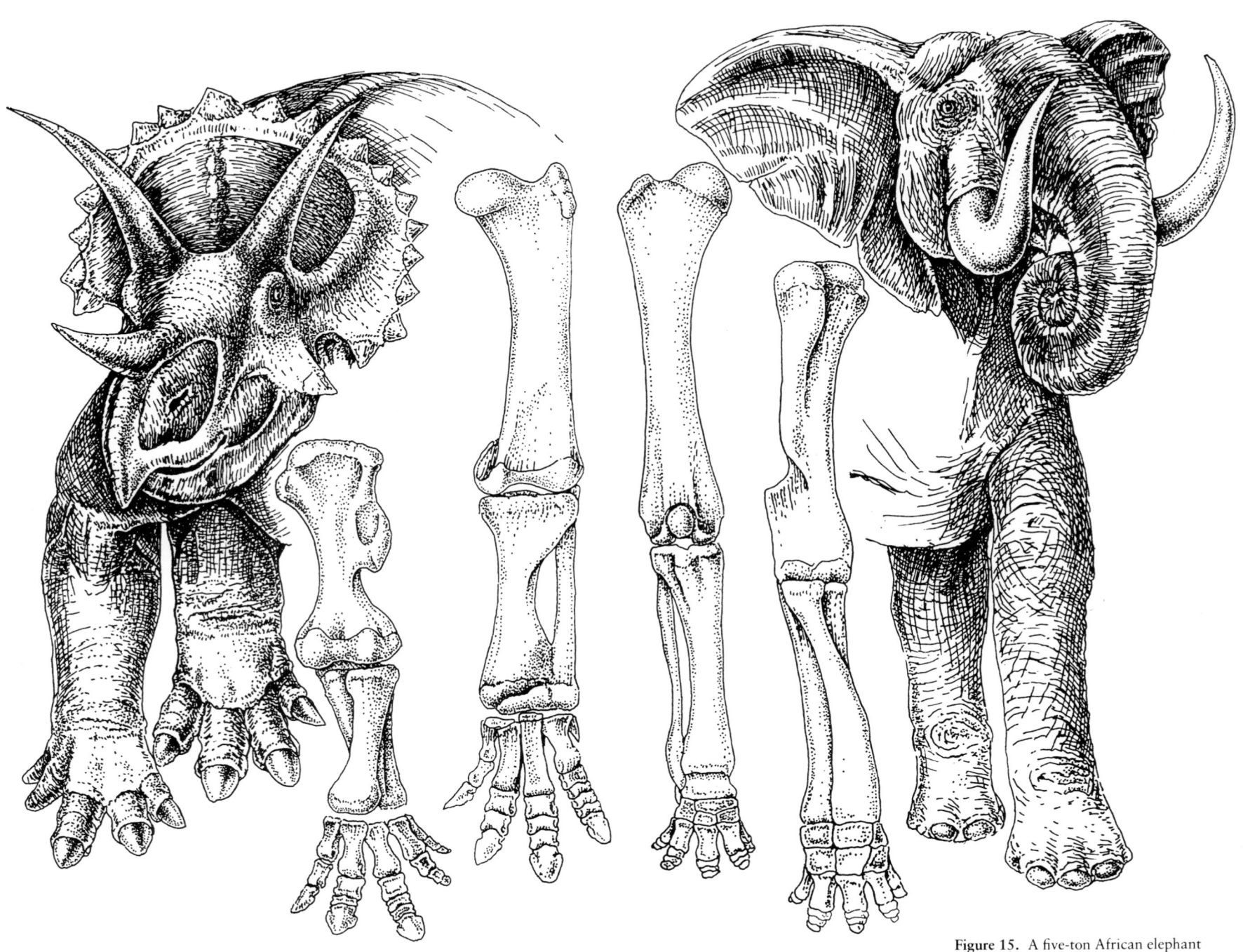

Figure 15. A five-ton African elephant and a five-ton *Triceratops* drawn to the same scale to show the girth of the limbs and length of the limb segments.

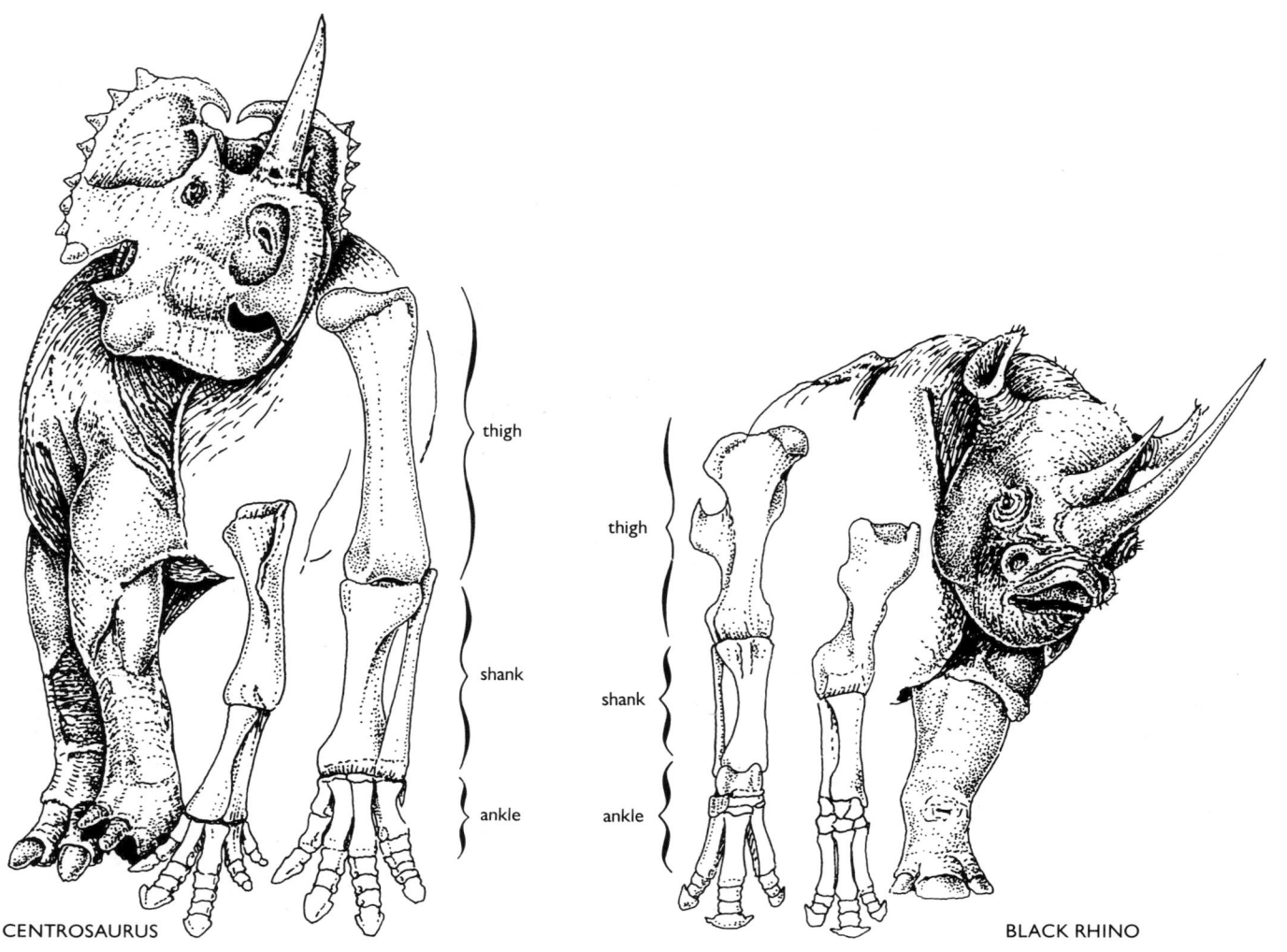

thigh

shank

ankle

thigh

shank

ankle

CENTROSAURUS

BLACK RHINO

Figure 16. A two-ton black rhino and a two-ton centrosaur drawn to the same scale. Note that the total foot length, from mid-astragulus to hoof tip, is greater in the centrosaur.

this primitive state the lower edge of the coracoid can slide a bit in a groove in the sternum, but the short clavicle prevents this movement from contributing much to the fore-and-aft stroke of the glenoid (Fig. 12a). Typical lizards increase the fore-and-aft swing of the glenoid by raising the joint between clavicle and scapula far above the glenoid, to a point near the upper corner of the scapular blade (Fig. 12b). Chameleons eliminate the clavicular brace entirely, so that the elongated, straplike scapular blade has free play over the chest (Fig. 13). The shape of the chameleon chest is strongly modified to accentuate the scapular swing. Instead of being wide side to side and depressed top to bottom as in many terrestrial lizards the chameleon chest is very deep and narrow, like that of a horse.

The big quadrupedal dinosaurs all have an

exceedingly long and narrow scapular blade, the clavicle is reduced to a rudimentary splint or absent entirely, and the chest is relatively deep and slab sided (Fig. 13). The posterior body cavity in these quadrupeds is usually wide and capacious, as indicated by the strong outward curvature of the posterior dorsal ribs, but the first four or five dorsal ribs are nearly always relatively straight and extend downward vertically from the rib heads. Compared to the body bulk, the scapulocoracoid of stegosaurs, horned dinosaurs, ankylosaurs, and sauropods is much, much larger than that of chameleons or any other lizard or crocodilians. The hypertrophy of the shoulder blade can be interpreted as evidence of an evolutionary trend to amplify the role of shoulder swinging. When the length of the scapula is added to the total fore limb in *Triceratops*,

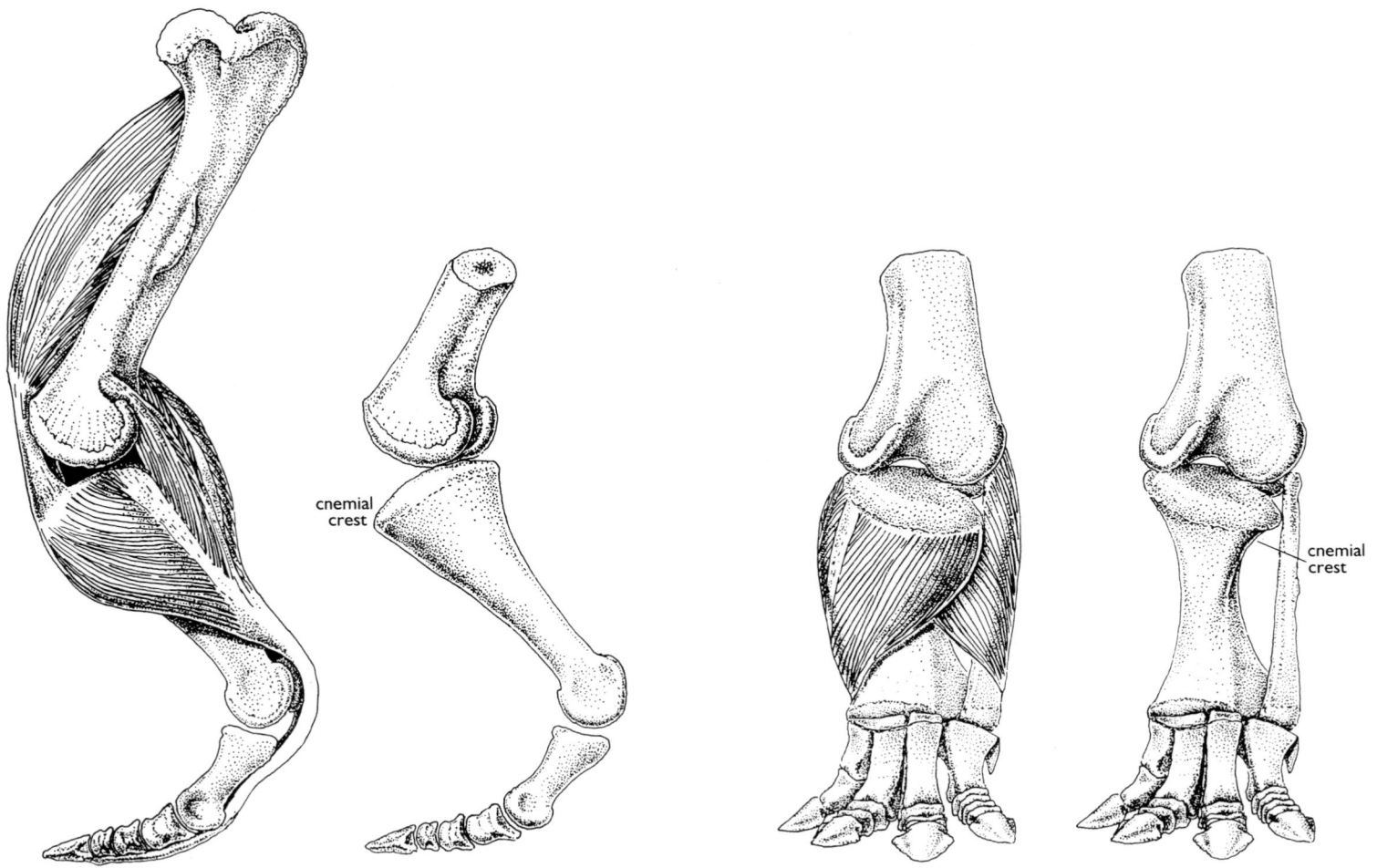

the length of the combined moving segments is only slightly less than that of the hind limb.

Deep chests in quadrupedal dinosaurs offer another insight into dinosaur locomotion. Extant lizards have on average much smaller hearts than do the active terrestrial Mammalia, such as canids, horses, rhinos, and the artiodactyl ungulates (Bakker 1972b). The large hearts of the mammals reflect their bioenergetic economy, which includes prolonged periods of high, sustained, aerobic exercise (Bartholomew and Tucker 1964). By contrast all living reptiles and amphibians have only a very modest capacity for aerobic exercise (and some very primitive mammals are similarly limited; a case in point is the common Virginia opossum).

Fortunately for the paleophysiologist the an-

terior thoracic anatomy records important parameters of heart size and aerobic scope. The heart and its surrounding tissue fit quite snugly inside the arc of the first thoracic ribs, and the third rib usually spans the maximum girth of the pericardial cavity. The active mammalian carnivores and ungulates have much deeper anterior thoracic chambers than do lizards. Chameleon thoraxes are deep in the posterior part but shallow in the forward chamber because the heart is relatively very small. If the big dinosaurs were truly as slow footed in all their behavior as the Gilmorean paradigm preaches, then dinosaur thoraxes should be shallow. In fact, however, the third and fourth dorsal ribs in most large dinosaurs are very long and define a capacious cardiac compartment (Fig. 14). Therefore, the capacity for sustained, aerobic exercise among the Di-

Figure 17. The calf muscles of a *Triceratops*.

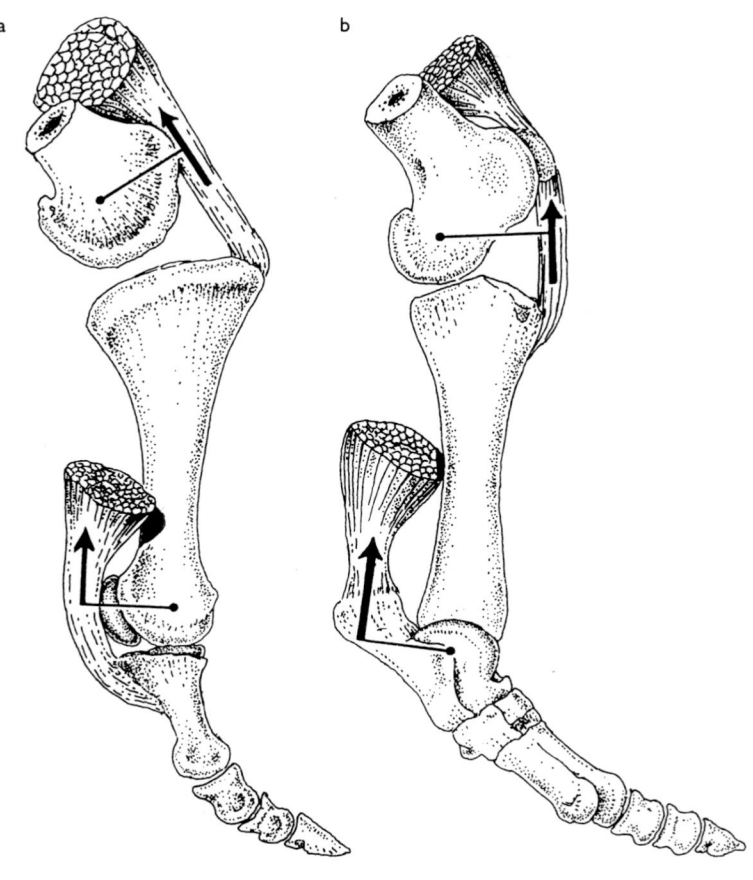

muscle action is to realign the forces incurred during locomotion so that the net compression is directed along the long axes of the limb bones (Basmajian 1964). The maximum load a limb bone can resist is largely dependent on the minimum shaft cross-section. A medium-size adult *Triceratops* had a body weight (calculated from clay scale models) of about five metric tons, equal to that of a large bull African elephant (the largest elephants and *Triceratops* reached twice this weight; Table 1). The circumference of the humerus is about equal in the *Triceratops* and elephant (Fig. 15), but the dinosaur femur is much thicker. The maximum thrust from the hind leg, therefore, must have been significantly larger. The fastest gait of African elephants is a running walk at about thirty kilometers per hour; the dinosaur should have been faster if simple limb-shaft strength was the limiting factor.

A subadult of the smaller horned dinosaur *Centrosaurus* would weigh about two metric tons, equal to that of a bull black rhino; the dinosaur limbs, especially the hind limbs, are much thicker (Fig. 16). The black rhino can gallop at forty-five kilometers per hour; the centrosaur should have been faster if judged by limb-shaft strength.

Any sort of fast gait requires a suspended phase when all four feet are off the ground and the body mass is propelled upward and forward by the limb thrust. All modern large runners capable of a suspended phase—fast mammals and giant ground birds—have very powerful knee extensor muscles that insert onto strongly developed crests on the tibia (cnemial crests) (Muybridge [1887] 1957; Sukhanov 1974). Elephants never get all four limbs off the ground, and the elephantine knee extensors and cnemial crests are very weak compared to those of a rhino.

If big dinosaurs were gallopers, then their knee extensor apparatus must have exceeded the scale of development seen in elephants. The cnemial crests in horned dinosaurs are indeed immense compared to those of elephants of the same size and exceed those even of rhinos of the same weight. The leverage of the common knee extensor tendon is fifty percent or more, greater in a centrosaurid horned dinosaur than in a black rhino of the same body mass (Table 1); a big *Triceratops* had nearly

Figure 18. The arrangement of the knee extensor and ankle flexor tendons in a five-ton *Triceratops* (a) and a three-ton white rhino (b). Leverage of the tendons is given in a light solid line; the line of pull of calf and knee extensor muscles is shown by heavy arrows. The shanks are drawn to the same length (the dinosaur has a longer shank relative to its body size).

nosauria may have been equal to, or superior to, that of the large Carnivora and hoofed Mammalia.

The arguments I have just summarized present a strong case that the quadrupedal dinosaurs had fully erect posture fore and aft and were well equipped for long swings of the powerful scapular blades; dinosaur aerobic capacity may well have been very high. Returning to the problem of uniformitarianism, I would ask: Were elephant-sized dinosaurs capable of much faster locomotion than present-day elephants? If the big quadrupeds were in fact much faster than modern elephants of the same weight, then dinosaurian limbs should be stronger and muscle mechanics more powerful. Experiments in limb muscle physiology during the last two decades have shown that one key function of

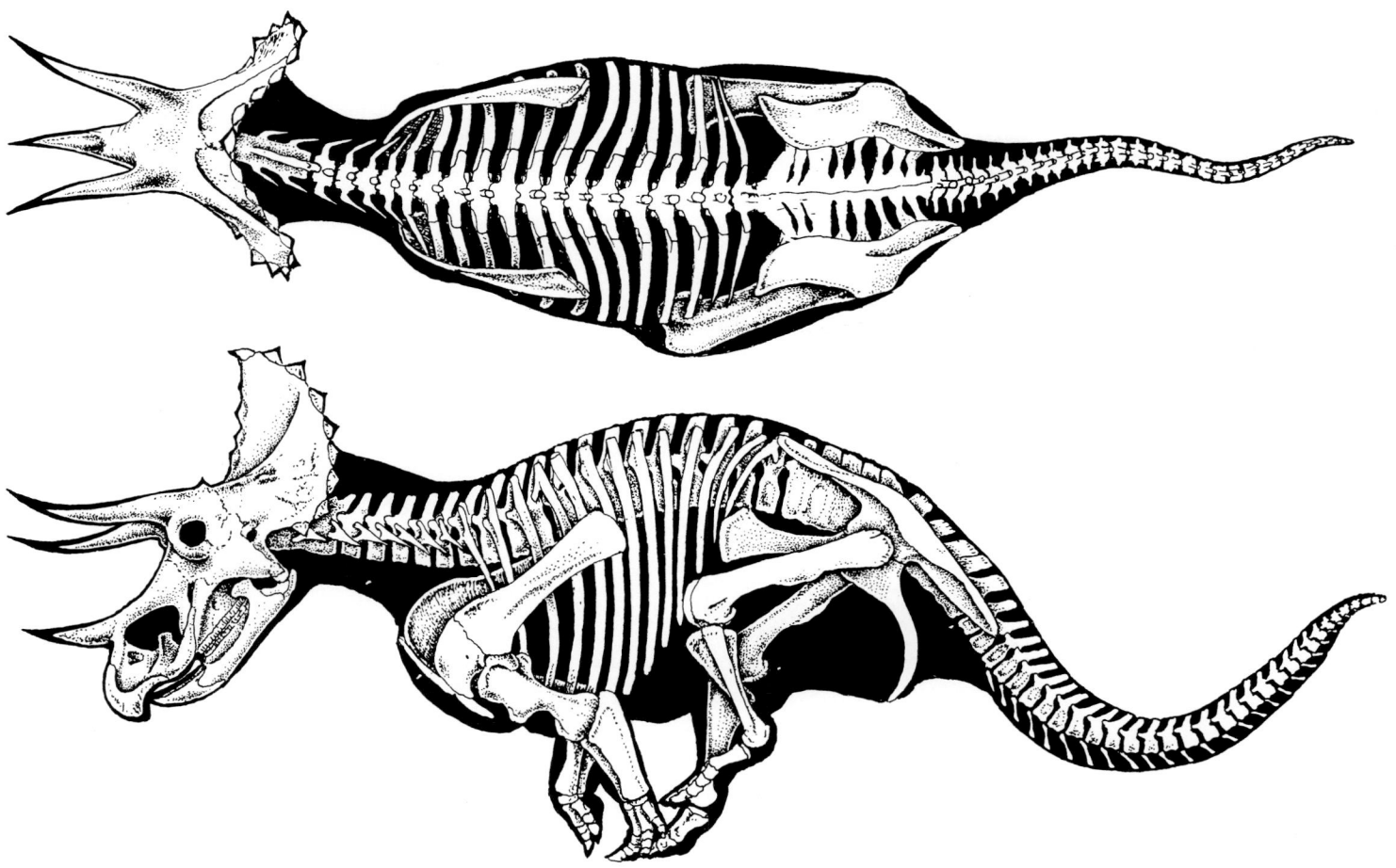

twice the extensor leverage of a bull African elephant (Fig. 17). Even stegosaurs and nodosaurs have much larger cnemial crests than either rhinos or elephants in the same weight class. The locomotor thrust at the knee in all these dinosaurs must have been far superior to that of all the multiton mammals today, both gallopers and walkers.

Dinosaurian knees have another property that gives evidence for exceptional hind-limb thrusts—the attachment site for the calf and foot flexor muscles is relatively gigantic compared to that of elephants and other nongallopers. In most dinosaurs, sauropods excepted, the cnemial crest is very birdlike and has a spacious area for the origin of the calf muscles on the inner side (gastrocnemius) and foot flexors on the outer side (peroneus longus). Galloping in a heavy animal requires a

short, very strong backward flexure of the foot at the very end of the stroke, and the pedal thrust of stegosaurs, ankylosaurs, and horned dinosaurs must have been much stronger than that of rhinos or elephants of the same bulk. Even sauropods, who have small cnemial crests by dinosaur standards, have larger muscle attachment sites than do elephants of the same size class.

Gilmore (1915) restored the calves of stegosaurs and other ornithischians and sauropods as skinny and emaciated. In fact, stegosaurs must have had bulging calf muscles like that of a short-legged version of an ostrich, and even sauropods must have had well-endowed calves.

The ankle apparatus of dinosaurs has been criticized as lacking the leverage present in big mammals, but this objection too can be shown to

Figure 19. A five-ton *Triceratops* in full gallop.

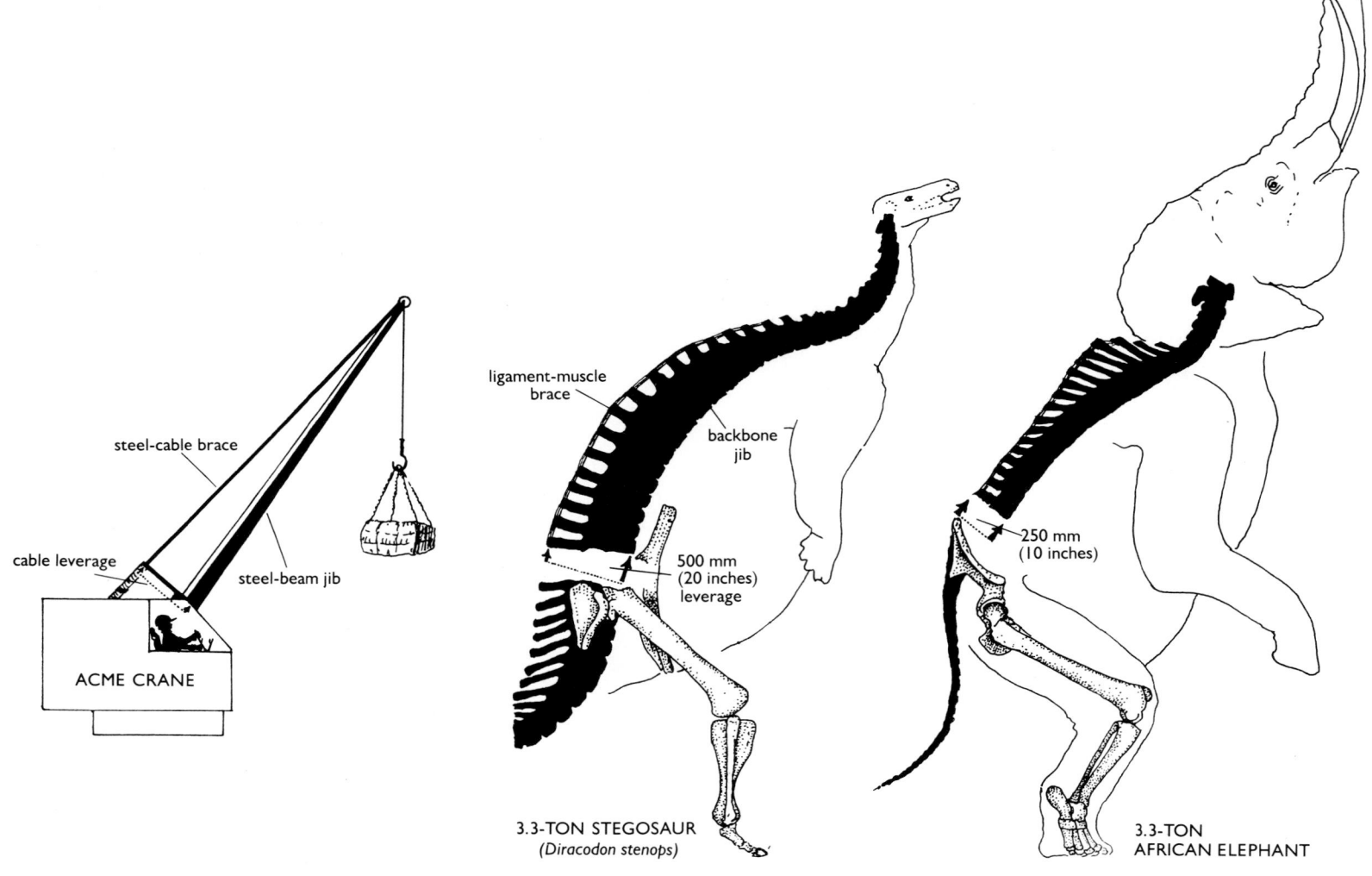

steel-cable brace

cable leverage

steel-beam jib

ACME CRANE

ligament-muscle brace

backbone jib

500 mm (20 inches) leverage

3.3-TON STEGOSAUR
(Diracodon stenops)

250 mm (10 inches)

3.3-TON AFRICAN ELEPHANT

Figure 20. Body-raising leverage in a stegosaur (USNM 4934) and an elephant, drawn to the same scale. The interspinous ligaments and muscles act like the steel-cable brace of a crane; the column of vertebral bodies acts like the jib of the crane.

be unfounded (see Fig. 11). Dinosaurs do not have a projecting heel bone (calcaneal tuber) that in mammals sticks up and backward to receive the insertion of the calf muscle tendon. Dinosaurs did have a birdlike ankle device that provided as much leverage as a calcaneal tuber. Birds have a pulley-like pad of cartilage that slides along a groove at the posterior surface of the lower end of the shank. The common calf tendon passes over the cartilage pad, and the peroneal muscle passes through the pad, and both muscles enjoy a notable increase in leverage with this arrangement. One great advantage of the pulley-pad system is that the leverage of the muscles remains constant as the foot flexes at the ankle. The mammalian heelbone rotates up and toward the shank as the ankle flexes, and hence the leverage of the calf tendon decreases as the foot

flexes backward, a distinct disadvantage since the greatest power is needed at the end of the stroke.

Triceratops and all other dinosaurs clearly had an ankle pulley pad, because the telltale bony architecture shows the presence of the avian ankle system (Fig. 18). There is a distinctive low groove in the back surface of the lower end of the tibia, and the inner and outer edges of the groove usually are roughened where the guiding ligament sheath would attach. The leverage at the calf tendon in *Triceratops* and other big quadrupedal dinosaurs would have been twice that of an elephant of the same weight and thirty percent greater than that of a white rhino scaled up to the same body size.

A final traditional misconception about dinosaur ankles is that the long bones of the ankle (the metatarsus) were too short for fast locomo-

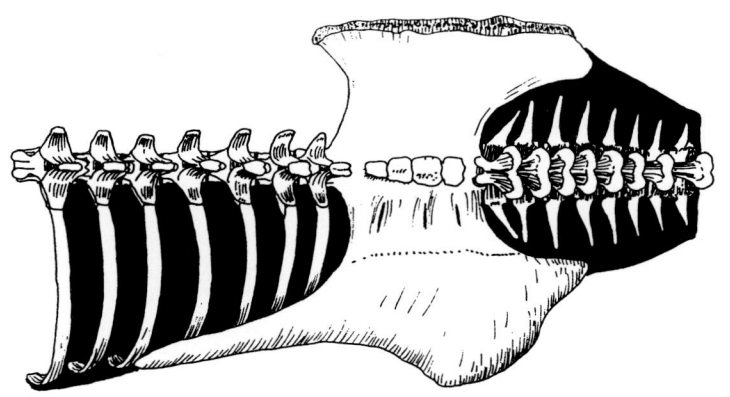

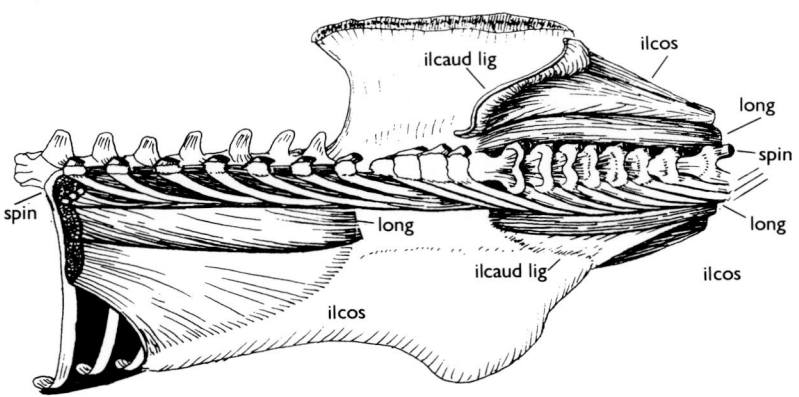

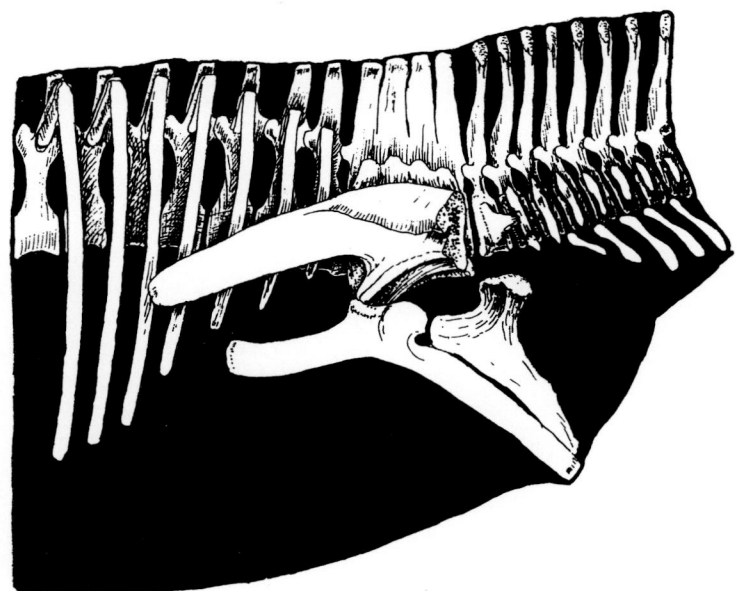

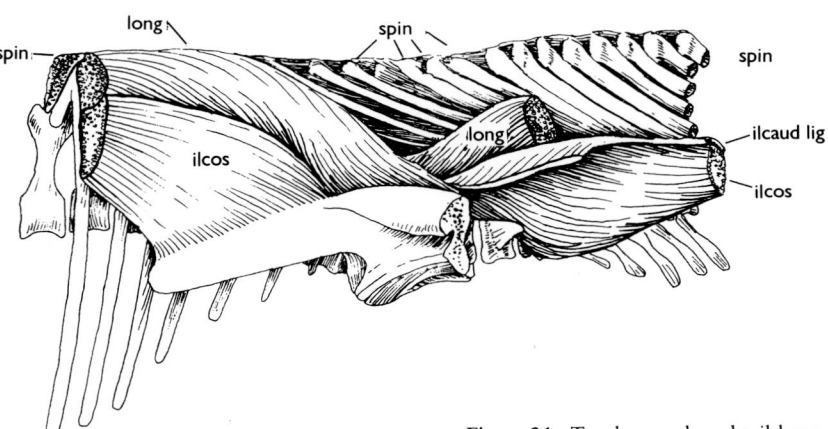

Figure 21. Trunk, sacral, and tail-base muscles of *Stegosaurus ungulatus*. Top, the lateral view of the left side of the last dorsal vertebrae, sacrum, and tail base, drawn from YPM 1888 and 1889; the posterior part of the ilium is cut off to show the first caudal vertebra, and the major axial muscles are shown (the thin costal muscles are omitted). Bottom, the top view of the same region. Abbreviations: ilcaud lig, iliocaudal ligament sheet; ilcos, iliocostalis; long, longissimus; spin, spinalis and semispinalis group.

TABLE 1. MEASUREMENTS THAT REFLECT LIMB STRENGTH, MUSCLE LEVERAGE, AND TRUNK-RAISING POTENTIAL

All weights for dinosaurs taken from scale models; weights for extant species calculated from the sources listed in Bakker (1984)

SPECIES	WEIGHT (TONS)	HUMERUS SHAFT CIRCUM. (MM)	FEMUR SHAFT CIRCUM. (MM)	KNEE LEVERAGE (MM)	ANKLE LEVERAGE (MM)	FOOT LENGTH (MM)	LAST LUMBAR HEIGHT (MM)	SPECIMEN NUMBER
African Elephant	5.00	425	425	151	152	402	288	USNM 163318
Triceratops sp.	5.00	416	539	223	198	671	557	USNM 4842
White Rhino	2.80	280	227	94	96	499	201	USNM 164587
Centrosaurus sp.	2.80	271	320	168	96	501	290	YPM 2015
Black Rhino	2.00	230	209	81	82	381	173	USNM 161925
Centrosaurus sp.	2.00	230	299	140	80	455	244	USNM uncat.
African Elephant	3.3	328	303	130	133	301	250	USNM uncat.
Diracodon stenops	3.3	335	370	200	135	275	500	USNM 4934
Diracodon laticeps	2.6	315	330	159	111	221	421	USNM mtd. compos.
Stegosaurus ungulatus	3.8	350	401	257	140	301	523	YPM 1888-1887
Indian Rhino	2.2	240	210	125	131	382	181	USNM 49639

YPM—Peabody Museum, Yale University
USNM—United States National Museum
USNM uncat. centrosaur material is subadult from the Two Medicine Formation.

tion. Fast-running extant mammals usually have a relatively long metatarsus relative to the femur length (Coombs 1978). For example, a white rhino has a longer metatarsus but a shorter femur than an elephant of the same weight. A *Triceratops* seems to have a relatively short metatarsus (Fig. 18), but this impression is misleading. The correct way to measure the length of a limb segment is from one center of rotation (hinge line) to another. The center of rotation at the mammal ankle lies within the upper ankle bone (astragulus), which is part of the foot. In dinosaurs the astragulus is fixed to the end of the shank and is not part of the foot; the center of rotation, however, lies within the astragulus. Most studies of dinosaur limbs have measured the foot length without including the astragulus, and this way of measuring ignores a significant component (Coombs 1978). Furthermore, the toe joints in *Triceratops* and other large dinosaurs were compact, stiff, and cylindrical, like those of ostriches and other giant ground birds. These stiff toe segments were part of the thrust-delivery apparatus, and so the true functional length of the dinosaur foot should be measured from the tip of the hoof to the hinge line within the astragulus.

When foot length is measured in this manner horned dinosaurs have feet as long relative to body size as do big rhinos. Shank length is also very important in evaluating dinosaur speed. The extension of the knee at the end of the stroke was very powerful in dinosaurs, and horned dinosaurs have much longer shanks relative to their body weight than do modern rhinos.

The entire dinosaur hind limb, hip to hoof, was an adaptively sophisticated mechanism designed for giving short, massively strong backward thrusts. Sauropods had the weakest limbs for their size among dinosaurians, but even sauropods had stronger knees and calves than do elephants (Bakker 1984).

There is yet one more traditional problem of dinosaur limbs to deal with, the alleged "thick pads of cartilage." Gilmore (1915, 1920) stated that most dinosaur limbs were ill fitting and the bony surfaces must have been separated by weak zones of thick cartilage. This conclusion is not correct. The overall shape of a humeral head in *Triceratops* is that of a cylindrical hinge rather like that of a giant rhino. The dinosaur differs from the rhino in having half-centimeter-deep pits all over the articular surface. These pits would have been filled in with cartilage in life, but each cartilage-filled pit was surrounded by bone and there was not a continuous pad of cartilaginous tissue. Would the pit-

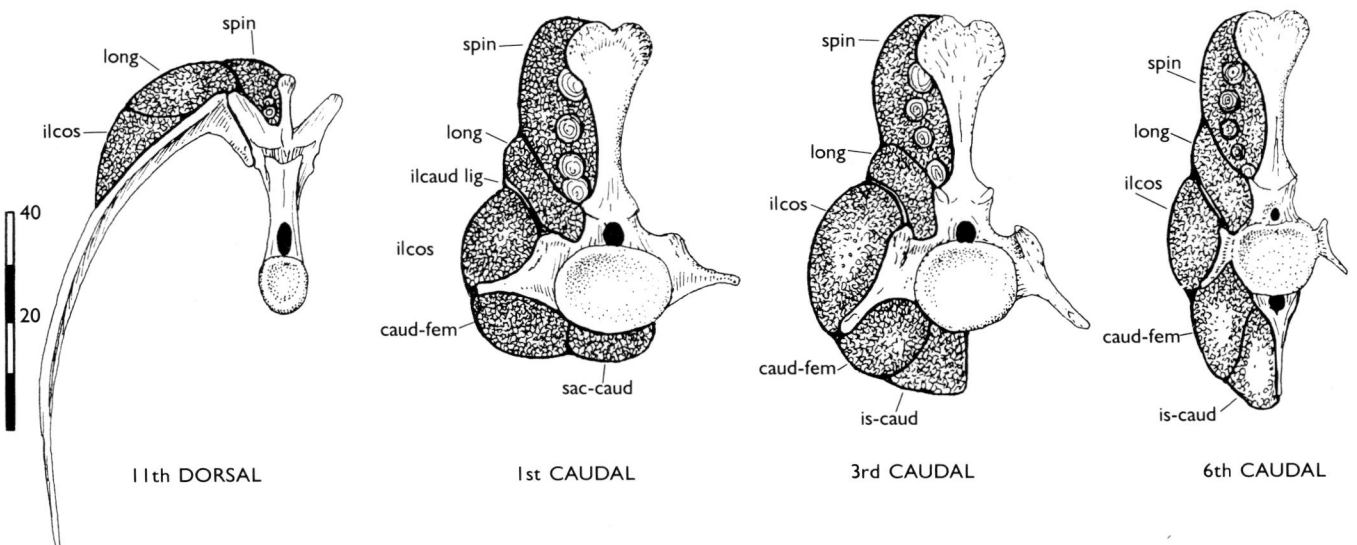

11th DORSAL   1st CAUDAL   3rd CAUDAL   6th CAUDAL

ted humeral head have been weaker than that of a rhino? Probably not. Cartilage confined in a bony recess would have very great powers of resistance to compression, which limb-joint surfaces must resist. Articular cartilage also serves as a porous reservoir for the lubricating capsular fluid, and the pit-filling cartilage plugs would exude lubricant when compression increased. I, therefore, do not believe in the traditional idea that the hard, shiny, continuous articular surfaces of most mammal bone is mechanically superior to the pitted articular surfaces of dinosaur bone.

So what is the locomotor bottom line for a five-ton *Triceratops?* The answer may be a maximum speed much higher than that of a charging African elephant or white rhino (Fig. 19). A top speed of more than fifty kilometers per hour is not an exaggerated estimate.

If you were raised on dinosaur books full of Gilmorean restorations as I was, it is startling to see the drawings of upright bipedal stegosaurs and diplodocine sauropods made in the early days between 1890 and 1910. It just does not seem right to have *Diplodocus* standing upright on its hind legs (Osborn 1904). When I was at Yale in the 1960s the learned professors and cocky graduate

students derided those quaint restorations, because we knew that all the big quadrupedal dinosaurs were confined to locomotion on all four feet. We were wrong.

Take the example of *Diracodon stenops,* the big-plated stegosaur from the lower Morrison Formation at Oil Creek, Colorado (usually referred to as *Stegosaurus stenops).* A clay model based on the excellent type specimen indicates a weight of about 3.3 metric tons (Table 1), about equal to a young African elephant bull. African elephants in the wild frequently rise up on their hind limbs to pluck fruit from selected trees, much as Indian elephants can be trained to perform bipedal circus tricks (Hanks 1979). These proboscidean excursions into bipedality usually last only a half minute or so, and the elephant can be said to be at the outer fringe of two-legged locomotion. When a quadruped rears up, its vertebral column obeys many of the engineering rules of the jib-and-tensile brace seen in derricks and cranes (Fig. 20). The jib of a crane is the lower compressive strut; the steel-cable brace is the upper tensile member. The greater the distance between the base of the jib and the steel cable, the greater the leverage the cable has for supporting the weight being lifted by the crane. In the vertebrate backbone the column of vertebral bodies (centra) and

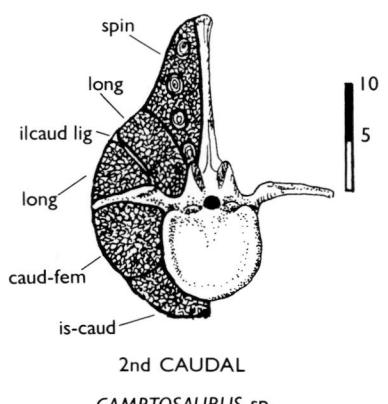

2nd CAUDAL

CAMPTOSAURUS sp.

Figure 22. Cross-sections of the major axial muscles in *Stegosaurus ungulatus.* Note how the outer tip of the caudal rib is bent downward, increasing the girth of the iliocostalis musculature. Also note the great height of the dorsal neural arch below the ribs and the upwardly bent transverse processes, two characters that increase the leverage of the iliocostalis and longissimus muscles for raising the body. A cross-section through the tail of a normal ornithischian, *Camptosaurus,* is shown (far right) for comparison.

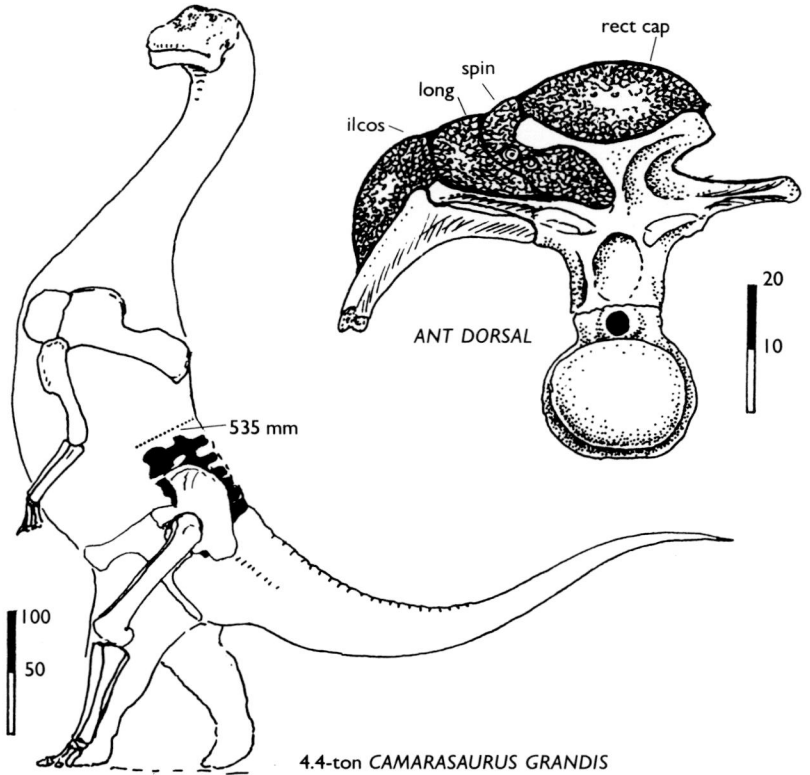

rect cap

spin

long

ilcos

ANT DORSAL

20

10

535 mm

100

50

4.4-ton *CAMARASAURUS GRANDIS*

Figure 23. Body-raising leverage in *Camarasaurus grandis* (YPM 1900 and 1901). Shown also is a cross-section through a middorsal vertebra and its axial muscles: note the stegosaurlike tall neural arch.

cartilaginous disks between the bodies constitute the compressive member, the jib of the trunk. The ligaments and muscles connecting the vertebral spines (neural spines) are the tensile members. To compare the structural strength available for rearing up, we need to start with the size of the vertebral bodies and length of the leverage at the last dorsal vertebra.

Diracodon stenops has a much larger vertebral body than does an elephant of the same weight; the height of the last dorsal centrum is almost twice that of the proboscidean (Fig. 20). The difference in leverage is even greater: the total height of the last dorsal vertebra in the stegosaur is 500 millimeters; in the elephant, only 250 millimeters. The entire configuration of the stegosaur vertebral column is that of a very specialized biped. The height of the vertebrae increases uninterruptedly going aft from shoulder to hips, exactly as in the bipedal tyrannosaurs or the giant ground birds of today. The stegosaur tail bore very large transverse processes and deep ventral spines (chevrons), showing that the musculature was very heavy (Figs. 21 and 22). Thus the tail could serve as a counter-

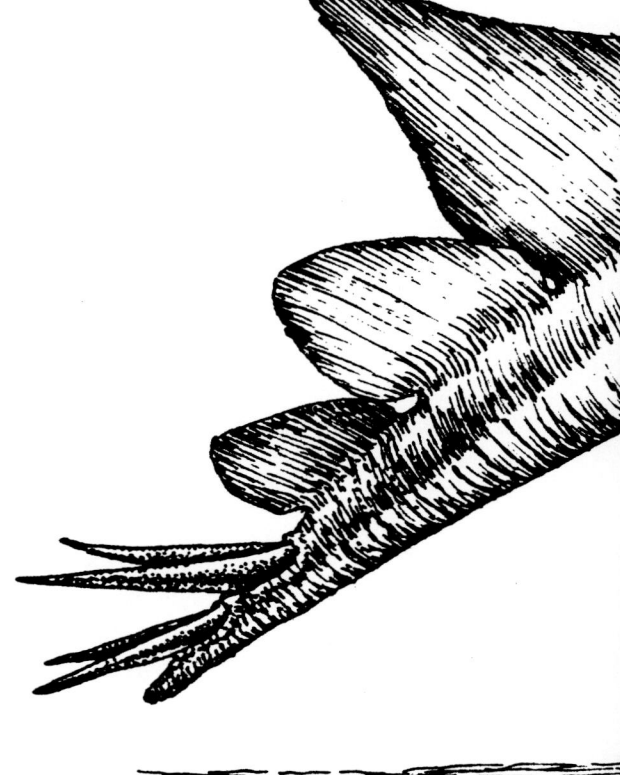

Figure 24. The short-legged, big-plated stegosaur, *Diracodon laticeps*, in bipedal mode.

balance to the trunk when the animal reared up. In an upright posture the thrust of the femur would be directed into the upper-anterior corner of the hip socket (acetabulum), a region formed by the anterior peduncle of the ilium in stegosaurs. This peduncle is massively braced by the very stout first sacral rib.

If a stegosaur were to rear up and support much of its weight on the tail, the tail musculature would brace the body from side to side and top to bottom. The tall neural spines and deep chevrons show that there was ample musculature to stabilize the body in the vertical plane. What of horizontal stability? Stegosaurs show great thickening at the outer corners of the summits of the neural spines in the first dozen tail vertebrae (Fig. 22). These thickenings are at the sites of origin of the tendons of the semispinalis muscles and show that these muscles were developed to an unusually high degree. The semispinales pull down and outward, from neural spine summit to the base of the neural spines of vertebrae five to ten segments farther aft. The height of the neural spines and breadth of the summit thickenings would give the muscles great leverage for raising the sacrum upward and for steadying the whole body from side to side.

A second caudal adaptation in stegosaurs is hypertrophy of the iliocostalis muscle group, the long, thick muscle column that passes aft from the sacral ribs to the outer part of the caudal ribs (transverse processes). In most dinosaurs the caudal ribs stick out sideways and slightly upward. But in stegosaurs the second through eighth caudal ribs are bent downward, so that the vertical thickness of the iliocostalis is increased and the muscle extends much farther below the rib base (Fig. 22). Since it is the caudal muscle located farthest from the midline plane, the iliocostalis has the greatest leverage for bracing the body from side to side.

Stegosaurs are not alone in having bipedal adaptations in the pattern of neural spine height and in the enlargement of semispinalis and iliocostalis. The diplodocid sauropods—*Barosaurus, Brontosaurus*, and *Diplodocus*—evolved the very same pattern (Riggs 1903, 1904).

The trunk of the stegosaurs shows unprecedented adaptations for an upright stance. The posterior dorsal vertebrae have very elongated arches that raise the rib heads to a level as high as the summit of the neural spine. The trunk iliocostalis and longissimus muscle bundles run forward from the sacrum to the outer tips of the transverse processes and the inner parts of the ribs. The leverage for raising the vertebrae relative to the sacrum is increased dramatically by the elevated position of the rib articulations. Unlike most other ornithischian dinosaurs, the dorsal vertebrae of stegosaurs were not held rigidly together by ossified tendons, and the zygapophyses (upper articular surfaces) were large and permitted extensive flexion and extension of the dorsal column. The job of raising the trunk to a near-vertical attitude could be performed, in part, by the back muscles raising the trunk relative to the sacrum.

It is especially intriguing to find a moderately strong degree of bipedal adaptation in some sauropod dinosaurs that rarely were considered bipeds even during the 1890s. *Camarasaurus grandis* has dorsal vertebrae with neural spines that are short compared to those of stegosaurs and diplodocid sauropods. The last dorsal vertebra of the camarasaur is much taller than that of an elephant of the same weight. The camarasaur tail, though thinner than that of a diplodocid, is still a very powerful organ by mammalian standards. The middorsal vertebrae of *C. grandis* have elevated rib articulations that approach in a less-exaggerated fashion the stegosaur condition (Fig. 23). The zygapophyses of camarasaurs, unlike those of diplodocids, permitted a wide range of vertical movement in the back, so that the iliocostalis and longissimus muscle groups could elevate the trunk relative to the sacrum and tail. It seems to me that it is quite defensible to restore the Grand Camarasaur as an upright biped.

I always come away from handling a *Triceratops* humerus with a sense of awe. I have measured and photographed dozens of rhinos and elephants from all the extant species and have seen both black and white rhinos galloping at full speed. The greater strength of the *Triceratops* at every joint is to me very persuasive evidence that this dinosaur had broken out of the adaptive limits we see today. *Tri-*

Figure 25. Two bull *Brontosaurus excelsus* in tripodal combat.

67

Figure 26. The three-ton nodosaur *Edmontonia rugosidens* at cruising speed.

ceratops could gallop, of that I am convinced by the evidence available from limb-shaft strength, muscle size and arrangement, and limb proportions. The other big dinosaurian quadrupeds—the sauropods, stegosaurs, ankylosaurs, and nodosaurs—also exceeded the boundaries of locomotor activity imposed on extant multiton species (Figs. 24–26). By the standards of modern giant land vertebrates, the Dinosauria are truly surprising.

ACKNOWLEDGMENTS

Two men sparked my interest in dinosaurs. Rudie Zallinger's wonderful painting in the Great Hall at Yale, "The Age of Reptiles," caught my imagination in 1954 when it was printed as a foldout in *Life*. Edwin Colbert provided food for thought in his series of popular books of the 1950s and 60s. Although some modern research—including my own—has led me to question some of the assumptions implicit in the work of these two men, their contribution to successive generations of dinosaurophiles is still unmatched by anyone of their epoch.

WORKS CITED

Alexander, R. McN. 1976. Estimates of the speeds of dinosaurs. *Nature* 261: 129–30.

Bakker, R. T. 1968. The superiority of dinosaurs. *Discovery* 23:11–23.

————. 1971. Dinosaur physiology and the origin of mammals. *Evolution* 25: 636–58.

————. 1972a. Anatomical and ecological evidence of endothermy in dinosaurs. *Nature* 238: 81–85.

————. 1972b. Locomotor energetics of lizards and mammals compared. *Physiologist* 15: 278.

————. 1975. Dinosaur renaissance. *Scientific American* 232, no. 4: 57–78.

————. 1984. The deer flees, the wolf pursues. In *Coevolution*, ed. D. Futuyama and M. Slatkin, 201–45. New York: Sinauer.

Bartholomew, G. A., and V. A. Tucker. 1964. Size, body temperature, thermal conductance, oxygen consumption, and heart rate in Australian varanid lizards. *Physiological Zoology* 37: 341–54.

Basmajian, J. V. 1964. *Muscles alive*. Baltimore: Williams & Wikins.

Beecher, C. B. 1901. The reconstruction of a Cretaceous dinosaur *Claosaurus annectens* Marsh. *Transactions of the Connecticut Academy of Science* 11: 311–24.

Bennett, A. F., and B. Dalzell. 1973. Dinosaur physiology: A critique. *Evolution* 27: 170–74.

Bird, R. T. 1944. Did Brontosaurus ever walk on land? *Natural History* 53: 61–67.

Buckland, W. 1824. Notice on the Megalosaurus, or great fossil lizard of Stonesfield. *Transactions of the Geological Society of London* 2: 1–390.

Coombs, W. P., Jr. 1978. Theoretical aspects of cursorial adaptation in dinosaurs. *Quarterly Review of Biology* 53: 393–418.

Currie P. J. and W. A. Sargeant. 1979. Lower cretaeous dinosaur footprints from the Peace River Canyon. *Palaeogeography, Palaeoclimatology, and Palaeoecology* 28:103–115.

Farlow, J. O. 1981. Estimates of dinosaur speeds from a new trackway site in Texas. *Nature* 294: 747–48.

Gambayran, P. P. 1974. *How mammals run*. New York: Halsted Press.

Gilmore, C. W. 1915. Osteology of *Thescelosaurus*, an orthopodous dinosaur from the Lance Formation of Wyoming. *Proceeding of the United States National Museum* 49: 511–616.

————. 1920. Osteology of the carnivorous Dinosauria in the United States National Museum, with special reference to the genera *Antrodemus (Allosaurus)* and *Ceratosaurus*. *Bulletin of the United States National Museum* 110: 1–159.

Gregory, W. K., and C. L. Camp. 1918. Studies in comparative myology and osteology. No. 3. *Bulletin of the American Museum of Natural History* 38: 447–563.

Hanks, J. 1979. *The struggle for survival.* Capetown: Mayflower.

Harkness, H. W. 1882. Footprints in the Carson City Penitentiary. *Proceedings of the California Academy of Sciences* 14:8–32.

Haubold, H. 1974. *Die Fossilen Saurier Fahrten.* Vittenberg: A. Ziemsen Verlag.

Jaeger, E. 1948. *Trails and trailcraft.* New York: Macmillan.

Kool, R. 1981. The walking speed of dinosaurs from the Peace River Canyon, British Columbia, Canada. *Candian Journal of Earth Science* 18: 823–25.

Lull, R. S. 1933. A revision of the Ceratopsia, or horned dinosaurs. *Memoirs of the Peabody Museum of Yale University* 3, no. 3: 1–135.

Mantell, G. 1844. *The medals of creation.* London: R. Clay.

Marsh, O. C. 1896. Dinosaurs of North America. In *Sixteenth Annual Report of the United States Geological Survey,* pt. 1: 186.

Murie, O. J. 1964. *A field guide to animal tracks.* Boston: Houghton Mifflin.

Muybridge, E. [1887] 1957. *Animals in motion,* ed. L. S. Brown. Reprint. New York: Dover.

Osborn, H. F. 1904. Fossil wonders of the West. *Century Magazine* 68: 680–94.

Ostrom, J. H. 1976. *Archaeopteryx* and the origin of birds. *Biological Journal of the Linnean Society* 8: 91–182.

Owen, R. 1841. Report on British fossil reptiles. Part 2. *Reports of the British Association for the Advancement of Science,* 60–204.

———. 1849. *A history of British fossil reptiles.* London: Palaeontographical Society.

———. 1879. *Memoirs on the extinct wingless birds of New Zealand.*

Petersen, J. 1972. PhD thesis, Dept. of Anatomy, University of Chicago.

Peterson, W. 1924. Dinosaur tracks in the roofs of coal mines. *Natural History* 24: 388–91.

Ricqlès, A. 1974. Evolution of endothermy: Histological evidence. *Evolutionary Theory* 1: 51–80.

Riggs, E. S. 1903. Structure and relationships of opisthocoelian dinosaurs. *Field Columbian Museum, Geology* 2: 165–96.

———. 1904. Structure and relationships of opisthocoelian dinosaurs. Part II: The Brachiosauridae. *Field Columbian Museum, Geology* 2: 229–48.

Riley, H., and S. Stutchbury. 1836. A description of various fossil remains of three distinct saurian animals discovered in the autumn of 1834, in the Mannesian Conglomerate of Durgham Down, near Bristol. *Proceedings of the Geological Society* 2: 397–99.

Romer, A. S. 1922. The locomotor apparatus of certain primitive and mammallike reptiles. *Bulletin of the American Museum of Natural History* 46: 517–606.

Russell, L. S. 1935. Musculature and functions in the Ceratopsia. *Bulletin of the National Museum of Canada* 77: 39.

Russell, D. A., and P. Béland. 1976. Running dinosaurs. *Nature* 264:486.

Sternberg, C. M. 1921. Dinosaur tracks from Peace River, British Columbia. *Bulletin of the National Museum of Canada* 68: 59–85.

Sukhanov, V. B. 1974. *General system of symmetrical locomotion of terrestrial vertebrates.* New Delhi: Amerind.

Williams, W. L. 1871. On the occurrence of footprints of a large bird. *Transactions of the New Zealand Institute* 4:124–127.

SMALL PROBLEMS: BIOLOGICAL IMPLICATIONS OF TINY DINOSAURS

GEORGE CALLISON

The recognition of tiny adult dinosaurs weighing about one kilogram enriches our understanding of dinosaurian diversity. Diminutiveness presents opportunities for unexpected utilization of Mesozoic environments by dinosaurs. Review of the literature on the biology of size suggests approaches to the study of some of these opportunities. Consideration is given to ecomorphological and physiological implications as predicted by allometric and other means. Besides describing the liabilities and assets of being tiny, attention is given to constraints for the prediction of feeding and locomotor behavior and general external appearance of diminutive adult dinosaurs.

Some dinosaurs are quite small as adults and are called tiny relative to usual dinosaurian standards (Callison and Quimby 1983). Included among these tiny dinosaurs are both saurischian and ornithischian representatives. *Compsognathus longipes*, a theropod (Fig. 1), and *Echinodon* sp., a fabrosaurid, are examples. Each is the size of a small chicken and probably had an adult body weight of less than one kilogram. Both are bipeds; one is car-

nivorous, the other an herbivore. Still other tiny dinosaurs (i.e., those with presacral body lengths of about seventy centimeters or less) are the theropods *Segisaurus* and *Avimimus* and the ornithopods *Heterodontosaurus*, *Lesothosaurus*, and *Scutellosaurus*. The early bird *Archaeopteryx lithographica* is presumed to have ancestry among theropodous dinosaurs—ancestry of tiny size. Mammals, birds, and other small terrestrial vertebrates surely must

Figure 1. *Compsognathus longipes* by Gerhard Heilmann (Heilmann 1926).

have been abundant at various times and in many places during the Mesozoic but are poorly represented in the fossil record. Together, these observations signal the probability of other similarly small dinosaurs whose existence is now marked only by fossil fragments if marked at all. The rarity of hatchlings and small size-class representatives of growth series of large dinosaurs is consistent with the argument that tiny dinosaurs may have been fairly abundant and that there are many more species of tiny dinosaurs yet to be discovered.

Despite the fact that there are hatchlings of both quadrupedal and bipedal dinosaur species that grow to become large adults, it is curious and may be significant that there are no known adult obligate quadrupeds (save, perhaps, the fabrosaurid *Scutellosaurus)* yet to be counted among the tiny. This observation is most likely biased by the

sparse record of tiny dinosaur fossils. Size seems to have no similar quadrupedal constraints among other reptiles or mammals.

Dinosaurs are best known for their enormity, and Hotton (1980) estimates that the body weight of known species averaged well more than a metric ton. Much emphasis is placed on dinosaurian bigness; there are profound consequences of being big. Large size limits dinosaurs to the same physiological, biomechanical, and ecological boundaries that limit large living land animals. But emphases on enormity have tended to lead us to think of dinosaurs in near-monolithic terms. With information indicating that adult dinosaurs have a considerably greater range of sizes than previously thought we can now begin to recognize the biological implications of their smallness.

Small Is Beautiful by E. F. Schumacher

(1973) calls to the attention of society some advantages (yea, necessities) of smallness in economic, technical, social, and political matters. Small can be "beautiful" in biological matters as well. I refer specifically to adult dinosaurs; beauty, as it must, remains in the eyes of the beholder.

Size carries much information about biological attributes of animals, fossil or not. As learned from living species there are many biological correlates with size that may not otherwise be indicated by the fossil record (McMahon 1973; McMahon and Bonner 1983; Calder 1984). Haldane ([1928] 1958: 322) reminds us of at least one advantage of being small when he states: "You can drop a mouse down a thousand-yard mine shaft; and, on arriving at the bottom, it gets a slight shock and walks away, provided that the ground is fairly soft. A rat is killed, a man is broken, a horse splashes."

Calder (1984: 1) notes that "size has until recently been one of the most neglected aspects of biology," but literature on the relationship of size to biology is burgeoning. Most has been published in the past ten years; fifty-seven percent of the 641 citations in the comprehensive synthesis and review by Calder (1984) were published since 1974. These studies show that "size has an effect not only on shape but also on all the activities of an organism, including its ability to move and the way it is influenced by physical forces, such as surface tension, friction, and inertia" (McMahon and Bonner 1983: 241)." Paleontologists, painters, sculptors, illustrators, animators, filmmakers, writers, and others who interpret fossils can benefit from an awareness and understanding of this new information.

Lest the reader think this a panacea, there are caveats. Animals do many things for which they do not appear to be particularly adapted. Kangaroo rats clamber around in bushes, foxes on small islands are insectivorous, polar bears eat algae, and hummingbirds eat small arthropods. It is difficult to predict from morphology what an animal is limited from doing. In addition, many observations in this report are based on allometric relationships. Allometric relationships are simply the comparison of the growth relations of two measurements. These

measurements can be of sizes, physiological properties, or other quantifiable features of organisms. These are empirical correlations; they do not establish cause and effect but may be instructive in such establishment.

The statements that follow apply most directly to adults but also apply in mixed measure to tiny juveniles of species destined to grow much larger into adulthood.

External shapes of tiny dinosaurs are indicated more or less by the skeleton. The skeleton provides the framework around which the other body masses are developed. The way these masses are organized and function relates to their shapes. Shapes of certain regions of the body are more completely reflected in the skeleton than are others. Distal legs and feet, distal forelimbs and "hands," snout, and tail have minimal other-mass components (*viz.*, other than the skeleton) and, by consequence, are regions that are shaped most like the skeleton. Shapes of more proximal regions have more other-mass components and thereby are less reliably predicted by the skeleton. An underlying physical cause of these relationships is that of minimizing mass to reduce inertia; this in turn reduces the amount of energy required to accelerate and decelerate these appendages to the body proper and at the same time increases the rapidity with which these changes in motion can occur (Heglund, Taylor, and McMahon 1974; Fedak, Heglund, and Taylor 1982). Soft and some hard elaborations (such as wattles, pinnae, frills, lips, eyelids, trunks, nostril covers, genitalia, scales, hair, feathers, claws, and horns) are rarely represented and difficult to estimate because of their variability and lack of skeletal scarring.

Animals with relatively small body masses can have proportionately thinner leg skeletons and muscle masses to stabilize, support, and move the bone, appendage, and individual. With proportionately less bone and ligament mass as well as less muscle and tendon mass and smaller body size there can be less vascularization and shorter blood vessels to serve the reduced masses of these living tissues.

MacArthur and Wilson (1967) argue that on a continuous scale of reproductive strategies there are two extreme kinds. One is "*r* selection" (*r* stands for rate of increase by reproduction) in which an individual has many offspring either by having a few offspring at frequent intervals or by having large numbers of offspring at one time. One characteristic of organisms that exhibit *r* selection is that they are small. A good example among mammals is mice versus elephants; mice show *r* selection, elephants do not. A pair of mice will produce many generations in a short time, while a pair of elephants have few young and each generation takes more than ten years. Elephants show "*K* selection" (*K* stands for the carrying capacity of the environment, which becomes the limiting factor for these animals). Two features of animals that exhibit *K* selection are large size and long generation time.

K and *r* selections are the two extremes of a range of reproductive strategies. *K* selection is especially suited to stable climates in which the full resources of the environment can be exploited safely. The tropics are a good example. The tropics hold many *K*-selection organisms and an enormous number of species. In contrast, *r* selection is best suited to unpredictable environments, such as temperate and subpolar regions where the production of large numbers of offspring insures against environmental catastrophe, freeze, flood, or drought.

Clutch sizes correlate inversely with body size (Calder 1983). So tiny dinosaurs probably exhibited *r* selection: large clutch sizes, little parental care, and short generation time.

Because of their size small vertebrates have enormous choices of stations in habitats.

Shelter is critical to survival; small animals have an easier time finding shelter than large ones. This may be a cause of increased species diversity in environments with more topographic irregularities (Simpson 1980; 233–42). Calder (1984) reports that home ranges (the geographic area an animal normally frequents) for mammals (carnivores range farther than omnivores or herbivores) and lizards scale linearly (Turner, Jennrich, and Weintraub 1969); so, small animals have small home ranges.

Calder (1984: 294) states, "the allometry of population density and home-range size indicates that for animals up to the size of a hare (2 kg.), only one to five home ranges must fit in the same per capita share of available space calculated from population density. These smaller mammals would therefore be expected to live as solitary individuals, in pairs, or in small family groups. (Did you ever run into a herd of mice?)" In remarking on the more gradual scaling of per capita space (less than the linearity noted for home range) he then says that for herbivorous mammals, "from the size of a marmot (*Marmota flaviventris*, 3.6 kg.) to the size of the wapiti (*Cervus canadensis*, 300 kg.), even greater home-range overlap means that larger numbers of individuals are expected to occupy the same area (resulting in groups of 3 to 6 individuals for marmots and 10 to 21 individuals for wapiti)."

When writing of African antelopes and buffalo, Jarman (1974) relates five classes of social organization to five classes of feeding styles. Body-size dependence is the pattern in this diversity of classes, and the following tendencies accompany decreased body size: smaller social groups, smaller home range, less likely migration, more selective feeding, and higher nutritive food value.

Tiny herbivorous dinosaurs, birds, and mammals share terrestrial locomotor features and may share energetic similarities. They may share the aforementioned relationships of small home-range and per capita space as well, but then, there are coveys of quail to confound our confidence.

Because of their low mass small vertebrates have low inertia. Because of their low mass and inertia small vertebrates are less liable to injury from falling than vertebrates with higher mass. Because of their low inertia small vertebrates can start, turn, and stop rapidly; they have quick movements. Because of their size small vertebrates have short neuronal connections and rapid reaction and response times.

Movement has two components of interest here: rate and duration. Small animals tend to move more rapidly; head, jaw, tail, and limb movements all can exhibit an almost frenetic rapidity. These movements are a result of there being relatively little inertia to overcome during the excursion of the turning member.

With regard to duration (endurance) Coulson (1984) analyzes the relationship between metabolic rate, anaerobic glycolysis, and the locomotion of reptiles. He shows that a major difference between such physiological extremes as homeothermic endotherms (birds and mammals, here) and heterothermic ectotherms (reptiles) is the slowness with which reptiles repay their oxygen debt from anaerobically supported activity. And, because metabolic rates (per unit body weight) are higher in smaller species, he concludes that "the smaller the reptile, the more capable it will be in terms of sustained work performance . . . if the body temperature remains high" (437). Thus, small reptiles are more bird- and mammallike in this capability than are their larger cohorts. If, however, the ambient temperature falls, so does the assistance of aerobic metabolism, and heterotherms become more dependent on anaerobic energy.

Coulson (1984: 425) mentions other consequences of size:

In any reptile, metabolic rate will be of prime importance in determining the habits of the animal. It will affect directly the food and water requirements, the rate of locomotion over prolonged periods, the length of time aquatic species can remain submerged, etc. Unlike mammals, reptiles are always concerned with achieving a body temperature optimum for them. It is probable that if the means were available each reptile would maintain a temperature almost as constant as that of mammals and birds. . . . Metabolic rate is the average of the rates of all the oxidative reactions in the body of an animal. It is a variable, being lowest during sleep, or whatever condition approaches sleep, and highest during maximal physical exertion.

The larger the animal, the lower the metabolic rate per unit body weight. Although metabolic rate seems to be related to surface area, it is not. (Not all mammals are constantly warm; those that are not will lose heat to the air when the air is cooler than they are and gain heat when the air temperature exceeds their own. Yet, in heterotherms the larger the animal, the lower the metabolic rate and their metabolic rates also correlate with their surface areas.) Coulson (1984) theorizes that metabolic rate is determined principally by the distance blood has to travel from the heart to the capillary, and the greater the distance, the greater the resistance and the slower the flow through the capillaries and veins and return to the heart.

Coulson (1984) continues,

If, from a chemical standpoint, the work capacity of individual cells is similar in all, the actual work accomplished when those cells are incorporated in organs may vary considerably, depending on the rate at which the organ is perfused with blood. In both reptiles and mammals all systems are in balance. Those with low metabolic rates demand and produce less aerobic energy than their more energetic neighbours, but both react to an increase in energy demand in the same manner. Regardless of temperature, a large reptile cannot produce as much energy as a mammal of the same size for the reason that it can neither oxygenate the blood, nor pump it, fast enough to supply the required oxygen and substrates. The metabolic difference between a reptile and a mammal owes less to chemistry than to chemical engineering.

One can then conclude that should tiny dinosaurs have the proper heart and lung equipment, then they should be able to produce more aerobic energy and have greater endurance thus supplied. Birds have such improved hearts and lungs and so might their immediate and, perhaps more distant, dinosaurian antecedents; but verification is elusive.

A small, heterothermic dinosaur would spend much of its daily time thermoregulating in a behavioral way but accomplishing other tasks such as feeding between thermoregulation times. A small heterotherm and a homeotherm would differ in their energy budgets by whether or not they had to produce heat; they are identical in their energy demand for muscle contraction, protein synthesis, and gluconeogenesis from lactate. Coulson (1984) elaborates:

The amount of energy available from oxidative processes for any but the smallest alligators is very small, too small for them either to defend themselves or to catch food. As is also the case in very large mammals, significant power can only be developed by that remarkable series of reactions called glycolysis, reactions which proceed without the need for any oxygen and therefore without the need for blood flow. When the animal is working maximally, most of the glycogen in the muscle is converted to lactic acid and energy is produced at a rate up to hundreds of times as great as that which can be produced by oxidative processes. This burst of energy, common to all animals, lasts only about 2 minutes if they are at maximum exertion (Coulson 1979), but work of lesser intensity may be performed at a slower rate, with a lower rate of drain on the muscle glycogen supply. The lactate, which is formed instantaneously, is either oxidized (20%) or converted by the liver back into glucose, and from there carried back to be reconverted into glycogen.

McMahon and Bonner (1983: 120) observe that "in general, small animals tend to stand and move in a crouched position, with their backs and limbs relatively more flexed than those of larger animals." Small animals can travel just about as fast uphill as on a level plane, and when traveling small animals tend to choose steeper trail angles (Taylor, Caldwell, and Rowntree 1972; Reichman and Aitchison 1981). Tiny dinosaurs should have these qualities too.

Stepping frequency is inversely related to body size or limb length (Calder 1984). Stride length increases with size (Maloiy et al. 1979). The total energy cost of travel increases with size but is cheaper per kilogram (Bennett 1982, for reptiles; Taylor, Heglund, and Maloiy 1982, for mammals). We might therefore expect tiny dinosaurs to warm up more rapidly and to move more rapidly, frequently, and cheaply than larger ones.

Small vertebrates have large brain to body size and cannot remain submerged as long as larger ones.

Brains require oxygen at all times. Terrestrial animals carry oxygen underwater in their blood. Small heterotherms and homeotherms, with their relatively large brains, high metabolic rate, and relatively less blood, cannot spend much time diving underwater; large animals, having relatively small brains, low metabolic rate, and relatively more blood, can spend considerable time underwater (Coulson 1984). No dinosaurs appear to be solely obligated to aquatic life; but as with modern terrestrial vertebrates dinosaurs probably possessed aquatic habitats to varying degrees, with many being frequent swimmers. When tiny dinosaurs frequented the water, one would not expect them to be adapted to perform activities requiring long diving times.

An interesting correlate here is that of vocalizations, which can be considered another form of asphyxia during breath holding (Calder 1984) and thereby may scale with body size as does diving. Should this be the case, then a one-kilogram tiny dinosaur (with birdlike lungs and song mechanism where the inspired air oscillates back and forth through the syrinx until the end of the song) might sing for about two minutes. Should the tiny dinosaur have a vocalization mechanism that demanded the inspired air to expire then the duration of vocalization would be significantly shorter.

For mammals, at least, size is a significant factor in determining a sense of hearing. Mice can hear more than two octaves higher than elephants at an intensity level of sixty decibels. A strong inverse relationship can be recorded between the high-frequency cutoff (at sixty decibels) and the time difference between the arrival of sounds at the two ears in mammals (Heffner and Masterton 1980; Heffner and Heffner 1980). Birds do not seem to exhibit such a relationship with the high-frequency cutoff, but extremely large birds have not been examined (Knudsen 1980; Dooling 1980). Tiny dinosaurs would be expected to be more birdlike.

Small vertebrates have very high surface to volume ratios.

McMahon and Bonner (1983: 38ff.) have discussed the relationship of length, surface area, and volume. Volume is proportional to length cubed; surface area is proportional to length squared. If a simple geometric shape such as a cube doubles in length, it will acquire four times the original surface area and eight times the original volume. When we think of tiny dinosaurs, it is helpful to think of the converse of the consequences of such scaling where volume is dramatically reduced relative to surface area with a reduction in length (see Leighton, Siegel, and Seigel 1966). The result is a tiny individual with a high surface to volume ratio.

Because of their high surface to volume ratios and relative to their body mass small vertebrates absorb oxygen, water, and nutrients rapidly and lose water, carbon dioxide, and other metabolites rapidly.

Surface area provides a route for materials and heat into and out of organisms. Lungs are important for exchange of gases, stomach and intestinal walls for the absorption of nutrients, kidneys for the riddance of liquid wastes, and skin (plus the lining of nose, mouth, and air passageways) for heat exchange. Tiny vertebrates have proportionately high surface areas for their body size, and this most profoundly affects heat exchange and other exchange phenomena as well.

Because of their high surface to volume ratios tiny vertebrates warm up and cool off rapidly.

Porter and Gates (1969) note that "the smaller the animal the . . . [larger] the convection coefficient . . . and the animal surface temperature is coupled tightly to the air temperature." Their work also revealed that, because of larger body size, sheep-sized animals have temperatures that are decoupled from the air temperature.

Tiny animals are more likely to seek shelter when stressed by temperature change. Thus, if tiny dinosaurs were to be active over much of the day or night then they may be expected to have some sort of thermal insulation to help them control the absorption and dumping of heat and to modulate the amplitude of ambient temperature swings.

Regal (1985) notes that lizard scales are enlarged and raised where they protect them from solar heat. Although there is no direct evidence of such, tiny dinosaurs may have enjoyed similarly enlarged scales. Regal (1985) then argues for the appearance of feathers as heat shields to provide shade to the precursors of birds; but Feduccia (1985) asserts that feathers are too complex to have been insulators originally and that they evolved initially in an aerodynamic context. Notwithstanding their initial adaptive significance, protofeathers must have been present in the dinosaurian antecedents of birds and may have been present in other lineages of tiny dinosaurs.

Hearts of tiny vertebrates beat more rapidly than those of large vertebrates. Breathing rates of small vertebrates are higher than those of the large. Small vertebrates live shorter lives in absolute time than large ones.

Environmental factors such as tidal cycles, day and season length, and climatic fluctuations do not scale according to animal size; regardless of their size, all must cope with the environment. And, as Lindstedt and Calder (1981) document and Calder (1983) notes, "each animal lives its life faster or slower as governed by size, but accomplishes just as much biologically whether large or small."

Some generalizations may be applied to characterizations of tiny dinosaurs. The most familiar is the corollary: the smaller they are, the easier they fall.

Tiny dinosaurs would be quick, able to start, turn, and stop rapidly, while tending to move and stand in a crouched position. They would prefer uphill paths of travel. Long underwater diving times were probably not in their repertoire.

Reproduction strategies would emphasize infrequently laid, large clutches of eggs or smaller clutches produced at more frequent intervals; offspring would be provided with less parental care.

Small home ranges occupied by solitary individuals, pairs, or small groups would typify their social organization. They would not likely migrate. More selective feeding on food of high-nutritive value would also follow.

Should they vocalize, their vocalizations would be short.

They would warm up and cool off rapidly; species ancestral to birds would most likely have had integumentary thermal insulation.

High breathing rates and heart-beat frequencies would also be expected. Short absolute times conclude their lives.

Acknowledgments

This project was accomplished with the assistance of assigned time from the University Research Committee of California State University, Long Beach, and with additional support from the Center for Field Research/Earthwatch in Watertown, Massachusetts, and the Program in Biological Research Resources of the National Science Foundation, Grant BSR-8405598.

Works Cited

Bennett, A. F. 1982. The energetics of reptilian activity. In *Biology of the Reptilia*, ed. C. Gans and F. H. Pough, 13: 155–99. New York: Academic Press.

Calder, W. A., III. 1981. Scaling of physiological processes in homeothermic animals. *Annual Review of Physiology* 43: 301–22.

———. 1983. Ecological scaling: Mammals and birds. *Annual Review of Ecology and Systematics* 14: 213–30.

———. 1984. *Size, function, and life history.* Cambridge, Mass.: Harvard University Press.

Callison, G., and H. M. Quimby. 1983. Tiny dinosaurs: Are they fully grown? *Journal of Vertebrate Paleontology* 3, no. 4: 238–47.

Coulson, R. A. 1979. Anaerobic glycolysis: The Smith and Wesson of the heterotherms. *Perspectives in Biological Medicine* 22: 465–79.

———. 1984. How metabolic rate and anaerobic glycolysis determine the habits of reptiles. In *The structure, development, and evolution of reptiles*, ed. M. W. J. Ferguson, 425–41. Symposia of the Zoological Society of London, no. 52.

Dooling, R. J. 1980. Behavior and psychophysics of hearing in birds. In *Comparative studies of hearing in vertebrates*, ed. N. Popper and R. R. Fay, 261–85. New York: Springer Verlag.

Fedak, M. A., N. C. Heglund, and C. R. Taylor. 1982. Energetics and mechanics of terrestrial locomotion. II. Kinetic energy changes of the limbs and body as a function of speed and body size in birds and mammals. *Journal of Experimental Biology* 79: 23–40.

Feduccia, A. 1985. On why the dinosaur lacked feathers. In *The beginnings of birds*, ed. M. K. Hecht, J. H. Ostrom, G. Viohl, and P. Wellnhoffer, 75–79. Eichstätt, Germany: Freundes des Jura-Museums.

Haldane, J. B. S. [1928] 1958. On being the right size. In *A treasury of science*, ed. H. Shapley, S. Rapport, and H. Wright, 321–25. Reprint. New York: Harper.

Heffner, H., and B. Masterton. 1980. Hearing in glires: Domestic rabbit, cotton rat, feral house mouse, and kangaroo rat. *Journal of the Acoustical Society of America* 68: 1584–99.

Heffner, R., and H. Heffner. 1980. Hearing in the elephant *(Elephas maximus)*. *Science* 208: 518–20.

Heglund, N. C., C. R. Taylor, and T. A. McMahon. 1974. Scaling stride frequency and gait to animal size: Mice to horses. *Science* 186: 1112–13.

Heilmann, G. 1926. *The origin of birds.* London: H. F. & G. Witherby.

Hotton, N. H., III. 1980. An alternative to dinosaur endothermy: The happy wanderers. In *A cold look at the warm-blooded dinosaurs*, ed. R. D. K. Thomas and E. C. Olson, 311–50. Boulder, Colo.: Westview Press.

Jarman, P. J. 1974. The social organization of antelope in relation to their ecology. *Behaviour* 48: 215–67.

Knudsen, E. I. 1980. Sound localization in birds. In *Comparative studies of hearing on vertebrates,* ed. A. N. Popper and R. R. Fay, 289–322. New York: Springer Verlag.

Leighton, A. T., Jr., P. B. Siegel, and H. S. Seigel. 1966. Body weight and surface area of chickens *(Gallus domesticus). Growth* 30: 229–38.

Lindstedt, S. L., and W. A. Calder. 1981. Body size, physiological time, and longevity of homeothermic animals. *Quarterly Review of Biology* 56: 1–16.

MacArthur, R. H., and E. O. Wilson. 1967. *The theory of island biogeography.* Princeton, N.J.: Princeton University Press.

McMahon, T. A. 1973. Size and shape in biology. *Science* 179: 1201–4.

McMahon, T. A., and J. T. Bonner. 1983. *On size and life.* New York: Scientific American.

Maloiy, G. M. O., R. M. Alexander, R. Njau, and A. S. Jayes. 1979. Allometry of the legs of running birds. *Journal of Zoology* (London) 187: 161–67.

Porter, W. P., and D. M. Gates. 1969. Thermodynamic equilibria of animals with environment. *Ecological Monographs* 39: 227–44.

Regal, P. J. 1985. Common sense and reconstructions of the biology of fossils: *Archaeopteryx* and feathers. In *The beginnings of birds,* ed. M. K. Hecht, J. H. Ostrom, G. Viohl, and P. Wellnhoffer, 67–74. Eichstätt, Germany: Freundes des Jura-Museums.

Reichman, O. J., and S. Aitchison. 1981. Mammal trails on mountain slopes: Optimal paths in relation to slope angle and body weight. *American Naturalist* 117: 416–20.

Schumacher, E. F. 1973. *Small Is Beautiful.* New York: Harper & Row.

Simpson, G. G. 1980. *Why and how.* Elmsford, N.Y.: Pergamon.

Taylor, C. R., S. L. Caldwell, and V. J. Rowntree. 1972. Running up and down hills: Some consequences of size. *Science* 178: 1096–97.

Taylor, C. R., N. C. Heglund, and G. M. O. Maloiy. 1982. Energetics and mechanics of terrestrial locomotion. I. Metabolic energy consumption as a function of speed and body size in birds and mammals. *Journal of Experimental Biology* 97: 1–21.

Turner, F. B., R. I. Jennrich, and J. D. Weintraub. 1969. Home range and body size of lizards. *Ecology* 50: 1076–81.

DINOSAUR TRACKWAYS

MARTIN G. LOCKLEY

*P*aleontologists and artists concerned with the accurate reconstruction and restoration of dinosaurs and their habitats have tra-*ditionally used a combination of anatomical, floral, and faunal evidence to authenticate their work. One very important type of evidence, that of footprints, has almost always been overlooked, partly because the study of trackways has lagged behind other fields of research, particularly in recent years when almost every other discipline in soft-rock geology has been synergistically integrated for a much-improved understanding of paleoecology and paleoenvironments.*

Dinosaur trackways are an integral and often common part of the ichnological record in many Mesozoic continental facies. Not only do they provide paleobiological evidence concerning locomotion, behavior, and diversity, but they also offer considerable insight into the nature of local paleoenvironments by furnishing evidence pertaining to shoreline trends, sediment saturation, and depositional cycles. Detailed analysis at many sites permits the re-creation of an accurate picture of life in the past and indicates that field paleontology still has much new evidence to offer to science. Artistic restorations of such scenes offer a unique opportunity for an authentic blending of science and art.

In the restoration of dinosaurs and their habitats much recently discovered evidence regarding posture, metabolism, and social behavior has contrib-uted to an exciting new era of dinosaur interpretation. This renaissance (Bakker 1975) has been aided by revolutionary advances in our understanding of ancient environments arising from equally radical progress in the field of paleoenvironmental reconstruction. The subdisciplines of sedimentology (particularly facies analysis), paleoclimatology, and paleobotany enhance the potential for thoroughly authentic backdrops in any restoration. Thus the sciences have combined to produce realistically restored dinosaurs integrated into carefully re-created landscapes.

In this paper I will focus on the subdiscipline of ichnology, or trace fossil analysis, which has developed slowly and has rarely been effectively integrated into paleontological considerations of dinosaur habitats. This neglect, which precluded realization of the considerable potential of dinosaur (and other) tracks, is now being remedied. With the current reawakening of interest in ichnology (Mossman and Sarjeant 1983) the future of the subject looks bright, not only for providing much new ichnological data but also for enhancing the whole field of paleoenvironmental reconstruction.

While crediting the many fine artists, among them several renowned paleontologists, who have made dynamic and anatomically authentic dinosaur restorations a fine art and have spearheaded a new wave of dinosaur consciousness, it is worth pointing out that in many instances ichnology could add a significant, previously unexplored dimension.

Trackways are the actual record of animal activity at a specific location and time in the past, more of a true snapshot than almost any other kind of paleontological evidence. They can indicate how many animals passed in a particular direction and provide specific information on their size, speed, and diversity. They usually occur in moist sediments that were recently deposited or wetted by storm or flood events and may indicate behavioral patterns at such times. When coupled with the evidence of track depth and configuration, footprints also permit accurate reconstruction of local habitats such as river, lake, and sea shorelines, particularly when their position in relation to drainage systems and distribution of vegetation can be diagrammed. Data from a track site may quickly build into a picture of dinosaurs (or other animals) traveling a specific route or routes across a faith-

fully re-created habitat. A trackway map can be transformed into a perspective view of a group of dinosaurs as they actually traveled a particular terrain. As with photographic snapshots, however, multiple exposures (several episodes of one passage) on a single negative (substrate) may produce a confusing result.

Far from being an analytical intrusion into an otherwise creative composition of an ancient scene, trackway evidence offers an opportunity for a successful blending of scientific observation and artistic reconstruction. The study of trackways is the detectivelike reconstruction of the scene of ancient dinosaur activity.

There are very few artistic reconstructions based on trackways. Those presented by Bird (1944, 1985) and Langston (1979) for Cretaceous dinosaurs from Texas are simply cartoons addressing only a part of the available evidence (Fig. 1). Others (e.g., Paul in Bird 1985: 18) are not accompanied by detailed explanation of the trackway data except in rare cases (Coombs 1980).

Probably the most famous of the Texan footprints are the Albian Glen Rose Formation trackways, which include supposed evidence of a carnosaur attacking the left-rear flank of a sauropod (Fig. 1c; Bird 1985; Langston 1979: fig. 15). Because of the dramatic implications of this evidence, the segments were removed to the American Museum of Natural History, New York (AMNH) and Texas Memorial Museum in Austin. Unfortunately, however, a thorough analysis of the trackway data have never been undertaken. For example, the fact that Bird originally referred to a dozen sauropod trackways all trending in one direction (south) seems to be overlooked (see Bird 1985: 179). James Farlow recently discovered Bird's original map showing four of the parallel sauropod trackways (including the AMNH segment) as well as three carnosaur trackways, which trend southward, and one carnosaur trackway, which trends northward in the opposite direction. Such evidence clearly alters the picture of a one-on-one predator-prey altercation and could suggest the much wilder scenario of a "sauropod herd pursued by a carnosaur pack" (Bird and Farlow personal communication 1985). A recent Bolivian study by Leonardi (1984) docu-

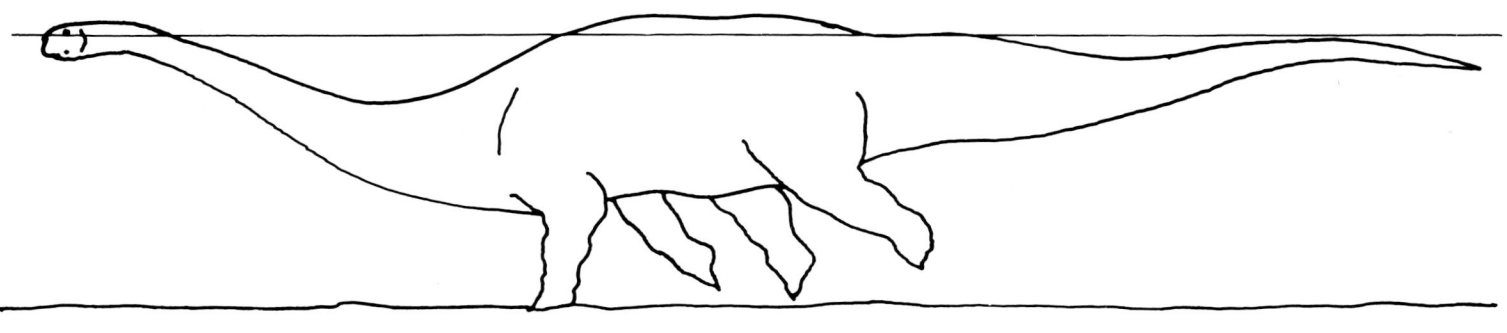

a

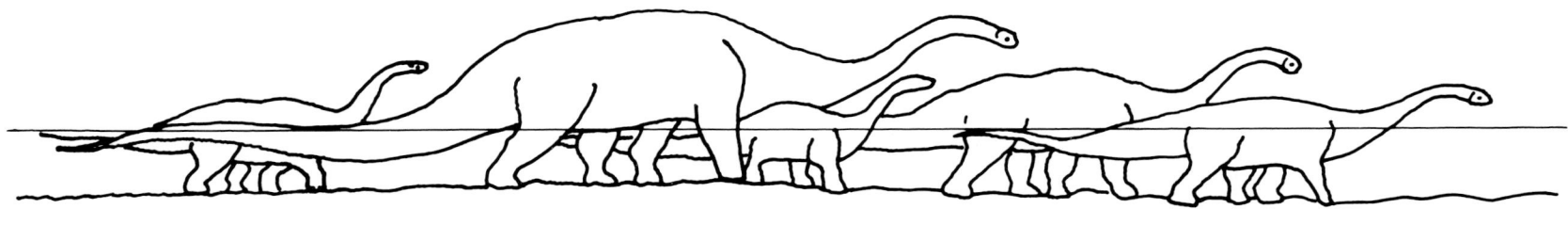

b

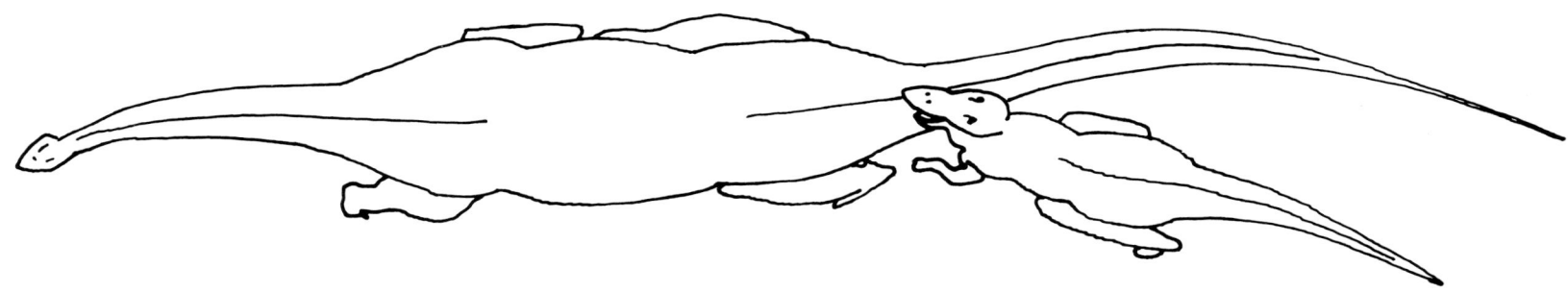

c

Figure 1. Dinosaur sketches by Roland T. Bird (redrawn here after Bird 1985) depict dinosaur activity inferred from trackways, including (a) the swimming sauropod, Mayan Ranch track site, (b) the sauropod herd, Davenport Ranch track site, and (c) the carnosaur-attacks-sauropod scenario, Paluxy River track site.

TABLE 1. SAUROPOD TRACKWAY DATA, DAVENPORT RANCH SITE, CRETACEOUS
OF TEXAS.[1]

TRACKWAY NUMBER	MEAN FOOTPRINT LENGTH: WIDTH (CM)	MEAN STRIDE (CM)	MEAN GLENO-ACETABULAR ESTIMATES[2]	ESTIMATED SPEED (METERS/SECOND)
1	55:40	194	134 (187)	1.37
2	45:35	178	119 (168)	1.38
3	45:35	173	136 (181)	1.32
4	56:44	208	149 (201)	1.37
5	39:27	160	98 (142)	1.57
6	78:53	252	186 (252)	1.52
7	60:46	226	- (191)	1.50
8	76:54	241	162 (224)	1.38
9	53:38	191	131 (180)	1.41
10	55:46	201	144 (203)	1.23
11	61:48	207	149 (190)	1.23
12	46:35	172	126 (156)	1.31
13	35:26	150	100 (139)	1.47
14	52:41	200	154 (178)	1.40
15	51:39	199	150 (194)	1.47
16	51:38	206	138 (188)	1.60
17	51:38	204	141 (190)	1.58
18	50:37	198	140 (189)	1.55
19	52:39	184	137 (172)	1.29
20	58:42	238	154 (213)	1.81
21	52:37	193	150 (187)	1.48
22	43:32	177	108 (158)	1.52
23	61:43	228	161 (226)	1.85

1. Statistical parameters given were estimated from measurements of an enlarged copy of Bird's map of the Davenport Ranch site.

2. Mean glenoacetabular estimates are derived using both the "primitive alternate pace" method and the "alternate pace" method (in parentheses); see Leonardi (in press) for details. The latter method gives values which average thirty-five percent higher than the former method.

OPPOSITE:

Figure 2. An interpretation of the Davenport Ranch trackway assemblage of 23 sauropod trackways (bottom), numbered from left to right. The circles at top represent individual animals and have diameters proportional to foot width (shown in 5-cm size intervals). The time sequence on the vertical scale is inferred from the overlapping trackway relationships indicated by arrows between circles. Thus in the right group, animal 21 passed by first, followed by 20, then 19, and so on, with animal 9 being the last. At an average speed of 1.5 meters per second (see Table 1), each animal would take at least one second to walk its own body length (shoulder to hip distance). Even with necks erect, the spacing between animals would be on the order of several body lengths to allow space for their tails. If each animal took several seconds to pass, before the next followed, the minimum time for passage of animals 21 through 9 would be on the order of 30 to 60 seconds.

Dotted lines indicate that the time relationships between the left and right groups and individuals 8 and 23 are unknown. The central inset shows percentage of substrate trampled in area 1 (left group) and area 3 (right group); the values are 26 and 29 percent, respectively, and combine to produce a total of 23 percent when untrampled area 2 is included.

mented a similar scenario in which a group of carnosaurs had followed a herd of sauropods.

The outcome of the supposed Texan dinosaur skirmish is also never discussed. While it may be true that a missing footprint of the carnosaur at the point where it appears to have attacked the sauropod's left flank could be genuine evidence for collision or physical contact, the data are only now being thoroughly analyzed from a quantitative viewpoint (Farlow personal communication). Many issues need to be considered. Why did the carnosaur trackway subsequently cross the sauropod trackway from left to right, implying that it fell in behind the sauropod after only four or five strides? Similarly why does another sauropod trackway to the left of the AMNH trackway also veer thirty degrees to the left at the point at which the

attack is supposed to have occurred? Hopefully such questions can be addressed by Farlow's work, which has recently uncovered new trackway evidence at the original Paluxy River site.

Similarly the Davenport Ranch trackways (Glen Rose Formation of Texas) indicate at least twenty-three sauropods all progressing in the same direction as a herd heading toward a common objective (Bird 1944). Since Bakker (1968: 20) first observed that the trackway evidence had the potential for suggesting a "structured" herd, with the "very largest footprints made only at the periphery of the herd; the very smallest . . . only in the center," several other authors have studied the data (Alexander 1976; Haubold 1984; and Lockley 1986a, b), and some (Ostrom 1972, 1985) have questioned the validity of Bakker's interpretations, even though Bird (1985: 162, 216) evidently concurred with Bakker. A detailed analysis, however, has never been undertaken. Because of my interest in Jurassic sauropod trackways and the unknown potential of the Texas data I have undertaken just such an analysis. The results seem to suggest the considerable potential for what is at first sight a confused and overprinted assemblage of trackways.

It is highly significant that Bird (1944) referred to his map as the "all important foot chart." He was uniquely qualified in such detailed cartography after months of work producing the exquisite Howe Quarry site map (Morrison Formation of Wyoming; see Bird 1985), and in reference to the Davenport Ranch site modestly stated that "few charts of such complexity have been made" (Bird 1985: 163). Careful analysis from an enlarged map of foot, step, and stride size, and overlap relationships (Table 1), consistently show that Bird's cartography was extremely accurate. For example, left and right footprints within a given trackway are consistently the same size and within the range of variation that might be expected from the differential response of the substrate to successive footfalls. Similarly step and stride measurements and glenoacetabular estimates are consistent in each trackway and illustrate predictable relationships to footprint size, and speed estimates all fall within a narrow range of 1.23 to 1.85 meters per second.

By color coding and numbering each trackway, resolving the overlapping relationships, and measuring relevant parameters, I was able to resolve all twenty-three trackways with almost no ambiguity (Fig. 2). Only one or two individual tracks either appear to be missing or are not obviously associated with the numbered trackways.

For consistency I numbered the trackways from left to right so that the centrally located large trackway is 8 (cf. Bird 1944: 67) and the one on the far right is 23. Based on the published map, these two are the only ones that neither overlap nor become overstepped by other trackways, and for this reason they cannot be interpreted unequivocally. (Note, however, that Bird stated that 8 was the "only one . . . that did not cross another." Taken literally this might mean that it was overlapped, and that 23 crossed another trackway. Although

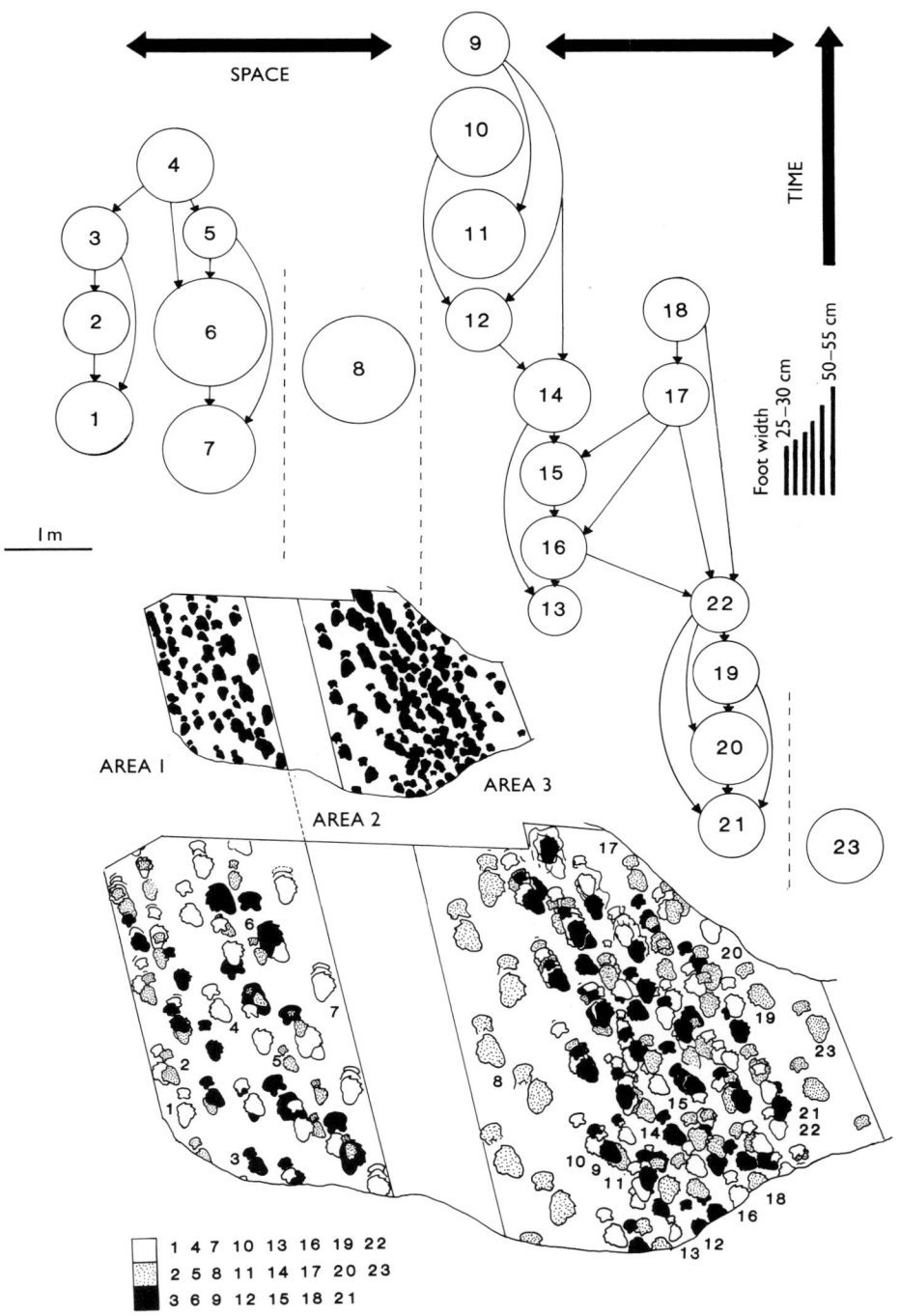

Bird probably meant "intersect with" rather than cross, further guesswork is fruitless.) Concentration on what can be accomplished makes it possible to analyze all other trackways in terms of those that they overlap or are overprinted by. Thus a sequence of events begins to emerge. Add to these data on trackway orientations, which vary by as much as fifteen degrees, the fact that overlapping trackways on the same trend imply at least one animal length for each overlapping relationship, and it is possible to determine that the herd must have been strung out at least four or five deep (Fig. 2). Twenty-three animals with glenoacetabular dimensions in the range of about 98 to 162 centimeters (and hence body widths of at least 50 to 80 centimeters) passing through an area only about fifteen meters wide cannot have been progressing on a "broad front" as Currie (1983) inferred for a hadrosaur herd.

Although there may be some truth in Bakker's inferences (1968) on herd structure, his statements cannot be substantiated. If we treat the whole group as a herd, the largest track makers (6–8, 11, 23) are, with the exception of 23, centrally located. The location of the larger individuals, however, must be understood in the context of a chronological sequence of events, as proposed in this interpretation. The herd appears to have consisted of several laterally spaced subgroups (e.g., 21, 20, 19, 22; 12, 11, 10, 9; and 7, 6, 5) with individuals following in line. There is some indication both that the larger individuals led the way followed by smaller ones and that the speed of the individuals in each subgroup was remarkably consistent. The scenario of small individuals following larger ones has been suggested before based on Cretaceous ornithopod tracks (Sarjeant 1981; Lockley, Young, and Carpenter 1983).

It is also possible to determine accurately that the herd trampled twenty-three percent of the area it traversed, and that in the right-hand group, successive animals consistently passed farther to the left than those ahead of them (Fig. 2).

The data derived from such an analysis obviously have the potential for enhancing the authenticity of an artistic restoration by placing animals in correct relative positions. Clearly the evidence is not unequivocal but does provide certain constraints that allow one to eliminate false scenarios. Such potential exists at many sites where accurate trackway maps and analyses are available.

Dale Russell (personal communication) observed that if certain Cretaceous deposits in England were subject to the arid climatic regimes that produced badland topography, they would produce the type of fossil bonanza found in parts of Asia, Africa, and the western United States. The same is true of the eastern United States (Hitchcock 1958; and Lull 1904, 1953), where the potential is confined by the limitations of exposure. Fortunately in the western United States such limitations are less of a problem, and extensive track sites appear to be quite common and considerably more accessible than in regions such as North Africa and South America where startling potential also exists (Jenny and Jossen 1981; Leonardi 1981; and Lockley 1986a). Lack of knowledge about western track sites simply reflects lack of previous interest, which in turn resulted in a literature so impoverished as to suggest that such sites are rare. Nothing could be farther from the truth. Important track sites ranging in age from late Triassic to late Cretaceous span the whole dinosaurian era.

Many of these sites are currently being studied by a research group at the University of Colorado at Denver and by others in the West (see Lockley 1986b). Of the several dozen sites documented only a few will be mentioned here as examples of sites with considerable potential for providing authentic restorations. Those chosen are mainly from classic vertebrate-bearing deposits and include examples from the Triassic Chinle Formation and Dockum Group, the Jurassic Morrison Formation, and the Cretaceous Dakota and Mesaverde Groups.

While the old adage that a picture is worth a thousand words holds true for many restorations of the past, words of scientific wisdom are also useful to convince the reader of the authenticity of a restoration. It is particularly important to appreciate this point in connection with the type of restorations discussed here. An attempt is being made to place constraints on the orientation and relative positioning of animals and localize them in paleoenvironments for which accurate base maps exist. Caution must be exercised in determining the nature of constraints suggested by footprint data, especially where factual ambiguity exists. (For example, what are the time relationships between the right and left subgroups in the Davenport assemblage? [Fig. 2].) The leeway found in most data sets encourages the essential freedom of artistic expression, and it is in this spirit that I hope exciting restorations will arise from the new phase of trackway work currently underway in the western United States.

Until recently trackways were virtually unknown in late Triassic formations of the western United States, despite the fact that deposits like the Chinle are among the best-known and best-exposed vertebrate-bearing formations of this age (Colbert 1985). Recent discoveries at several sites have provided significant evidence of the activity of dinosaurs and other animals. Among the ichnogenera recognized at these sites (with possible track makers in parentheses) are *Coelurosaurichnus* and *Agialopus* (procompsognathid dinosaurs), *Rhynchosauroides* (a lizard or sphenodontid), *Apatopus* and *Gwyneddichnium* (protorosaurids), *Brachychirotherium* (an aetosaurid), *Pentasauropus* (a dicynodont), a ?poposaurid trackmaker, and a chirotheriid form probably representing a phytosaur. The first five trackway types represent an assemblage of smaller animals often associated with well-preserved invertebrate trails and ecologically separated from most other large forms. Such a distinction between assemblages of large and small track makers may reflect preservational differences, and there can be little doubt that more data are needed to substantiate these ecological generalizations. Based on current evidence, however, two particularly fruitful sites provide interesting ichnological insights into early dinosaur habitats.

The first, in the Popo Agie Formation of Moffat County, Colorado, contains an exquisitely preserved assemblage of invertebrate and small vertebrate traces whose occurrence strongly suggests feeding activity. The presence of abundant arthropodlike traces (cf. *Pterichnus* and *Scoyenia*) with tracks of chicken-sized dinosaurs and lizard-sized quadrupeds surely suggests some kind of foraging scenario worthy of reconstruction. Although the trackway evidence is largely confined to isolated slabs, with no in situ area yet mapped, the assemblage of trace fossils provides as good an overall picture of the small vertebrate and invertebrate fauna as any contemporary western assemblage of body fossils.

A second track site in the Chinle Formation of eastern Utah contains a very different in situ trace fossil assemblage dominated by the trackways of large pseudosuchians (*Brachychirotherium*), dicynodonts (*Pentasauropus*) and large ?poposaurid trackmakers. The tracks occur as impressions in the upper surface of an extensive (five hundred square meter) clean-washed, well-sorted sandstone bed exposed in the floor of a dry wash. Sedimentological indicators suggest that the sandstone was deposited in the waning stages of a flood that carried water northwestward into the Central Utah Basin and deposited considerable plant debris as the water subsided. Such deposition would presumably be closely linked to flooding of a major perennial river and could represent a sand sheet draping a point bar or other bank environment. Trackways at the upstream end of the site show a very strong bimodal trend thought to indicate shore-parallel progression in opposite directions. This inference is strongly substantiated by the coincidence of trackway orientations with the main flow direction indicated by sedimentological current evidence. This type of integration of biogenic trackway data with purely physical geologic evidence has rarely been accomplished in paleoenvironmental studies, despite the fact that considerable potential exists (Lockley 1986a).

The Sloan Canyon Formation (Dockum Group) of eastern New Mexico and Texas, which is in part equivalent to the Chinle Formation, has also yielded a remarkable trackway assemblage at a locality previously known only for a few isolated coelophysid and rhynchosaur tracks of the type described from Moffat County, Colorado (Baird 1964). Just as it is surprising to find dozens of trackways in the Chinle Formation where none was previously known, it is equally astonishing to find that the Sloan Canyon Formation exhibits almost one hundred trackways dominated by forms differ-

Figure 3. Interpretation of the conditions leading to the perservation of phytosaur tracks at a Dockum track site in New Mexico. Block diagram sequence shows (a) preflood fluvial system with terrestrial track makers predominating along the river banks, (b) flood stage obliging phytosaur migration to margins of swollen river, and (c) waning flood stage when phytosaur tracks are made on newly deposited sand sheets. Note upright or high walk inferred from trackways. (See Lockley 1986b for map of track site.)

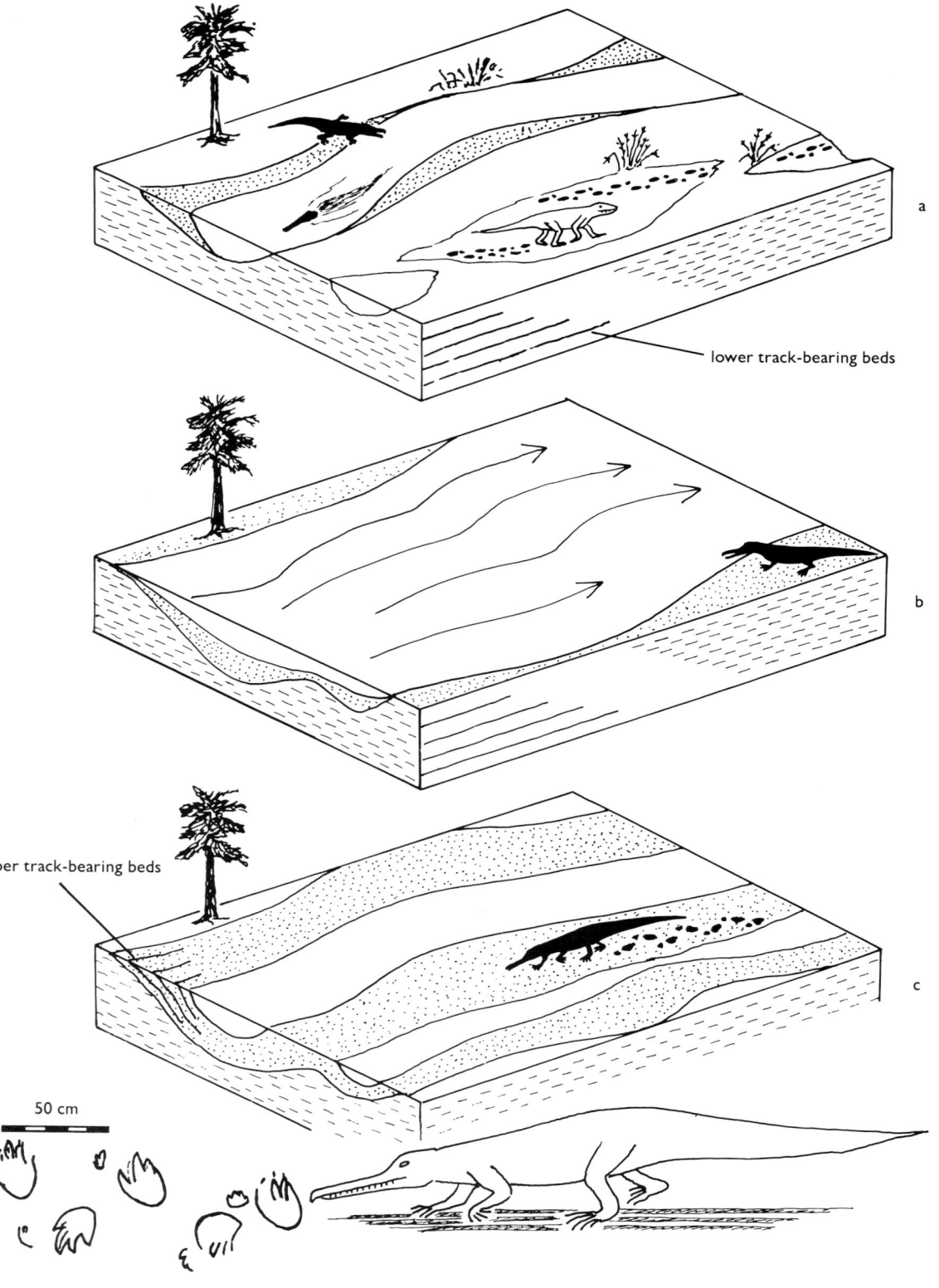

lower track-bearing beds

upper track-bearing beds

50 cm

ent from the isolated and rarer specimens described by Baird.

Based on the occurrence of approximately fifty large presumed phytosaur trackways in association with an exhumed river channel complex the site has been dubbed "Phytosaur Gulch." According to Parrish (in press), "Previously trackways of phytosaurs have not been recognised." This is presumably largely due to the predominantly aquatic mode of life of phytosaurs. The conclusion that these particular trackways represent phytosaurs can be substantiated in many ways. The trackways are found associated with, and to large degree oriented parallel to, an exhumed fluvial channel (Fig. 3; see also Lockley 1986b: fig. 17). The site also yields fish-bearing coprolites and phytosaur teeth, an unusual coincidence of trace and body fossil evidence. Aquatic animals would not be expected to stray far from fluvial settings, whereas terrestrial track makers like chirotheres were evidently more active along the banks. Phytosaur tracks would be expected on land after a flood had deposited fresh sand and mud along the river bank: as the waters rose the phytosaurs would probably retreat to the margins to avoid the faster-flowing, turbid torrents; as the flood waned they would edge back to the river, possibly scavenging flood victims along the riverbank, before resuming river hunting once the flood had fully subsided. Such a plausible scenario explains the presence of flood-derived sediment with the walking trackways of predominantly aquatic animals.

Other important evidence substantiating the phytosaur interpretation comes from the configuration of the trackways. As suggested by Parrish (in press) in his assessment of the structure and function of the phytosaur tarsus, these animals had a sprawling gait. The pace angulation, which measures the degree of sprawling, is generally lower for the manus (front foot) (90 degrees) than for the pes (back foot) print (130 degrees). The midline of the pes and manus tracks also turns out at quite a high angle from the midline of the trackway as predicted by Parrish. This seems to be consistent with an aquatic adaptation, in which propulsive and steering strokes are more in a horizontal lateral plane than they are parallel to the vertical midline (sag-gital) plane as in most terrestrial quadrupeds. Phytosaurs, however, probably used their tails more than their limbs for propulsion. The generally large size of the tracks (pes length : width = 30 : 20 centimeters) also supports the phytosaur interpretation; in some instances trackways approaching the channel appear to end abruptly as if the animal had swum off in shallow water.

Such new trackway evidence enhances our ability to propose authentic restorations. For example, tail-drag impressions were not observed, implying that a phytosaur walked with its hind legs quite well adducted toward the midline, thus elevating and cantilevering the backbone over the raised hips. The bonanza of trackways at Phytosaur Gulch also indicates the potential of track sites for providing insight into the behavioral response of animals to the climatic and sedimentological events responsible for the deposition of footprint beds. Finally at this site in decreasing order of relative abundance we can also picture large quadrupedal pseudosuchians (chirotheres) and rare dicynodonts as part of the large vertebrate fauna. We know that smaller forms like coelophysids and lacertilians (lizards or sphenodontids?) were also present along the banks, although based on trackway evidence they may have not been common.

Jurassic track sites in the western United States are at least as abundant as those of the Triassic or Cretaceous age. Dinosaur trackways have been reported from the successive Wingate, Moenave, Kayenta, Navajo, Entrada, and Morrison Formations of Arizona, Colorado, and Utah, but dinosaurs are neither abundant nor well known from any but the Morrison Formation. Although this fact alone might encourage one to study the earlier trackway evidence to supplement a sparse record, at present the younger Morrison trackways command more attention. The reasons for this are that they are currently better known (Lockley 1986a; Lockley, Houck, and Prince 1986) and can be studied in the context of the world-famous and well-preserved Morrison dinosaur fauna known from skeletal remains (Dodson et al. 1980).

Above all others the Purgatory River site in southeastern Colorado stands as a remarkable example of a track site yielding a wealth of da-

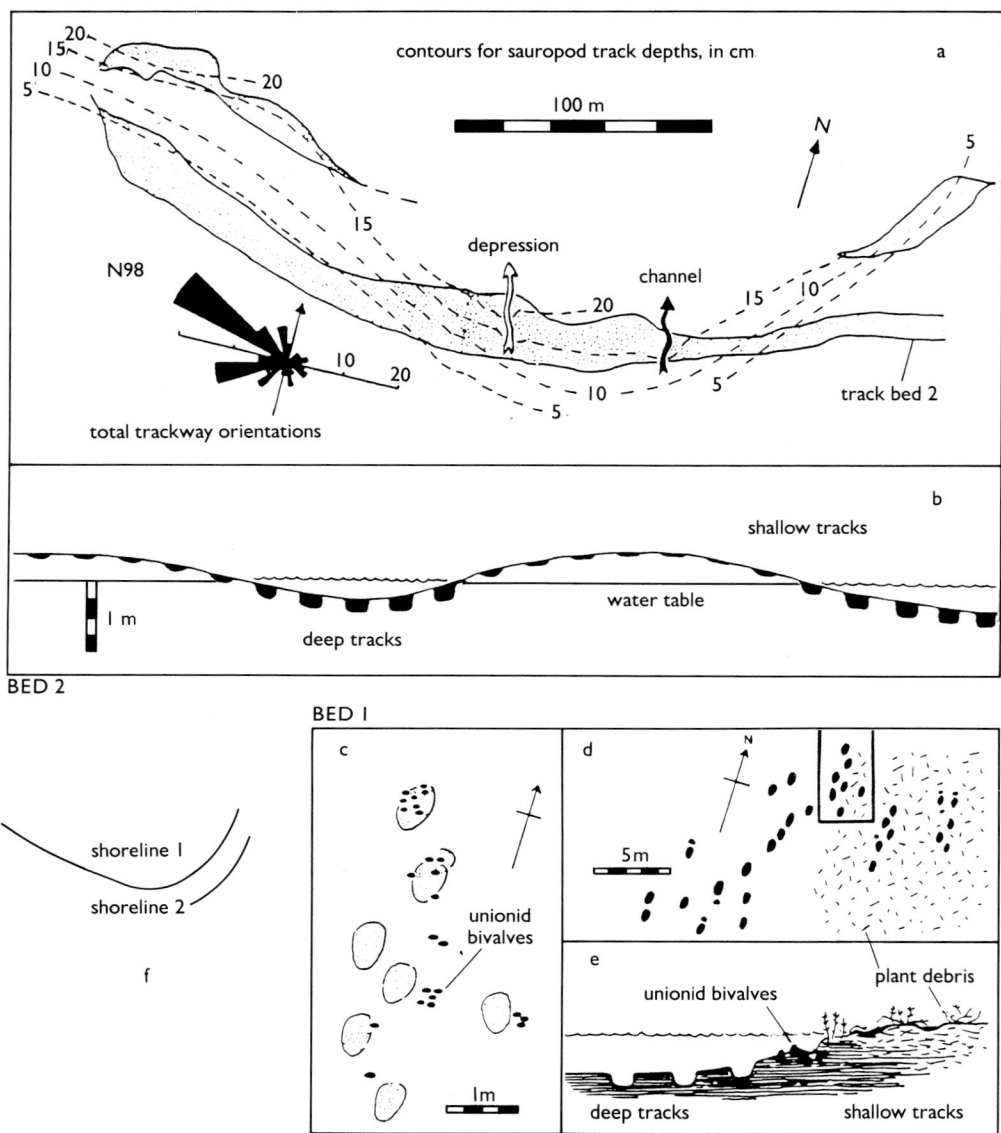

Figure 4. Trackway evidence for shoreline position in footprint beds 2 (a, b) and 1 (c–e) at the Purgatory River track site, Morrison Formation of southeastern Colorado (after Lockley 1986a, b). a. Contours of sauropod footprint depth show a northerly facing shoreline embayment with contours V-ing toward a depression and channel, which represent an ancient drainage, a classic pattern in geomorphology; the predominant trend of trackways follows the westward shoreline of the embayment. b. Schematic illustration of the relationship between track depth and water table, modified after the data in a. c. Distribution of trampled and disturbed bivalve shells along a sauropod trackway. d and e. Plan view and schematic cross-section of trackways and plant debris at the eastern end of trackbed 1; inset in d shows location of the trackway in c. f. Reconstructed shoreline positions for beds 1 and 2, showing coincidence of shoreline at the eastern end of the site at two different time intervals.

ta that invites detailed paleoenvironmental reconstruction. First discovered in 1935 and visited by Barnum Brown's assistant Roland T. Bird in 1938, the potential of the site was soon recognized (Maclary 1938; Bird 1985). Because of the discovery of the more accessible and somewhat better preserved Texas trackways, the site's potential was not comprehensively studied at that time.

Now that it has been investigated by the University of Colorado at Denver many interesting and remarkable facts emerge. It appears to be the largest mapped track site known anywhere in the world with more than thirteen hundred tracks comprising at least one hundred different trackways. The most obvious tracks occur in the second of four successive track beds. Beds 1 and 2 contain abundant footprints, and the trackway configurations are related to the lake shoreline and can help in its reconstruction (Figs. 4 and 5). For example, in bed 1 at the eastern end of the exposures a group of north to north-northwestward trending sauropod trackways appears to define the shoreline trend. This conclusion is based on several lines of evidence intimately related to the footprints. First as one progresses lakeward (northwestward) the micritic track-bearing bed dips slightly and the tracks become much deeper. On the shoreward (eastward) side abundant impressions of vegetation are found and the tracks are so shallow as to be almost without discernible relief, recognizable mainly by their distinctive purple color. Finally and most dramatically at the place where the plant zone gives way to the deep-track zone (Fig. 4c–e), one finds a north-south trending zone of trampled fresh-water clams. These presumably flourished in the periodically wave-agitated shoreline waters adjacent to the vegetated shore until they met sudden death. Sauropod herds had considerable impact on the environments they frequented. The cause of the clam carnage might be questioned on the basis of the evidence above but is hardly in doubt. As shown in Figure 4 the clams are found only in footprints or in the disturbed, bulged rims of sediment surrounding them. They are all articulated and spar filled, a sure sign of rapid (almost instant) burial and death. None is oriented in life position; instead they either lie flat and crushed in the tracks or are randomly oriented in the bulged rims, sometimes with long axes paralleling the inferred principal stress direction (Lockley 1986a, b).

From an artistic viewpoint the novel possibility of a clam's or snail's eye view of a passing brontosaur herd is suggested. Other, broader views might incorporate a group of brontosaurs traveling northward along a west-facing shoreline, some in the shallow water, others trampling through the lakeside vegetation.

Similar reconstructions are possible based on trackway data from bed 2. Here the abundance of brontosaur and other trackway data permits a more extensive base map and shoreline reconstruction indicating a northwestward-facing embayment at this time. Evidently the westward-facing shoreline followed the same geographic trend as during the time of bed 1, thus indicating some continuity of lake shoreline configuration through time. The main trackway trends, however, appear to be westward and associated with the east-west shoreline of this embayment. As shown in Doug Henderson's restoration (Fig. 5) sauropods followed this shoreline, traveling in gregarious groups, thus suggesting that trackway configurations are often controlled by a combination of factors. The evidence for the shoreline is clear, whereas the evidence for herding is based on the fact that the trackways are parallel (nonoverlapping with consistent intertrackway spacing), of approximately the same footprint size and depth, and indicate a consistent speed of progression at a walking pace. These criteria are unlikely to combine in the observed configuration as a result of the passage of separate individuals. In addition there is other sauropod track evidence from Texas (Bird 1944, 1985) and Arkansas (Pittman 1984), indicating gregarious tendencies in these dinosaurs.

The sediments of bed 2 are also different, consisting of a crudely graded, carbonate grainstone with well-developed wave ripples. This lithology, which includes ooids, broken-shell debris, and other heterogeneous material, indicates a high-energy shoreline deposit, which evidently accumulated as a result of storm activity. Apart from being one of the first lacustrine storm-generated deposits recorded from the Morrison Formation, this type of deposit may provide insights into the local climatic regime. Dodson et al. (1980) have suggested that a seasonal climate prevailed during Morrison time. If this is true, then storms may have been associated with the onset of the rainy season. Such an inference would be consistent with the fact that soon after the footprints were made, they were covered and preserved by shallow water sediment. For this to have happened the lake must have been replenished, by run-off and/or groundwater recharge, before the fresh tracks were eroded or destroyed by overprinting.

A similar scenario, involving different sediments, was reported from the Pliocene of eastern Africa by Hay and Leakey (1982: 55), who described a succession of footprint horizons "deposited over a short span, perhaps in a few weeks near the end of the savanna dry season and extending into the early part of the rainy season." They also reported "the abrupt appearance of footprints of elephants and other large animals in the upper unit" (Leakey and Hay 1979: 318), which could be "at least in part" related to "their migration which accompanies the rainy season." The same might be true for the brontosaur trackways in the Morrison.

If there is a close genetic relationship between patterns of climatic cyclicity, seasonality, sediment deposition, and animal behavior, certain types of trackway evidence could be expected to appear repeatedly in the footprint record. Observations by Moss (1975) suggest that elephants, for example, frequent lakeshores or water holes more during the dry season, and Bakker (1971) regards brontosaurs as ecologically like elephants. Thus the artistic restoration of the sauropod group might be viewed in the context of seasonal migration. Previous references to sauropod migration (Antunes 1976; Russell, Beland, and McIntosh 1980) lack convincing supporting evidence. Although tenuous, the link between modern observations of elephants, a Pliocene footprint site, and the sedimentology of the Morrison track site suggest another line of evidence.

Because of the attention given to the potential of Cretaceous track sites in Texas, it is unnecessary to dwell at any length on their usefulness in enhancing authentic reconstructions. Each site yields its own exclusive data set, and some are far more significant than others. Outside Texas a great wealth of Cretaceous trackway data has also emerged from the Rocky Mountain region (Currie 1983; Lockley, Young, and Carpenter 1983; Lockley 1985, 1986b), which has inspired artistic restorations (e.g., Paul in Bird 1985: 18).

In his discussion of Aptian-Albian tracksites in Canada Currie (1983) outlined the potential for recognizing herd structure among ornithopods. Track sites of approximately the same age in Colorado (Lockley 1985) also yield similar trackways indicating that ornithopods frequently progressed quadrupedally. The very name *ornithopod* conjures up a picture of a biped, and in most instances ornithopods such as iguanodontids (early Cretaceous) and hadrosaurs (late Cretaceous) have been restored in bipedal postures. More recently restorations by Gregory Paul and Eleanor Kish have included ornithopods (hadrosaurs) in quadrupedal progression. The reasons for this reassessment of ornithopod posture and locomotion have been succinctly outlined by Paul (in press) and are in part due to, or supported by, footprint evidence (e.g., Currie 1983). The Colorado trackway evidence (Lockley 1985) is entirely consistent with Paul's interpretations. As he points out, however, trackways can be misleading if not carefully interpreted. As a quadruped progresses it may overprint its front footprint with a hind footprint, thus leaving what appears to be a trackway attributable to a biped. Such a phenomenon has recently been documented for sauropods at the Purgatory River site where all gradations of overprinting occur (primary overlap sensu Peabody 1959). Great care should therefore be taken in the interpretation of ornithopod trackways, and students of ichnology should be aware of clear front footprint tracks (cf. Lockley 1985) or, better still, partially overlapped front footprint impressions that have yet to be documented. The probability of finding new trackways is very high, particularly in units like the Mesaverde Group where much untapped potential is known to exist (Lockley, Young, and Carpenter 1983; Lockley 1986b).

Failure to recognize the full potential of trackways and track sites has frequently been a contributing factor in the proliferation of incorrect reconstructions of dinosaur activity. Even where good trackway evidence existed and was well known the interpretation rarely was adequate. For example, the Texan track sites reviewed here tell us that sauropods did not drag their tails, yet probably ninety-nine percent of all sauropod reconstructions made in the last fifty years have suggested that they did. Even Bird (1939, 1944, 1985) who studied the site, was so conditioned by the "tail-dragging concept" that he devised an elaborate shallow-water scenario to float their tails above the substrate. This neither makes sense in the light of the evidence of mud clots that fell from the sauropod feet nor in the context of what we know of the poor-preservation potential of tracks made underwater (Lockley 1986a). It is ironic, however, that despite the considerable potential of trackways for changing such outdated notions the new restorations seem to rely heavily on revised interpretation of functional morphology. The fact that trackway evidence clearly points to the same conclusion and has sometimes been known for generations appears to be almost incidental and suggests a lack of faith in footprint evidence. Perhaps it is this lack of faith that has contributed to the poor progress of vertebrate ichnology. Hopefully the renewed interest in tracks, following in the wake of the new wave of dinosaur consciousness, will allow footprint evidence to be used to fuller advantage.

The potential of footprint evidence should be viewed in the broader context of track sites. Often these represent unique records of animal activity at a particular place and time and thus are as close to snapshots of the past as any known paleontologic evidence. The concept of the track assemblage, or ichnocoenosis, as a dynamic census of ancient communities should be of considerable interest now that ecological principles are effectively integrated into the study of paleontology.

The study of Triassic, Jurassic, and Cretaceous dinosaur track sites in the western United States emphasizes the hitherto unrecognized potential also evident in many other parts of the world (e.g., Leonardi 1984; see Lockley 1986a, b for other references). Track sites provide a valuable

Figure 5. Artistic reconstruction by Doug Henderson showing sauropods following a lake strandline. Based on trackway evidence in bed 2, Purgatory River site, Colorado. Checklist 103.

census of ancient communities and also shed light on behavior patterns in very specific paleoenvironments. The powerful combination of sedimentological and trackway evidence appears to have significant implications for anyone interested in artistic restorations, and it is hoped that many authentic compositions will arise from a creative blend of scientific track site evidence and artistic talent.

ACKNOWLEDGMENTS

I am grateful to my many colleagues in Colorado who have helped me in the field and lab, in particular D. Adelsperger, K. Conrad, K. Houck, and N. Prince and also to G. Leonardi for his generous and enlightened approach to our discussion of track sites. J. Farlow and G. Paul have also been most helpful in discussing with me Cretaceous tracks and track makers. The Triassic track sites in Colorado and Utah respectively were studied under Colorado permit C-42032 and Utah permit 3 issued by the Bureau of Land Management. Access to sites on private land was facilitated by the kind cooperation of Mr. and Mrs. C. Hughes and Mr. and Mrs. C. Taylor. Thanks also to D. Henderson for Figure 5.

WORKS CITED

Alexander, R. McN. 1976. Estimates of the speeds of dinosaurs. *Nature* 261: 129–30.

Antunes, M. T. 1976. Dinosaurios Eocretaceous de Lagosterios: Ciencias de terra 1: 1–35. Lisbon: Universidade Nova de Lisboa.

Baird, D. 1964. Dockum (Late Triassic) reptile footprints from New Mexico. *Journal of Paleontology* 38: 118–25.

Bakker, R. T. 1968. The superiority of dinosaurs. *Discovery* 3: 11–22.

———. 1971. Ecology of the Brontosaurs. *Nature* 229: 172–74.

———. 1975. Dinosaur renaissance. *Scientific American* 232, no. 4: 58–78.

Bird, R. T. 1939. Thunder in his footsteps. *Natural History* 43: 254–61.

———. 1944. Did Brontosaurus ever walk on land? *Natural History* 53: 61–67.

———. 1985. *Bones for Barnum Brown*. Fort Worth: Texas Christian University Press.

Colbert, E. H. 1985. The Petrified Forest and its vertebrate fauna in Triassic Pangea. *Museum of Northern Arizona Bulletin* 54: 33–43.

Coombs, W. P. 1980. Swimming ability of carnivorous dinosaurs. *Science* 207: 1198–1200.

Currie, P. J. 1983. Hadrosaur trackways from the Lower Cretaceous of Canada. *Acta Palaeontologica Polonica* 28: 1–2, 63–73.

Dodson, P. A., A. K. Behrensmeyer, R. T. Bakker, and J. S. McIntosh. 1980. Taphonomy and paleoecology of the dinosaur beds of the Jurassic Morrison Formation. *Paleobiology* 6, no. 2: 208–32.

Haubold, H. 1984. *Saurierfahrten: Die neue Brehm-Bucheri*. Wittenberg Lutherstadt, East Germany: A ziemsen Verlag.

Hay, R. L., and M. D. Leakey. 1982. The fossil footprints of Laetoli. *Scientific American* 246: 50–57.

Hitchcock, E. 1858. *Ichnology of New England: A report on the sandstone of the Connecticut Valley, especially its fossil footprints*. Boston.

Jenny, J., and J. A. Jossen. 1982. Découverte d'empreintes de pas de dinosauriens dans le Jurassique inférieur (Pleinsbachien) du Haut-Atlas central Maroc. *C. R. Academie Sci. Paris* 294: 223–26.

Langston, W., Jr. 1974. Nonmammalian Comanchean Tetrapods. *Geoscience and Man* 8: 77–102.

———. 1979. Lower Cretaceous dinosaur tracks near Glen Rose, Texas. In *Lower Cretaceous shallow marine environments in the Glen Rose Formation: Dinosaur tracks and plants*. American Association of

Stratigraphic Palynologists. Field Trip Guide 12: 39–55.

Leakey, M. D., and R. L. Hay. 1979. Pliocene footprints in the Laeotolil beds at Laeotoli, northern Tanzania. *Nature* 278: 317–23.

Leonardi, G. 1981. As localidades com rastros fosseis de tetrapodes ria American Latina. In *Anais II Congreso Latino-Americano. Paleonto. Porto Alegre,* 929–40.

———. 1984. Le impronte fossili di dinosauri. In *Sulle orme Dei Dinosauri Paleont.* Ricercatore CNOQ del Brasile.

Leonardi, G., ed. In press. *Glossary and manual of vertebrate paleoichnology.* Brasil: Dept. Nacional de Producão Mineral, Brasilia.

Lockley, M. G. 1985. Vanishing tracks along Alameda Parkway. In *Environments of deposition (and trace fossils) of Cretaceous sandstones of the Western Interior,* ed. C. K. Chamberlain et al., 3: 131–42. S.E.P.M. Field Guide.

———. 1986a. The paleobiological and paleoenvironmental importance of dinosaur footprints. *Palaios* 1: 37–47.

———. 1986b. A guide to dinosaur tracksites of the Colorado Plateau and American Southwest. *University of Colorado at Denver Geology Department Magazine.* Special issue 1, 56 pp.

Lockley, M. G., B. H. Young, and K. Carpenter. 1983. Hadrosaur locomotion and herding behavior: Evidence from footprints in the Grand Mesa Coalfield, Colorado. *Mountain Geology* 20: 5–14.

Lockley, M. G., K. Houck, and N. K. Prince. 1986. North America's largest dinosaur tracksite: Implications for Morrison Formation paleoecology. *Bulletin of the Geological Society of America* 97: 1163–76.

Lull, R. S. 1904. Fossil footprints of the Jura-Trias of North America. *Memoirs of the Boston Society of Natural History.* 5: 461–557.

———. 1953. Triassic life of the Connecticut Valley. *Connecticut State Geological Natural History Survey* 81.

Maclary, J. S. 1938. Dinosaur trails of Purgatory. *Scientific American* 158: 72.

Moss, C. 1975. *Portraits in the wild.* Boston: Houghton Mifflin.

Mossman, D. J., and W. A. S. Sarjeant. 1983. The footprints of fossil animals. *Scientific American* 248: 74–85.

Ostrom, J. H. 1972. Were some dinosaurs gregarious? *Palaeogeography* 11: 287–301.

———. 1985. Social and unsocial dinosaurs. *Field Museum of Natural History Bulletin* 55: 10–21.

Parrish, M. In press. Structure and function of the Tarsus in the phytosaurs (Reptilia: Archosuria). In *The beginning of the age of dinosaurs,* ed. K. Padian. Cambridge: Cambridge University Press.

Paul, G. In press. Reconstructing hadrosaurian dinosaurs and their relations. Mesozoic vertebrate life, vol. 1,

Peabody, F. E. 1959. Trackways of living and fossil salamanders. *University of California Publications in Zoology* 63: 1–72.

Pittman, J. G. 1984. Geology of the De Queen Formation of Arkansas. *Transactions of the Gulf Coast Association of Geological Society* 34: 201–9.

Russell, D. A. 1980. Reflections of the dinosaurian world. In *Aspects of vertebrate history,* ed. L. Jacobs, 257–68. Flagstaff: Museum of Northern Arizona Press.

Russell, D. A., P. Beland, and J. S. McIntosh. 1980. Paleoecology of the dinosaurs of Tendaguru (Tanzania). *Memoirs of the Society of Geological Fr.,* n.s. 139: 169–75.

Sarjeant, W. A. S. 1981. In the footsteps of the dinosaurs. *Expl. Journal* 59: 164–71.

BRINGING DINOSAURS TO LIFE

Mark Hallett

Artists seeking to portray such extraordinary animals as dinosaurs have recognized the need to form an effective partnership with paleontologists and other researchers to distill and interpret the large new mass of data now available to dinosaur students. A synthesis of the artist's technical skills and intimate understanding of animal form, behavior, and ecology, supported by facts from the paleontologist's reservoir of extensive and specialized knowledge, is essential in showing how dinosaurs looked and lived. In addition, new technological tools such as computer-generated images offer the artist-paleontologist team valuable aid in more accurately restoring dinosaurs and their environments.

What did dinosaurs really look like? As an artist involved with the fascinating challenge of depicting dinosaurs and other prehistoric life forms in their environments, I am constantly reminded of how important access to accurate information is to the creation of a realistic, as well as artistic, restoration of long-extinct animals and their worlds.

Accurate information may lie buried, like the dinosaur fossils themselves, in a book, occasional paper, or in the mind of a research associate.

Much information has become available only relatively recently. Modern studies in biomechanics, behavior, and ecology, as well as innovative graphics technologies and an exciting menagerie of newly discovered dinosaurs are waiting to aid the artist intent on bringing the Mesozoic past back to life.

Paleoartists who strive for accuracy place the greatest importance in working closely with paleontologists and other specialists in planning a prehistoric animal restoration. The extensive knowl-

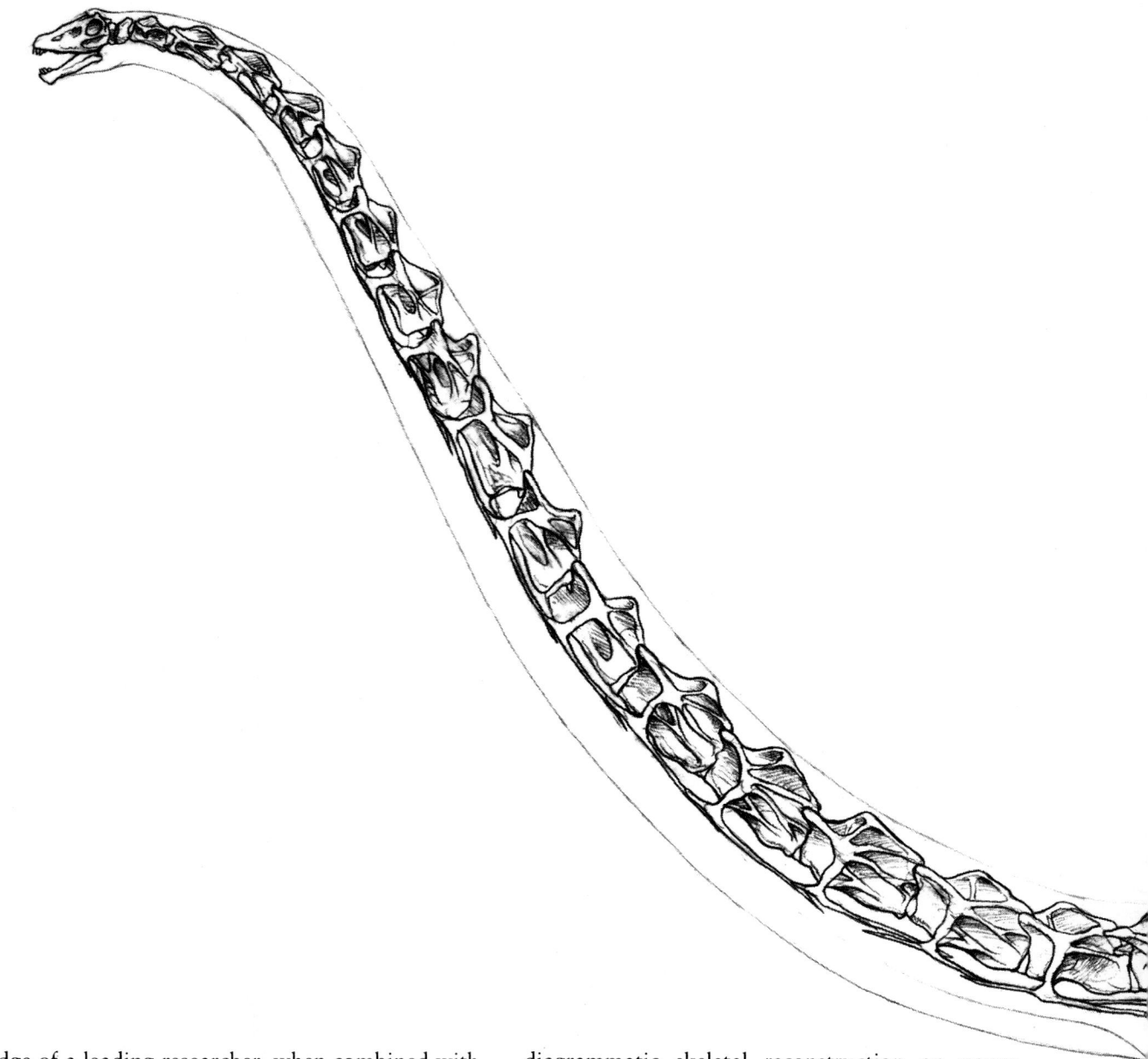

Figure 1. Skeletal reconstruction of *Mamenchisaurus hochuanensis,* based on photographs and drawings of original specimens and studies of other diplodocids, under the direction of John S. McIntosh.

edge of a leading researcher, when combined with the paleoartist's skills, independent research, and understanding of animal form and behavior, as well as the informed opinions of other specialists and fellow artists, is key to creating accurate renditions of a dinosaur or other extinct form.

I begin a restoration by surrounding myself with as much scientific literature on the species as possible and by interviewing or corresponding with a leading student of that particular dinosaur. In addition, I examine and photograph either the original fossil specimens or well-reproduced casts of this material. Since the bones are usually incomplete, a

diagrammatic skeletal reconstruction on paper must be worked out under the direction of the consultant. This was necessary in determining the extent and probable body proportions of the Chinese diplodocid *Mamenchisaurus hochuanensis,* which I undertook to reconstruct under the direction of John McIntosh in January 1986 (Figs. 1 and 2).

Any restoration begins with an accurately reconstructed skeleton (Fig. 3). Not only does the skeleton establish the animal's overall dimensions, it also indicates the posture, musculature, and possible habits. While an already existing mounted skeleton or published reconstruction would seem a windfall at this point, they must be looked on with a critical eye. The osteology of even some supposedly well-known dinosaurs has in the past been partially based on incorrectly restored bones, while skeletal mounts constructed from unequally sized individuals of the same or even different species have created longstanding misconceptions.

The artist and consultant must sometimes decide whether a restoration should be attempted at all. *Spinosaurus,* confidently depicted in popular illustrations as a megalosauridlike theropod with a "sail," is very poorly known and may not even be a dinosaur. When it was proposed as an illustration for a recent book, my consultant, Robert A. Long of the University of California, Berkeley, and I decided that a painting of this animal would be an exercise in pure fantasy and should not be attempted until more complete remains are described.

Direction from a well-informed consultant can not only help the paleoartist avoid these problems but can also provide shortcuts in interpreting scientific data. In starting a new restoration of *Iguanodon* I received simplified and timesaving summaries of technical descriptions about the kinetics of the skull in chewing and limits of the fore-limb movement in a personal communication from David B. Norman of Oxford University, a leading authority on this ornithopod. Based on new concepts of iguanodontid skeletal mechanics developed by Norman, I sketched a close-up of the skull (Fig. 4) and a reconstruction of the skeleton in a quadrupedal walking position instead of the more typically seen bipedal pose (Fig. 5a).

In addition to the informed opinions of paleontologists and other specialists, paleoartists obtain valuable ideas from each other. Like a scientific researcher, the artist can explore the possibilities of the anatomy and biology of dinosaurs through direct visual depictions. Sharing this information with each other, as Stephen Czerkas and Gregory Paul generously have done with me in the past, can help artists consider aspects of dinosaurs of which they may not have previously been aware.

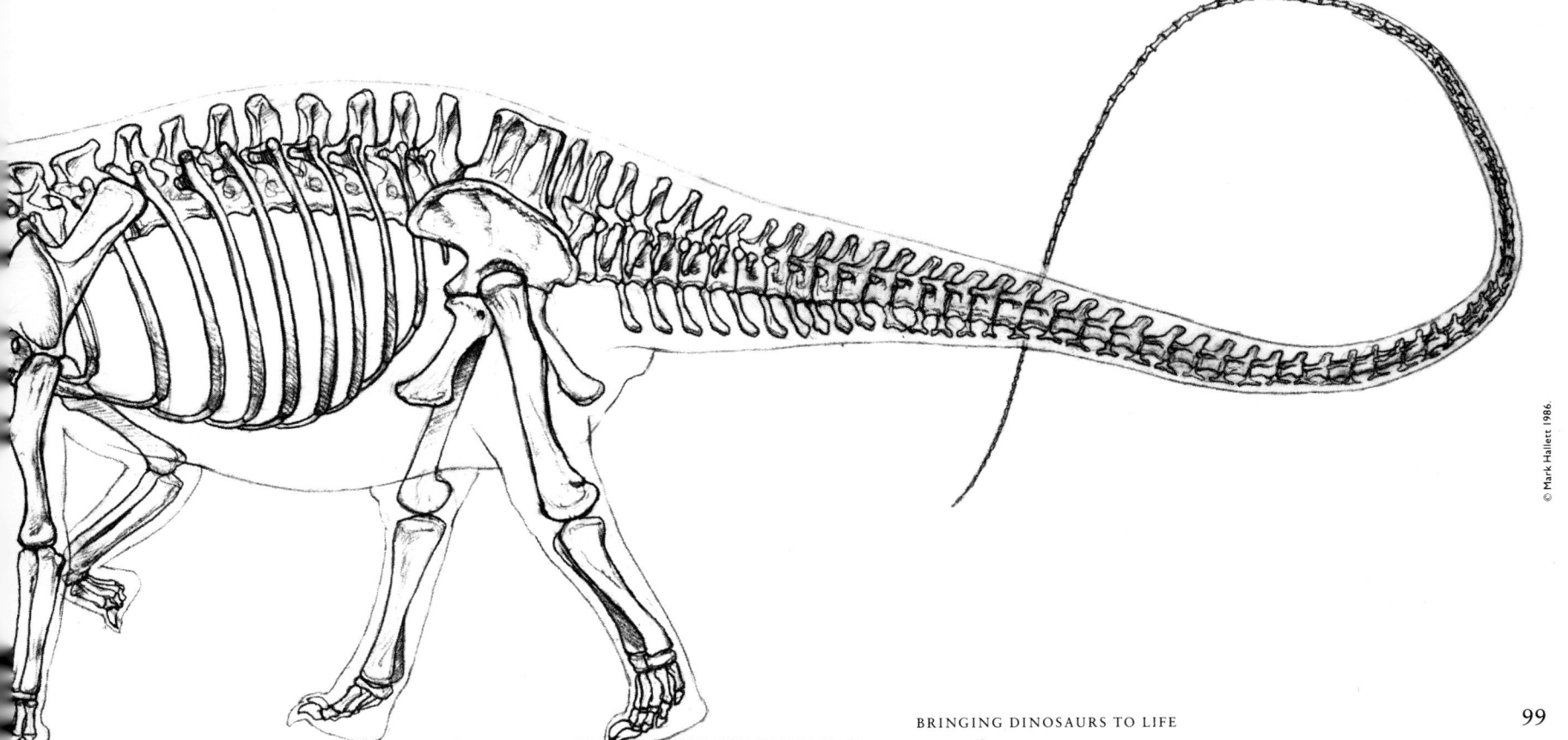

© Mark Hallett 1986.

Figure 2. "Crossing the Flat," a restoration of *Mamenchisaurus hochuanensis.* Checklist 140.

© Mark Hallett 1986.

The next stage, determining the dinosaur's vanished musculature, requires a careful study of the reconstructed skeleton, a cautious comparison with dinosaur relatives, and an artist's ability to model anatomy. Areas of muscle attachment often create distinctive surface features like scars, ridges, and rugosities, or rough places, on bone. These areas on dinosaur skeletons may often be very similar to known areas of muscle attachments on crocodilians and birds, the dinosaurs' closest living relatives (Fig. 6). By assuming that the location and direction of the main muscles on dinosaurs is roughly similar and considering the fossil species' skeletal proportions and possible range of movement, the artist can sketch or sculpt the probable extent of the major muscles.

This approach was the one I took in working out the musculature of *Iguanodon,* whose thoracic and limb morphology I based on the recent studies of Norman (1980), Walter P. Coombs (1979), Paul (personal communication), and the earlier work of R. S. Lull and N. E. Wright (1942) as well as my own notes from dissecting crocodilians and birds. Although the proportions and osteology of the neck suggested similarities to the myology of large birds and some mammalian ungulates, the head was a more difficult area to restore because the ornithopod's distinctive skull and chewing mechanism was unique and is not readily comparable with that of many known vertebrates. In this case Norman's analysis of skull kinetics was vital and helped me arrive at a final tentative version of the musculature (Fig. 5b).

The integument, or hide, is the final stage of reconstructing a dinosaur's soft anatomy. While fossilized skin texture is unfortunately either very incomplete or nonexistent, the paleoartist can draw on logic and his knowledge and observations of living types to complete the animal's outer form. On medium-sized and large dinosaurs prominent compression and stretch folds would certainly have developed around parts of the skin that flex and extend, similar to those developed in modern mammals such as rhinoceroses and elephants (Fig. 2). As in living reptiles like crocodilians and lizards, these areas would be expected to have a smaller scale or tubercle pattern than elsewhere on the body to permit flexibility, while larger areas that did not flex would have had a broad pattern of large scales, or scutes.

The widely debated issue of dinosaur endothermy and ectothermy has a direct bearing on the question of whether smaller dinosaurs like dromaeosaurids or hypsilophodontids should be shown with an outer insulating fur or featherlike pelt. To date no direct evidence exists that any known dinosaur had such a covering: The positive indication for the presence of such insulation in active archosaurs like birds and pterosaurs, however, makes this logical and perhaps even probable. If it is discovered I predict that the pelt will have a furry or hairy look, like the fine, long feathers of living ratites or the fur of mammals instead of the broad, flattened body contour feathers of flying birds. Feathers that no longer have a flying function quickly revert to this type of structure, and I explored this possibility in a restoration of the small Australian coelurosaur *Kakuru kijani* (Fig. 7f).

Birds, the dinosaurs' living descendants, often provide clues to other external details. The scale and claw shapes on the hind and fore feet of many bipedal dinosaurs may have been similar to those of large ground-dwelling birds like ostriches and bustards. The beak, nostrils, and eyelids of birds ranging from condors to emus are good models for dinosaur types like ornithomimids, hypsilophodontids, and others, and I used some of these as references for forms like *Fulgurotherium* in a 1981 painting showing known dinosaur species from Australia (Fig. 7b).

While sketching animals at zoos and pet shops one may become familiar with the way the skin, fur, and feather patterns of living animals behave. In my studio I supplement these studies with an extensive scrap file of clippings, photographs, and other references that provide ideas for the lifelike details that make a drawing or painting look convincing. These and other sources helped me arrive at a final solution for the skin of *Iguanodon* (Fig. 5c).

Until recently most restored dinosaurs were either drab gray, drab brown, or drab green. The assumption was that since the actual colors were unknown, these were "safe" colors. No one seemed to realize, with the exception of some paleoartists like Zdeněk Burian and Rudolph Zallinger, that to survive in their world dinosaurs may have depended on all the colors and patterns found in modern vertebrates (Fig. 7). I have always been intrigued by theories of animal coloration, and many of the ideas developed by the zoologist A. Portmann (1952) and the artist-naturalist Jonathan Kingdon (1977) can be applied to dinosaurs.

As in hatchling ostriches or crocodilians, for example, most baby dinosaurs would almost certainly have needed cryptic markings to help them hide from predators. In some large herbivorous forms like hadrosaurs these markings might have changed as the animals grew larger to a disruptive pattern to break up their body outlines, thus helping these types avoid detection from a distance by predators. Solitary hunters probably depended on concealment by spots or stripes in ambushing prey, like tigers or leopards, while those that hunted cooperatively may have had bold, random markings to help pack members know each others' identities and locations while maneuvering for an attack, as one finds in African hunting dogs.

Like morphology, color in dinosaurs might have evolved in tandem to reinforce specific types of behavior, such as those that promote recognition or bonding between the sexes or parents and offspring; other colors may have functioned to signal the onset of breeding condition or as an aid to intimidation during periods of intraspecific rivalry (Fig. 8).

At present there is no proof for pattern or colors in dinosaurs. Considering the likelihood that their lives were governed by the same behavioral principles as modern vertebrates, it seems probable that most of these animals may have had patterns and colors of almost any kind rather than being drab and patternless.

To ascertain a dinosaur's possible behavior and habits, after preparing a formal anatomical study I often make small behavioral sketches that help me visualize its posture, weight, and body movement. After making the anatomical renderings of *Iguanodon,* for example, I wanted to determine the appearance and flexibility of the hand. For this I drew upon Norman's recent studies (1980) of

potential joint movement and original research by Phil Currie (personal communication) and Stephen Czerkas (personal communication) of mummified hadrosaur hands (Fig. 9).

The re-creation of the vanished environment in which the dinosaur lived requires the same combination of artistic skill and application of scientific knowledge as does the restoration of the animal itself. The paleoartist sometimes draws on knowledge obtained from several specialists in such areas as geology, paleobotany, and taphonomy, the study of what happens to an animal between its death and ultimate burial. If the painting is to be of a particular locality at a relatively specific geological period, I first work with a consultant to obtain a precise idea of the conditions prevailing in the area during that time. For a 1977 panorama of the Dinosaur National Monument area during the Morrison Formation of the Upper Jurassic, the late paleontologist Russell King worked with me on developing an aerial scene showing the then existing river that meandered eastward over a floodplain and the known chain of active volcanoes toward the west. Magazine photographs of modern river and subtropical forest scenes, plus detailed information on the fossil flora of the time and surviving similar plants, helped me re-create the appearance of this 140 million-year-old landscape (Fig. 10). Further research and King's knowledge of the site finally permitted depiction of the correct position of the sauropod carcasses on the sandbank that later became the fossil-bearing lens.

Such a working partnership between paleoartist and paleontologist is much easier when both are comfortable with each other's professional language. A researcher who uses simple drawings or diagrams to express concepts can greatly aid illustrators like myself, who often think in terms of visual or spatial concepts. For an artist, getting in the habit of using the proper scientific terms not only facilitates working with a specialist but allows one to more easily gather and understand data from the scientific literature.

In the future the artist and paleontologist may find themselves working with a new partner in their efforts to bring the past to life, the computer programmer. The developing technological art of

Figure 3. Reconstructed skeleton of *Stegosaurus stenops* (a) based on a recent find at Dinosaur National Monument, Utah, and a restoration of *S. stenops* (b) shown defending itself against predator *Ceratosaurus nasicornis* (Checklist 138). From *Ranger Rick's Dinosaur Book*, with permission of the National Wildlife Foundation.

a

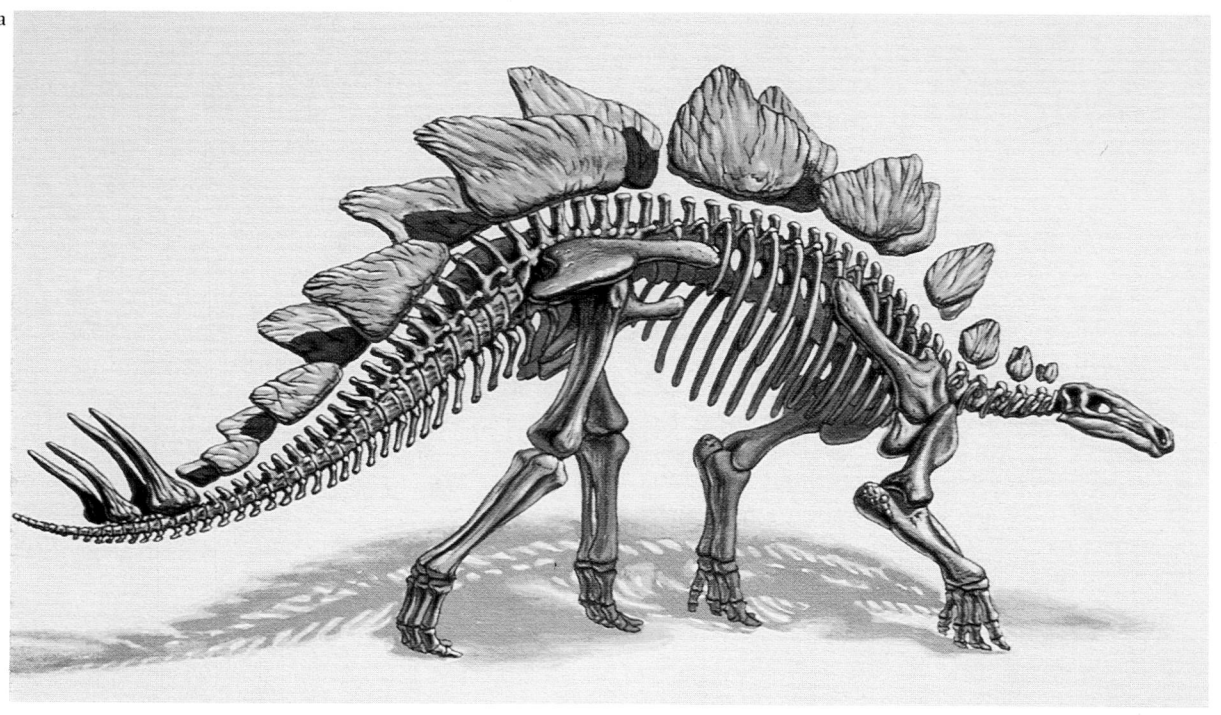

© Mark Hallett 1983

b

computerized graphic images, which already uses processes such as three-dimensional modeling, texture mapping, shading programs, and animation to create special effects for flight-simulation films and television commercials, could eventually become an invaluable tool for depicting dinosaurs and other ancient life forms.

To better understand the three-dimensional form of a skull or skeleton as an aid to sculpting or painting, an artist, after consulting with a paleontologist, might work with a computer technician, who, from a set of orthographic line drawings, could create a wire-frame image of the skull or other skeletal element on a vector-graphic system. This wire-frame image would then be progressively refined as a "solid" form by either building over the image with tiny polygonal shapes or projecting simple mathematically defined shapes, or primitives, onto the image. The resulting "three-dimensional" picture of the skeleton could be manipulated on the screen to provide the paleoartist with any desired view and close-up needed.

This same imaging process could be used to accurately determine how dinosaurs might appear at different ages. In forms like *Maiasaura*, in which extremely young and mature skull morphology is known, models of adult and hatchling skulls could be sectioned and measured to establish two systems of corresponding points, programmed for different perspective planes. By programming assumed progressive or allometric growth factors (such as the size of the orbit) the artist could follow the gradual changes between the juvenile and adult on the screen, allowing construction of a model of the ontogeny of *Maiasaura*, comparable to that known for other dinosaurs like *Protoceratops*.

An even more fascinating possibility would be to re-create as a computer-animated simulation an event like the Glen Rose Sauropod Migration or Lark Quarry Dinosaur Stampede from Australia described by Thulborn and Wade (1979). To do so a map of the trackway assemblage would be recorded on a data tablet and programmed as a perspective view on a computer screen. Since the size, depth, and angle of the tracks can often furnish information about the size, weight, and approximate speed of an animal, the data from a sin-

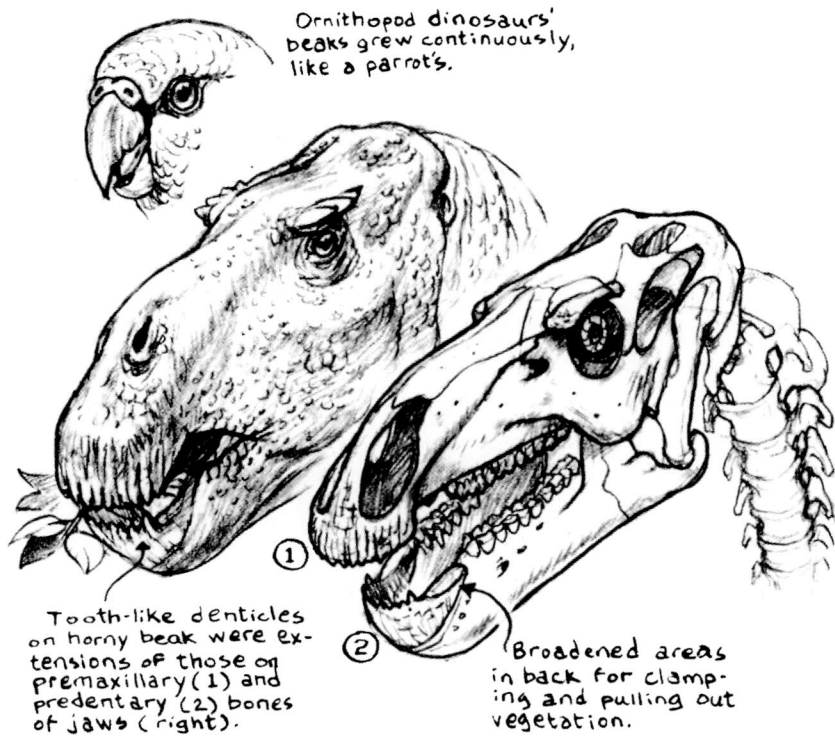

Ornithopod dinosaurs' beaks grew continuously, like a parrot's.

Tooth-like denticles on horny beak were extensions of those on premaxillary (1) and predentary (2) bones of jaws (right).

Broadened areas in back for clamping and pulling out vegetation.

Figure 4. Detail of the skull of *Iguanodon bernissartensis*, comparing its horny beak with that of a parrot.

c

Figure 5. Skeletal reconstruction and muscular and integument restorations (a–c, respectively) of *Iguanodon bernissartensis.*

HALLETT

a

b

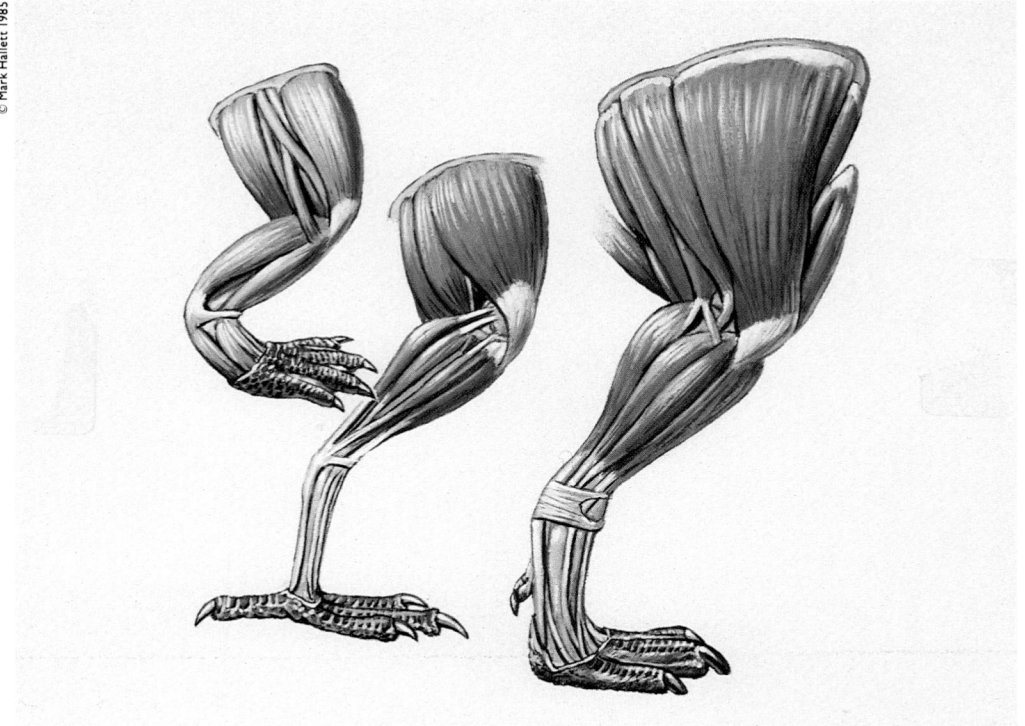

Figure 6. Comparison of hind-limb musculature in *Tyrannosaurus rex,* an alligator, and a pigeon.

Figure 7. "Australian Dinosaurs," 1981. In this composite scene of Early Cretaceous animals from different times and places, ornithopods are represented by *Muttaburrasaurus* (a) and *Fulgurotherium* (b). The herbivores include *Minmi* (c), two sauropods, *Austrosaurus* (d), and an unnamed brachiosaurid (e). The predators depicted are a coelurosaurid, *Kakuru* (f), and the megalosaurid *Rapator* (g), shown here chasing an eagle-sized pterosaur (h) from its kill. From *Science Digest* with permission of the Hearst Corporation.

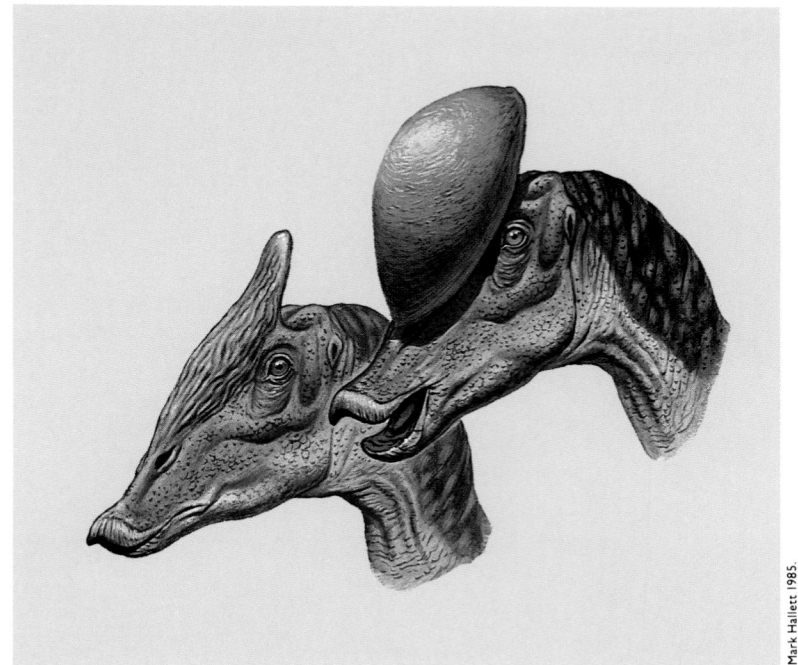

Figure 8. As in some modern birds, certain dinosaurs may have had areas of bright color to aid in individual recognition or bonding between the sexes or parents and offspring. The hadrosaur, *Saurolophus angustirostris,* suspected of having an inflatable nasal skin, may also have signalled the onset of breeding condition with the aid of color.

109

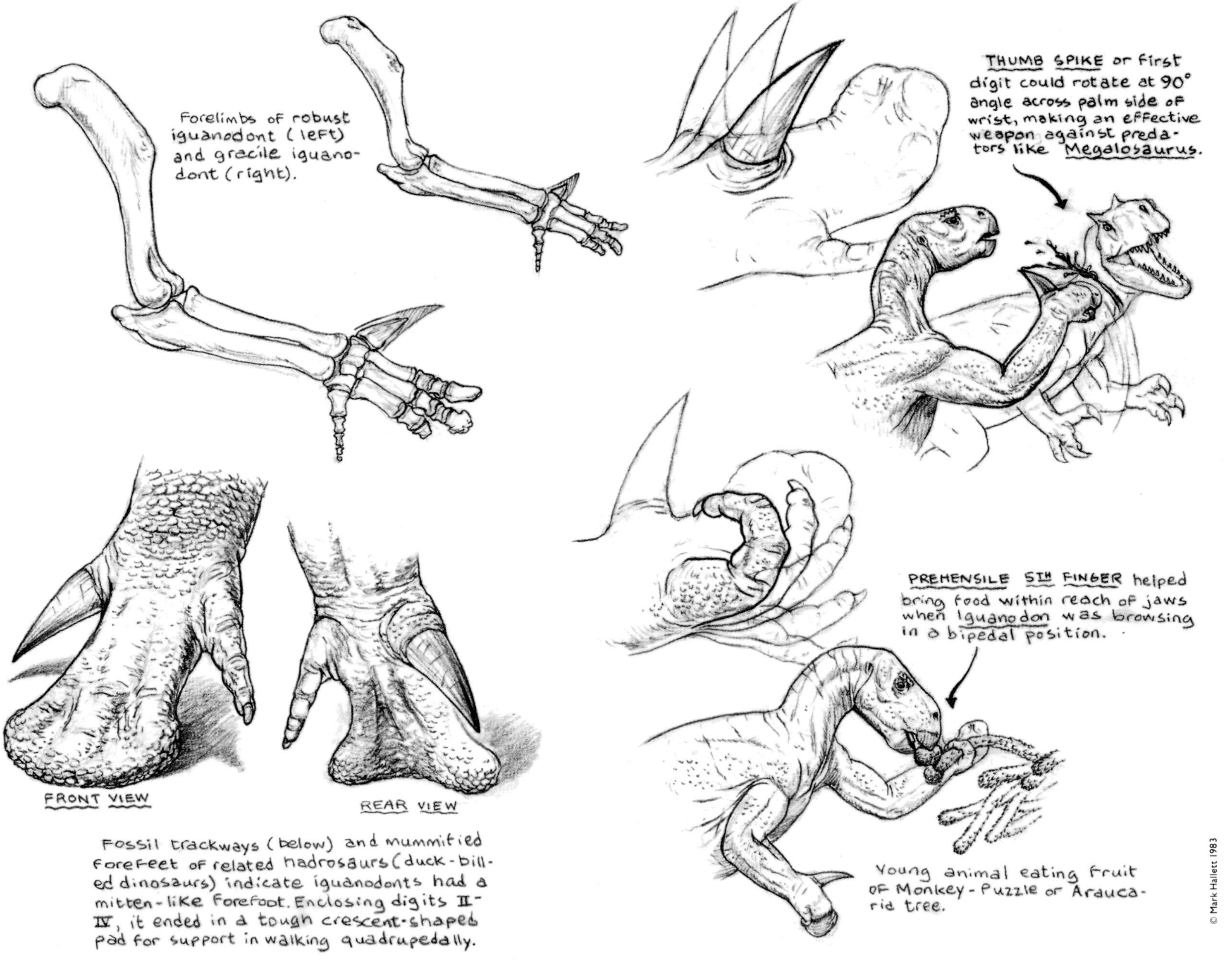

Forelimbs of robust iguanodont (left) and gracile iguanodont (right).

THUMB SPIKE or first digit could rotate at 90° angle across palm side of wrist, making an effective weapon against predators like Megalosaurus.

FRONT VIEW

REAR VIEW

Fossil trackways (below) and mummified forefeet of related hadrosaurs (duck-billed dinosaurs) indicate iguanodonts had a mitten-like forefoot. Enclosing digits II-IV, it ended in a tough crescent-shaped pad for support in walking quadrupedally.

PREHENSILE 5TH FINGER helped bring food within reach of jaws when Iguanodon was browsing in a bipedal position.

Young animal eating fruit of Monkey-Puzzle or Araucarid tree.

© Mark Hallett 1983

Figure 9. Behavioral sketches can often aid in visualizing a dinosaur's movements. Checklist 126.

gle individual's footprints, if these could be isolated, could be used to construct and program dinosaur images that would fit the size of each set of tracks. Combined with texture mapping and shading techniques, these images could be animated to show the sauropod herd migrating from a moving "camera-eye" vantage point in a simulated Jurassic landscape.

While at present such an experimental project would be enormously time-consuming and expensive, this and other imaging technologies like holography could someday become a valuable and routinely used technique for re-creating scientifically accurate scenes and animated films of dinosaurs in their environments. These could serve either as models for paleoartists or as ends in themselves. Such a Mesozoic time machine may be years away, but its fuel, the combined knowledge, skills, and imagination of the paleontologist and artist, already exists.

Acknowledgments

I wish to thank the many people who either directly or ultimately contributed toward making this article possible. These are David B. Norman, John McIntosh and Phillip Currie, who provided me with much of the material used in my various dinosaur studies and restorations, my fellow paleoartists Gregory S. Paul and Stephen and Sylvia Czerkas for their generous help in sharing information and for providing critiques of work in progress, my wife Veronica for her excellent work in photographing transparencies of the drawings and paintings used in this volume and finally my mother Joan G. Hallett, who started me on my long and happy path through the world of prehistoric life.

Works Cited

Coombs, W. P., Jr. 1979. Osteology and myology of the hindlimb in the Ankylosauria (Reptilia, Ornithischia). *Journal of Paleontology* 5, no. 53: 666–84.

Kingdon, J. 1977. *East African mammals (An atlas of evolution in Africa)*. Vol. 1114. London: Academic Press.

Lull, R. S., and N. E. Wright. 1942. *Hadrosaurian dinosaurs of North America*. Geological Society of America, Special Paper, no. 40.

Norman, D. B. 1980. *On the ornithischian dinosaur Iguanodon bernissartensis of Bernissart*. Brussels: Institute royal des Sciences naturelles de Belgique.

Portmann, A. 1952. *Animal forms and patterns: A study of the appearance of animals*. New York: Faber & Faber.

Rivlin, R. 1983. Filming by computer. *Technology Illustrated* (February): 28.

Thulborn, R. A., and M. Wade. 1979. Dinosaur stampede in the Cretaceous of Queensland. *Lethaia* 12: 275–79.

OVERLEAF:
Figure 10. "The River," a panorama of late Jurassic Morrison landscape in Utah. Depicted (see key below) are *Brachiosaurus* (a), *Dryosaurus* (b), *Diplodocus* (c), *Ceratosaurus* (d), *Apatosaurus* (e), *Camarasaurus* (f), *Stegosaurus* (g), *Ornitholestes* (h), *Allosaurus* (i), *Camptosaurus* (j), *Barosaurus* (k), and *Goniopholis* (l). Checklist 122.

HALLETT

© Mark Hallett 1977

MODELS AND PAINTINGS OF NORTH AMERICAN DINOSAURS

DALE A. RUSSELL

*I*n technical paleontological writing un-constrained speculation is not encouraged. Artistic restorations of dinosaurs and their environments nevertheless require a use of inference not unlike first-order approximation in astrophysics. Questions are posed during this process that provoke reflection. A major benefit of artist-scientist collaboration, these avenues of thought should not lightly be dismissed for they approximate the self-correcting exercise lying at the root of the advancement of knowledge.

One artist-paleontologist interaction resulted in the fabrication of a hypothetical highly encephalized dinosaur. Initially a model was made of a small Cretaceous dinosaur with a relatively large brain. A logical question suggested by the model was, "What would this animal have evolved into had the dinosaurs not become extinct?" This question might have been answered by nonpaleontologists in a relatively unconstrained manner if the professional response were, "This question cannot be answered." The reaction of the public to the "dinosauroid" indicates that the second model was humanly quite interesting. The academic response was relatively shy. In spite of the fact that improvements could be made to both models, they have not attracted an unusual amount of academic criticism. Perhaps paleontologists are more tolerant than the peer-review process leads them to suspect.

Figure 1. Two of the great horned dinosaurs, *Triceratops,* beside a small lake in a forest of bald cypress and gum trees south of Wood Mountain, Saskatchewan. Painting by Eleanor Kish. From Russell 1977. Courtesy National Museum of Natural Sciences, National Museums of Canada.

Artists are the eyes of paleontologists, and paintings are the window through which nonspecialists can see the dinosaurian world. Paleontologists usually do not paint, and artists do not usually read paleontological treatises; teamwork can be advantageous. A paleontologist must discipline himself to assemble all of the available data needed and thoughtfully translate it from a technical vocabulary into the vernacular, and the artist must discipline himself to be paleontologically (not compositionally) obedient. Words often fail, and a joint effort making scale models can replace words as a means of communication. When models are based on scale skeletal reconstructions it is amazing how the anatomical individuality of an extinct creature emerges. Appropriate environmental images are necessary to construct the setting for a painting, but searching for them in publications is inefficient and frustrating. It is better, and probably cheaper, to travel to living-equivalent environments (and vegetation), and take suitable photographs.

Artists want their paleontological colleagues to commit themselves deeply to any joint endeavor in reconstructing the past. They know that achievement is the result of a mobilization of personal talent to express a concept. One indication of authentic commitment is the presence of a personal quality in art. The remarks which follow are a bit more personal than is usual in paleontological writing. Perhaps this is a result of the gentle and long-sustained encouragement of my artist colleagues to be a bit more involved.

There have been other results. I have found artists to be spontaneous and creative people who identify deeply with their vocation, and they have helped me feel the same way about mine. They tend to approach life in a holistic manner and can be rather unappreciative of the narrow perspective of a specialist. The whole truth is better, but being someone who is often puzzled by what he studies, I usually lack a clear paleontological perspective (this will shortly become obvious). These notes were nevertheless made in the assumption that I am not unique, and in the hope that they might instill patience within the bosom of an artist and courage within the bosom of a paleontologist as they embark upon some future collaboration.

It is possible to imagine two extremes in reconstructing dinosaurs. In one, a cinematographic version, a young lady clad in an interesting bearskin is pursued by a bellowing tyrannosaur. Fortunately a volcano explodes, the earth trembles, and the young lady is snatched to safety (by a blond caveman with a grecian profile) as the tyrannosaur falls off the edge of a cliff. One may ask how do we know that tyrannosaurs were attracted to young ladies clad in bearskins and so begin a process of placing constraints on speculation. At another extreme are countless pages of professional paleontological literature in which an organism's fossilized remains are described and classified with minimal attempt to show how the fossils are related to the organic world from which they were derived. We are tempted to believe that a rigorous scientific approach can not advance beyond the identification of bones.

Working with artists in reconstructing the past requires a willingness to extrapolate combined with a perspective gained through paleontological experience. It can be useful to approach a reconstruction in the way astronomers approach a problem in astrophysics, by bringing information to bear that is understood with varying degrees of precision. Constrained speculation is inherently interesting because it suggests solutions that are plausible but remain to be proven. A self-correcting exercise is thereby initiated that leads to the advancement of knowledge. University students are taught to question the hypotheses of their predecessors but are not discouraged from the humbling and exciting task of identifying useful new hypotheses. The filling in of gray areas is a major preoccupation of artist-paleontologist collaboration which partakes of the same style of approach found in our best graduate schools.

Figure 2. The ostrich dinosaur *Dromicei-omimus* in a redwood grove in central Alberta. Painting by Eleanor Kish. From Russell 1977. Courtesy National Museum of Natural Sciences, National Museums of Canada.

Figure 3. The duckbilled dinosaur *Saurolophus*, with a plesiosaur in the background, along a brackish-water bayou in central Alberta. Painting by Eleanor Kish. From Russell 1977. Courtesy National Museum of Natural Sciences, National Museums of Canada.

I am a paleontologist who neither paints nor makes models, so it has been my good fortune to find these talents in two colleagues with whom I have worked at the National Museum of Natural Sciences in Ottawa, Ontario. These are Eleanor Kish and Ron Seguin. The lessons learned from a series of paintings that are being made to illustrate a general history of the dinosaurs of North America will be discussed first followed by those gained from the fabrication of models suggesting a theme in dinosaurian evolution.

Painted restorations of dinosaurs in their Mesozoic environments are immensely popular, and it is not surprising that during the past century many museums have complemented programs of dinosaurian research with dinosaurian restorations. Museums would perhaps do well to invest more heavily in "state of the art" (and science) reconstructions. Artists can be the eyes of paleontologists; they help them experience a world with which they are intimately concerned but would otherwise never see. But paleontologists must work with artists if the product is to be all it can be. On the average it has taken Kish about one month to produce a painting: it has taken me an average of two weeks to find the supporting information for a painting. A paleontologist must thus discipline himself to assemble all of the available data needed for a restoration and translate it from a technical vocabulary into the vernacular. The translation should be discussed, with its implications, in an ongoing collaboration. It then becomes the task of the artist to faithfully express the translation on canvas. The maxim for the paleontologist is "Thou must not meddle with the composition" and for the artist "Thou must be paleontologically obedient."

In working on *A vanished world: The dinosaurs of western Canada* (Russell 1977; see Figs. 1–5, 7) Kish and I learned that it is not possible to frame anatomical restorations from drawings alone. Words cannot adequately describe the modifications needed to bring an image to a suitable degree of accuracy. Models served as a basis for the restorations of Charles R. Knight, which were supplemented by sketches of living animals (Czerkas and Glut 1982). The interplay between light and shadow is extremely useful in imparting a three-

dimensional effect to paintings. As an aside, Knight's use of birds as well as reptiles in re-creating the form of dinosaurs is compatible with current thinking on dinosaurian-avian relationships and the existence of metabolic rates higher in some dinosaurs than those typical of reptiles. Using mammals as a source of insight for homeothermic dinosaurs is probably less well justified. We have also found that the construction of scale-model skeletons upon which the myology is directly restored is an essential endeavor. It is often amazing how the "personality" of an animal emerges as a consequence of working from a skeletal frame.

During the Mesozoic era herbaceous plants were less abundant than they now are. Larger plants produce less new growth in proportion to their weight than do herbs. Plant biomass must therefore have been more highly visible in dinosaurian landscapes and imparted much "character" to ancient terrestrial ecosystems. Complete plants are seldom found in the fossil record, and whole-plant restorations are rarely made. It is thus very difficult to estimate the appearance of ancient plantscapes. One can consult photographs of living plants of ancient lineage, preferably in their natural surroundings. However, I have spent so many hours fruitlessly scanning illustrations in journals and books that this exercise must be considered as dubiously cost effective. People who study dinosaurs often have an opportunity to travel and thereby may find themselves in vegetational or topographic settings that may provide useful images for restorations. They should take advantage of such opportunities to assemble a collection of resource photographs. Photographs taken in the course of field work in Zambia or on holiday in the Florida Keys are worth much more than a thousand words spoken to a painter, and much less time is required to take a photograph than to find a similar picture in a library.

Every painting with which I have been involved has been the occasion of a special learning experience. Some of these may be of general relevance. One experience concerned the giant late-Jurassic sauropod *Apatosaurus*. My prejudice about the anatomy of the animal at the outset involved three points: that the neck was lean (exceedingly light neck vertebrae would not be in keeping with large, heavy muscles), that the evidence for a strong tendon extending along the top of the neck to the head was tenuous, and that the animal has usually been restored in overly obese proportions (the slenderness of elephants tends to be obscured by their large size). A scale model of the type *A. louisae* skeleton was constructed, and the musculature was carefully restored following the general skeletal contours (Fig. 6). The resulting model was used as the basis for the painted restoration of the living animal.

After the model was made I coauthored a study relating limb bone circumference to body weight in living and extinct animals (Anderson, Hall-Martin, and Russell 1985), which indicated that the *A. louisae* skeleton belonged to an animal weighing thirty-five metric tons. With the able assistance of Bruce Pratte of the Hydraulics Laboratory, National Research Council (Canada), we determined that the scale model displaced a quantity of water equivalent to that indicating a full-sized animal weighing only nineteen metric tons. This was barely within the ninety-five percent confidence limits of the regression used to determine body weight from the bones. At least three possibilities suggest themselves: the model represents an *Apatosaurus* that is atypically lean, the line of regression was skewed because the heaviest point was from a young, raw-boned animal, or the force of gravity at the surface of the earth was stronger because the planetary radius was less 140 million years ago (cf. Stewart 1977). Which option is closest to the truth?

A complex problem set is depicted in a restoration of Dinosaur Provincial Park in Alberta, Canada, as it was during the late Cretaceous. The set can be summarized by the question, "What was the population density of dinosaurs?" To the extent that the herbivorous dinosaurs had reptilian metabolic rates, a given quantity of vegetation could support a greater number of large dinosaurs than of equally large mammals. The carbon dioxide content of the atmosphere may well have been higher than at present during the late Cretaceous (Berner, Lasaga, and Garrels 1983). Living plants grow more rapidly under comparably elevated carbon-dioxide concentrations (Rogers, Thomas, and Bingham 1983). Cretaceous floras were more primitive anatomically and may also have been more sluggish metabolically. Would an atmosphere richer in carbon dioxide have enabled these ancient plants to grow as rapidly and thereby produce as much food for plant-eating animals as do modern plants? With these and other considerations in mind, it has been assumed that dinosaurian populations were usually denser than modern big-game populations, and this option is being shown in a restoration now in preparation (an earlier illustration of this scene [Fig. 7] shows the lush environment but fewer animals).

One vexatious problem was rapidly resolved with a grand first-order approximation. The flora of the early-Cretaceous Cloverly Formation from Wyoming and Montana has never been studied in detail, although the dinosaurs have. On the island of New Caledonia in the southwestern Pacific archaic conifers and lower vascular plants grow in profusion. Some are distantly related to plants that have been collected in strata surrounding the Cloverly Formation. A slide from the New Caledonian bush was simply adapted to the Cloverly scene to present an impression of the appearance of cone-bearing trees, which do not possess the conical shape typical of modern northern conifers.

Another problem could not be resolved. A restoration with a sunset on a bayou along the New Jersey coast during the late Cretaceous shows soft, wet clouds so typical of the tropics and so untypical of Canada. The modern atmospheric analogy used for the setting represents the failure of an attempt to discover whether or not the atmosphere was denser at that time and if its aerodynamic properties were therefore different as well. To evaluate this possibility the diameter for 1,116 species of wind-dispersed spores and pollen belonging to three different basic shapes (monoletes, triletes, bisaccates; see Jansonius and Hills 1976) were plotted against geologic time. In all three cases there was a statistically significant decrease in the diameter of the pollen and spores to about forty percent of the mean diameters of some four hundred million years ago. Are these trends evidence of long-term changes in atmospheric density? Or had natural selection

Figure 4. The duckbilled dinosaur *Edmontosaurus* in a bald-cypress swamp in south central Alberta. Painting by Eleanor Kish. From Russell 1977. Courtesy National Museum of Natural Sciences, National Museums of Canada.

Figure 5. The tyrannosaur *Daspletosaurus* and a fleeing *Champsosaurus* near the edge of a braided streamcourse in south central Alberta. Painting by Eleanor Kish. From Russell 1977. Courtesy National Museum of Natural Sciences, National Museums of Canada.

produced relatively tiny grains that compete better with larger grains in the struggle for existence? In an attempt to resolve the dilemma an aerospace engineer, Parvez Kumar, Space Station Programme Coordinator for the National Research Council (Canada), and I spent more than a year trying to derive atmospheric density from the actual or estimated flight characteristics of birds, bats, and flying reptiles. The effects of various uncertainties prevented us from coming to any conclusions; animals can alter their shapes and aerodynamic properties too freely. It was a fascinating if inconclusive exercise.

In recent years there has been much animated discussion about the impact of an asteroid and the extinction of the dinosaurs. What would the collision have looked like from the surface of the Earth? The matter was resolved in a straightforward way through the assistance of Eric Jones of the Los Alamos National Laboratory (USA) and Ian Halliday and Peter Millman of the Herzberg Institute of Astrophysics (Canada). An evening impact was chosen for a site located four hundred kilometers off the west coast of North America as a satisfactory compromise between geochemical and visual requirements. Two seconds before impact the asteroid would resemble a disk of light four times the diameter of the sun and fourteen times as brilliant. Ten seconds after impact the ejecta plume would be one hundred kilometers high, but because of the curvature of the Earth at that distance it would appear only twenty-eight moon diameters above the horizon. The plume would appear twenty-three moons wide. The artistic problem was greater. How do you portray on canvas an object that is fourteen times brighter than the sun? After several preliminary studies, Kish effectively solved the problem by depicting not the brightness but the strain that is produced in the eye by an intensely bright object. Photographs and telephone calls passed between Los Alamos and Ottawa. The surface of the ejecta plume became smoother, squatter, and oranger at the apex. Later time restorations from the vantage point by the sea would have been rendered impossible because of the more rapid arrival of the shock wave first through the water and then through the air and finally the impact of the

very hot material from the collapsing aprons of the ejecta plume.

Although the hypothesis that the impact of an asteroid exterminated the dinosaurs has recently been supported experimentally and quantitatively (Alvarez et al. 1980), its plausibility was already suggested in 1937 by the passage of the asteroid Hermes within eight hundred thousand kilometers of the Earth. M. W. de Laubenfels later proposed (1956) that had the asteroid collided with the Earth a heat flash much more powerful than the one generated by a cometary fragment that struck Siberia in 1910 (Halliday 1982) would have been generated. He postulated that such an event might have been the cause of terminal Cretaceous extinctions. I am indebted to Donald Wolberg of the New Mexico Bureau of Mines and Mineral Resources for this reference.

Relative to six other international groups (Hoffman and Nitecki 1985), vertebrate paleontologists are the least supportive of the asteroid-impact hypothesis and the most confident that there was not a Cretaceous mass extinction. In a survey taken during the annual Society of Vertebrate Paleontology meetings in the fall of 1985 (Browne 1985), twenty-seven percent of the respondents saw no evidence for a mass extinction at the end of the Cretaceous and forty-three percent believed that the approximately coincidental impact of an asteroid did not cause the extinctions. Although there was a general consensus that the popularity of the topic had benefited paleontology, some felt that the careers of those who favor a gradualistic view might be jeopardized by dissenters through the peer-review process. Although I have been an advocate of extraterrestrially induced catastrophism for more than a decade, I do not feel my career has thereby been impeded. The point of view I hold cannot have been popular, for only four percent of the respondents at the 1985 meeting (I was unable to attend) felt that an asteroid impact resulted in the extinction of the dinosaurs. Here is evidence of academic tolerance.

A compromise position might be that the effects of an asteroid impact were analogous to those of nuclear weapons used at the end of World War II. One alliance of nations was clearly in a military decline, and the nuclear explosions only provided a "coup de grace." The compromise might be credible if late-Cretaceous dinosaurs were morphologically stereotyped and represented by only a few, rare forms. From my perspective, however, this was not the case, and it is highly probable that something unusual occurred at the end of the Cretaceous. If the dinosaurian era ended in a sudden stress of nonbiologic origin ("external abiotic forcing factor", Jablonski 1986: 132), a natural question would be, "What would have happened had the dinosaurs not become extinct?" One response to the question, achieved with the collaboration of Ron Seguin, has aroused a greater amount of interest than any other dinosaur-related speculation in which I have been centrally involved (Figs. 8 and 9).

It could be argued that the question posed above cannot be answered paleontologically, but then others would have answered it who were not paleontologists. Seguin and I had worked together on a model of a dinosaur that possessed a relatively large brain (*Stenonychosaurus,* a junior synonym of *Troödon* [P. Currie, personal communication 1985]), and felt qualified to make an extrapolation. We evaluated the adaptive meaning of the human form and reassessed the proposition (cf. Simpson 1964) that there is a vanishingly small probability of it being a target for natural selective pressures. Like my colleagues at the meetings of the Society of Vertebrate Paleontology who were concerned about the comments of peer reviewers who did not share their opinions on dinosaurian extinction, I was not enthusiastic about the prospect of facing my peers with a model of a highly encephalized bipedal dinosaur. Several times I nearly had it destroyed before it was cast. However, Seguin was less disturbed about embarking on a project that might lie within the area of an academic "taboo," and gave me the courage to see it through. I am also very grateful to my colleagues in our Museum for their firm support on what at the time seemed to me to be a rather dubious venture. Our model was termed a *dinosauroid.*

The origin of the dinosauroid extends many decades into the past. In 1917 the veteran fossil collector Charles H. Sternberg collected a skull cap of

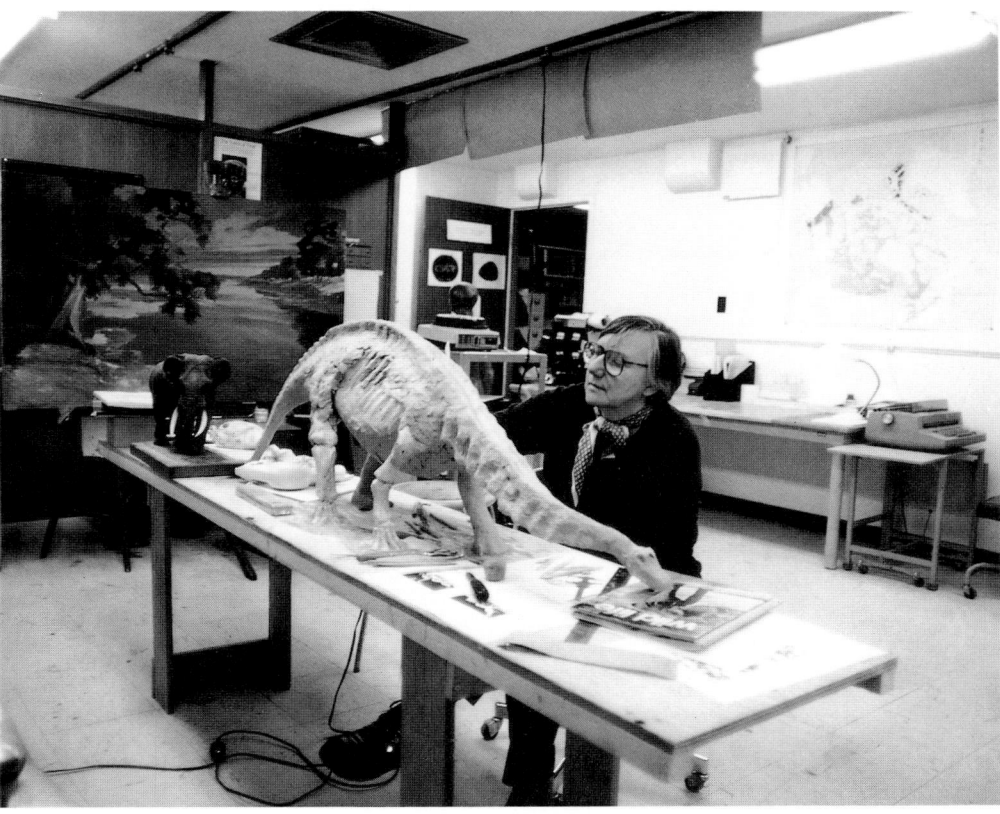

Figure 6. Eleanor Kish sculpting a model of *Apatosaurus louisae*, which was used as the basis for a painted restoration. Courtesy National Museum of Natural Sciences, National Museums of Canada.

a small theropod in what was to become Dinosaur Provincial Park in southern Alberta. It was offered for sale to the American Museum of Natural History (AMNH), New York, on April 23, 1918, was purchased soon after, and received the number AMNH 6174. I noticed the specimen at the museum late in 1965 and at the time accepted its identification as a skull cap of an ostrich dinosaur. During a visit in May 1968 I realized that the specimen was not an ornithomimid and later in the summer collected another specimen (NMC 12340) that demonstrated that the AMNH specimen belonged to an animal formerly named *Stenonychosaurus inequalis* on the basis of a hind foot (Russell 1969). Its relatively enlarged brain (by dinosaurian standards), opposable hand digits, and bipedal posture were reminiscent of human attributes (Russell 1971).

Figure 7. The duckbilled dinosaur *Hypacrosaurus* in a broad-leaved forest near Trochu, Alberta. Painting by Eleanor Kish. From Russell 1977. Courtesy National Museum of Natural Sciences, National Museums of Canada.

Carl Sagan (1977: 135) specifically suggested that *Stenonychosaurus* (*Saurornithoides*) would have given rise to the dominant intelligence on Earth had the dinosaurs not become extinct. Sagan's immensely popular book was probably responsible for several science-fiction stories about intelligent dinosaurs surviving the Cretaceous-Tertiary extinctions. Harry Jerison presented the Fellows' Address, "Smart dinosaurs and comparative psychology," to the Division of Comparative and Physiological Psychology at the American Psychological Association meetings in Toronto on August 29, 1978. Jerison's *Dromiceiomimus sapiens* was postulated to have evolved from ostrich dinosaurs toward an intelligence more dominated by "useful compulsions" than in our own case. I was not aware of Jerison's unpublished address until several years later. Nevertheless, a certain level of curiosity about what highly encephalized dinosaurs might have looked like was clearly in the air during the late 1970s.

The *Stenonychosaurus* and dinosauroid models, together with an explanatory manuscript, were completed during the summer of 1981. Comments from two peer reviewers were at best ambivalent:

"The ideas and methods used in the reconstruction are thorough and even elegant. However, I do not see much value in the extremely speculative 'dinosauroid' discussion. Dinosaur studies today are already characterized by a prominent science fiction component."

"The (dinosauroid) model you caused into being with such surprising results would be difficult to display without encountering retorts you would probably not welcome. Among your peers you would stir much trouble, righteous ridicule and much tut-tutting. I would recommend that—after you have a sufficiency of good photographs—you keep it securely out of sight; or destroy it if the skilled artists will not be too hurt."

Nevertheless, the National Museum of Natural Sciences (Canada), for whom we had made the models, decided not to destroy them, and plans were made to publish the manuscript early in the following year (Russell and Seguin 1982). A preliminary article describing a long-term evolutionary trend toward relatively larger brain sizes in

Figure 8. Dinosauroid and *Stenonychosaurus* by Ron Seguin. Checklist 141 and 142.

Figure 9. The face of the dinosauroid. Checklist 142.

backboned animals had already appeared (Russell 1981), and it was my intention to examine this trend more thoroughly during a sabbatical year at the University of California, Berkeley (see Russell 1982, 1983, and Wyles, Kunkel, and Wilson 1983, who unknown to me were simultaneously working on a similar project). There was no contact with the producers of "ET" nor is there really much resemblance between the respective models. In any event, I was invited to present a seminar to the Department of Paleontology at Berkeley and decided to discuss our work on *Stenonychosaurus* and the dinosauroid in the hope of profiting from the anatomical insights of my colleagues. The seminar was attended by approximately forty-nine professors and graduate students and by one Charles Petit, an outstanding science reporter working for the *San Francisco Chronicle*. His story (Petit 1981) appeared on the front page of the *Chronicle* and was carried on news wires all over the globe. The greatest outpouring of interest I have ever experienced began, one relevant consequence of which was a very well-written article in *Omni* (Hecht and Williams 1982). The public owes a great debit to the intelligence, breadth of knowledge, and integrity that I have uniformly encountered among science reporters.

Reaction to the models was both mixed (Fig. 10) and interesting. Members of the media usually telephoned invitations to appear on television or radio, or requests for more information or photographs. The written responses, about half of which were from the United States and the remainder from twelve other countries, were typically either comments on the models or requests for relevant publications. About forty percent were from people in professional occupations. Only ten percent of all written communications were negative, and these were usually concerned about a possible threat to the special place of *Homo sapiens* in nature. It is a pleasure to report that at least one third of the latter respondents were most cordial in presenting their objections. The models were not made with the intent to offend anyone's philosophical outlook and can be interpreted as an argument that the humanoid form may be a special (nonrandom) solution to the biophysical problems posed by intelligence.

The almost complete absence of any response from those who are nearest to me in science seemed significant. Therefore, six well-respected colleagues who are experts in the evolution of backboned animals of the dinosaurian era were recently canvassed by telephone. These people are friends as well as colleagues, and it is because of this that their remarks were so open; their candor is deeply appreciated. As a group, they suggested that paleontologists were rather embarrassed by the dinosauroid model. One colleague observed that anyone can write science fiction if he wishes, another evaluated the exercise as scenario overkill, and a particularly critical commentator was convinced that the project was a disservice to its authors, to vertebrate paleontology, and to the journal in which it was published. Most vertebrate paleontologists probably first heard of the project through accounts in the press, which appeared several months before the more technical report. Hopefully to a small degree the charge of professional irresponsibility may partly be allayed if the exercise focuses academic attention on the very interesting areas of evolutionary parallelism and convergence.

A sampling of negative reactions includes the following:

"Leaving the restaurant, four blue collar workers noticed the picture (on the front page of the *Chronicle*); one briefly picked up the paper—perhaps for 40 seconds of reading. 'What is it? A dinosauroid. A sculpture? Yeah, some kid in Berkeley. A space cadet. [Berkeleyans] are weirdos anyway.'"

"I read an article in this morning's paper which not only shocked me, it revolted me as well. It was about this theory of yours that man could have developed from a reptile. It has been bad enough to have scientists saying all these years that man came from a monkey but this is *too* much."

A sampling of positive reactions includes the following:

"I think, on the basis of a fair amount of reading and observation in my rather tangential professional vantage point, that the place of intelligence in evolution gets all too little heed."

"I followed with some fascination and appreciation your creation of the dinosauroid. It makes an important point that (a colleague) and I want to make in a forthcoming book on the origin of mind."

For an unfavorable published paleontological reaction see Eldredge and Tattersall (1983), and for a favourable reaction see Norman (1985: 54–55).

When the *Stenonychosaurus* and dinosauroid models were placed on public display together for a few weeks in the reptile house of the Calgary Zoo in Alberta, they prompted a flurry of anatomical questions from visitors. On one occasion I had an opportunity to demonstrate the models before a group of five-year-old children. One boy reached for the dinosauroid's tridactylate hand and held it. One girl embraced the model. Perhaps these reactions were prompted by the movie "ET" which had been released by that time. Professional visitors to our laboratory have been amused and appreciative of the opportunity to compare the two models visually. Most seem to find the dinosauroid nonthreatening or even vulnerable. One colleague wrote:

"It is a remarkable and very touching construction. Intelligence declares its presence. There is something about the eyes and mouth and cast of the head which begs affection and even the trust of its kin. The stance is purest early twentieth-century 'museum reconstruction.' The age of innocence still lives."

Specialists and laymen alike posed a remarkably similar series of anatomical questions, many of which are discussed in Russell and Seguin (1982). All were interesting, but only a few can briefly be mentioned. From top to bottom: data from the fossil record of the last sixty-five million years predict with a probability of ninety-nine percent that creatures of human brain-body proportions would have appeared within the next twenty-five million years (Russell 1983; for a much earlier description of the same trend see Cailleux 1971). The depth of the chest in the dinosauroid reflects that of *Stenonychosaurus,* but this solution was probably unwise. In a goat born without forelimbs, but which learned to walk bipedally, the chest was much flatter than in normal goats. The same phenomenon occurs in tree kangaroos where the body

Figure 10. Cartoon courtesy William Stout.

is held more vertically than in ground kangaroos (Slijper 1942). The dinosauroid has a navel because it was felt that living young could pass through a smaller pelvic canal than that required by an egg with all the additional life-support structures. Placentas also occur in nine families of lizards and snakes (Bauchot 1965) as well as in some invertebrates (*Peripatus,* an onychophoran; see Ghiselin 1984). An upright, tailless posture was adopted because it is a very efficient locomotor system. The metabolic cost of transport in humans is less than the average cost in mammals of comparable body weight (Tucker 1975) and considerably less than the cost of transport in other large primates (Rodman and McHenry 1980).

Many have wondered how Seguin was able to impart a transparent, lifelike quality to the dinosauroid's eyes (Fig. 9). A Christmas-tree bulb was half filled with clear liquid plastic and after the plastic had set was broken. The iris and pupil were painted onto the flat inner surface. Disks were cut from the orbital region of the head, the eyes were attached to the eyelids from the rear, and the orbital disks were reattached to the model.

The *Stenonychosaurus* and dinosauroid models may have some anatomical merit, and people seem to be interested in them, but what relation can they bear to reality? David Raup, a distinguished paleontologist, asked (1985: 36–37), "Was [Russell] demonstrating, in effect, that the humanoid condition should be expected to evolve as an adaptive convergence?" The answer is that construction of the dinosauroid was a thought experiment, which tends to answer Raup's question in the affirmative. It simply implies that the dinosauroid-humanoid form may have a nonnegligible probability of appearing as a consequence of natural selection within the biospheres of earthlike planets. And that there may be something more to study in the biophysical configuration of man.

ACKNOWLEDGMENTS

I am extremely grateful to E. Kish and R. Seguin for their creative and enthusiastic collaboration. Our projects were much fun and remain a source of continuing satisfaction. I have greatly benefited from the perceptive suggestions and moral support of my colleagues in the Paleobiology Division, National Museum of Natural Sciences, and particularly C. R. Harington, D. M. Jarzen, and K. A. Pirozynski. Without the generous support of the museum staff the restorations would never have been accomplished. I am indebted to C. Seeger of the SETI Group at the National Aeronautics and Space Administration, Ames, and P. Feldman of the Herzberg Institute of Astrophysics for many stimulating conversations on the subject of extraterrestrial life. I particularly wish to thank my wife, J. A. Russell, for the happy invention of the word *dinosauroid,* and my former supervisors F. H. Schultz and L. Lemieux for the gift of academic freedom. Suggestions generously made by P. Dodson of the University of Pennsylvania and C. C. Gruchy, Assistant Director, Collections and Research, and by anonymous reviewers have greatly improved the manuscript.

WORKS CITED

Alvarez, L., W. Alvarez, F. Asaro, and H. V. Michel. 1980. Extraterrestrial cause for the Cretaceous-Tertiary extinction. *Science* 208: 1095–1108.

Anderson, J. F., A. Hall-Martin, and D. A. Russell. 1985. Long-bone circumference and weight in mammals, birds and dinosaurs. *Journal of Zoology* 207: 53–61.

Bauchot, R. 1965. La placentation chez les reptiles. *L'Année biologique* 4: 547–75.

Berner, R. A., A. C. Lasaga, and R. M. Garrels. 1983. The carbonate-silicate cycle and its effect on atmospheric carbon dioxide over the past 100 million years. *American Journal of Science* 283: 641–83.

Browne, M. W. 1985. Dinosaur experts resist meteor extinction idea. *New York Times*, October 29, 1985, 21–22.

Cailleux, A. 1971. Le temps et les échelons de l'évolution. In *Time and science in philosophy*, ed. J. Zeman, 135–45. Amsterdam: Elsevier.

Czerkas, S. M., and D. F. Glut. 1982. *Dinosaurs, mammoths, and cavemen*. New York: Dutton.

de Laubenfels, M. W. 1956. Dinosaur extinction: One more hypothesis. *Journal of Paleontology* 30: 207–18.

Eldredge, N., and I. Tattersall. 1983. Future people. *Science* 83: 74–77.

Ghiselin, M. T. 1984. *Peripatus* as a living fossil. In *Living fossils*, ed. N. Eldredge and S. M. Stanley, 214–17. New York: Springer Verlag.

Halliday, I. 1982. Looking back on the Tunguska event. *Syllogeus* 39: 138–39.

Hecht, J., and G. Williams III. 1982. Smart dinosaurs. *Omni* 4: 48–54.

Hoffman, A., and M. H. Nitecki. 1985. Reception of the asteroid hypothesis of terminal Cretaceous extinctions. *Geology* 13: 884–87.

Jablonski, D. 1986. Background and mass extinctions: The alternation of macroevolutionary regimes. *Science* 231: 129–33.

Jansonius, J., and L. V. Hills. 1976. *Genera file of fossil spores and pollen*. Special Publication, Department of Geology, University of Calgary, Canada.

Norman, D. 1985. *The illustrated encyclopedia of dinosaurs*. New York: Crescent Books.

Petit, C. 1981. Bizarre vision of 'human' dinosaurs. *San Francisco Chronicle*, October 12, 1981, 1, 5.

Raup, D. M. 1985. ETI without intelligence. In *Extraterrestrials: Science and alien intelligence*, ed. E.

Regis, Jr., 31–42. Cambridge. Cambridge University Press.

Rodman, P. S., and H. M. McHenry. 1980. Bioenergetics and the origin of hominid bipedalism. *American Journal of Physical Antrhopology* 52: 103–6.

Rogers, H. H., J. F. Thomas, and G. E. Bingham. 1983. Response of agronomic and forest species to elevated atmospheric carbon dioxide. *Science* 220: 428–29.

Russell, D. A. 1969. A new specimen of *Stenonychosaurus* from the Oldman Formation (Cretaceous) of Alberta. *Canadian Journal of Earth Sciences* 6: 595–612.

———. 1971. The disappearance of the dinosaurs. *Canadian Geographical Journal* 83: 204–15.

———. 1977. *A vanished world: The dinosaurs of western Canada*. National Museum of Natural Sciences, National Museum of Canada, Natural History Series 4.

———. 1981. Speculations on the evolution of intelligence. In *Life in the universe*, ed. John Billingham, 259–75. Cambridge, Mass.: MIT Press.

———. 1982. Quasi-exponential evolution: Implications for intelligent extraterrestrial life. In *Abstracts, Twenty-fourth Plenary Meeting, Committee on Space Research ("COSPAR")*, 517.

———. 1983. Exponential evolution: Implications for intelligent extraterrestrial life. *Advances in Space Research* 3: 95–103.

Russell, D. A., and R. Seguin. 1982. Reconstructions of the small Cretaceous theropod *Stenonychosaurus inequalis* and a hypothetical dinosauroid. *Syllogeus* 37.

Sagan, C. 1977. *The Dragons of Eden: Speculations on the evolution of human intelligence*. New York: Random House.

Simpson, G. G. 1964. The nonprevalence of humanoids. *Science* 143: 769–75.

Slijper, E. J. 1942. Biologic-anatomical investigations on the bipedal gait and upright posture in mammals, with special reference to a little goat, born without forelimbs. In *Nederlandse Akademie van Wetenschapen, Proceedings* 45: 288–95, 407–15.

Stewart, A. D. 1977. Quantitative limits to paleogravity. *Journal of the Geological Society of London* 133: 281–91.

Tucker, V. A. 1975. The energetic cost of moving about. *Scientific American* 63: 413–19.

Wyles, J. S., J. G. Kunkel, and A. C. Wilson. 1983. Birds: Behavioral and anatomical evolution. In *Proceedings of the National Academy of Sciences U.S.A.*, 80: 4394–97.

THE AGE OF TRANSITION: COELOPHYSIS AND THE LATE TRIASSIC CHINLE FAUNA

David D. Gillette

The earliest well-known dinosaurs in North America are from the Coelophysis quarry at Ghost Ranch, near Abiquiu, New Mexico, and elsewhere in the American Southwest in the Chinle Formation of late Triassic age. Knowledge of the fauna and flora of the Chinle Formation has accumulated slowly over the past century, with considerable expansion in the last two decades. Restorations of the Chinle landscape and biota prepared by artists working for the University of California, Berkeley, in the 1930s present a simple flora and fauna, dominated by Araucarioxylon forests and thecodont reptiles; although the existence of dinosaurs in the Chinle Formation had been established forty years earlier, dinosaurs were not presented in these exhibits, which were prepared for the Petrified Forest National Monument in northern Arizona.

With the establishment of National Park status for the Petrified Forest came a need to revise the exhibits in the visitor centers at the park. Artist Margaret Colbert was commissioned to prepare a large mural restoration of the Chinle animals and plants for the park, which she completed in 1978. The mural presents Coelophysis as a central figure in the fauna, with a greater diversity of animals and plants than had been depicted in the displays prepared earlier. In addition, the landscape in the Colbert mural is more varied and includes a prominent upland component. The concept of an age of transition during

Figure 1. Paul J. Fair, sculptor for a diorama for the Petrified Forest National Monument, at work on phytosaur reconstructions, early 1930s.

Figure 2. The Paul J. Fair diorama of the Chinle biota constructed in the early 1930s for the Petrified Forest National Monument. The diorama includes sculpted pieces—the large *Araucarioxylon* trunk (a, left) and phytosaurs in combat (not shown).

b

Figure 3. Studies on landscape and biota of the Chinle Formation by artist Carl P. Russell, prepared in 1932–1933. The ungainly metoposaur (b) reveals an inadequate knowledge of these giant labyrinthodont amphibians. These interpretations ultimately were not used in the production of the diorama.

the late Triassic was taking shape, demonstrating the change in faunal dominance from thecodonts to dinosaurs. The emergence of dinosaurs and a more varied fauna in the Colbert restoration reflects our expanded knowledge of the Chinle biota, owing especially to the discovery of the Coelophysis *quarry in New Mexico.*

In 1985 Colbert completed a second restoration of the Chinle biota and landscape, for the New Mexico Museum of Natural History, Albuquerque. That mural presents greater complexity in the fauna, with the addition of several forms that reflect a more evenly balanced composition in the transition fauna, including a mixture of both ancient forms and new animals. The age of transition as documented in this mural is distinctive, different from the earlier thecodont-dominated early Triassic without dinosaurs and from the later dinosaur-dominated early Jurassic without thecodont reptiles.

Current intensification of research on the Chinle biota will continue to add to the faunal list and generate more refinement in our understanding of the age of transition. Artists are now engaged in updating visual interpretations for the public, which will again call for revision in our concepts of this critical time in the history of the dinosaurs.

The age of dinosaurs began more than 225 million years ago, in the middle of the Triassic Period, the age of transition, when thecodont reptiles gave way to dinosaurs, their descendants and long-time contemporaries. In bringing dinosaurs to the public, museums and artists have generally passed over the Triassic beginnings, instead focusing on the Jurassic and Cretaceous dinosaurs that have become familiar to every household: *Allosaurus, Brontosaurus, Diplodocus, Hadrosaurus, Iguanodon, Stegosaurus, Triceratops, Tyrannosaurus,* and a multitude of others of lesser fame. Not so familiar is the cast of dinosaur characters in the Triassic period: *Coelophysis* is the best known of a select and limited group: *Fabrosaurus, Halticosaurus, Herrerasaurus, Heterodontosaurus, Ischisaurus, Lesotho-*

Figure 4. Studies on elements of the Chinle biota by artist Palik (given name and initials unknown), for a display in the Rainbow Forest Museum at the Petrified Forest National Monument, produced in 1936 to augment an exhibit on the process of petrification of the logs in the park.

Figure 5. Overview of the Colbert mural at the Petrified Forest National Park, completed 1976. The Chinle fauna and flora are set in a landscape that is drier and more open than had been shown in earlier reconstructions. Details are shown in Figures 7–9.

saurus, *Pisanosaurus, Plateosaurus,* and *Scutellosaurus* are the most frequently encountered.

Triassic dinosaurs inherited the landscape and biota that had been the domain of the thecodont reptiles, typified by the giant phytosaurs and armored aetosaurs in the northern continents and thecodonts and synapsid reptiles, including the early mammallike reptiles and ancestors of the mammals, in Africa and South America. Nowhere in the Triassic were dinosaurs diverse, and it is doubtful whether they were ever dominant until the close of the period. With the waxing of the dinosaurs in the late Triassic came the waning of the thecodont reptiles in a long and surely revolutionary ecological transition. A handful of formations around the world provide a glimpse into this, the remotest of times of the dinosaurs: the Ischigualasto and Los Colorados Formations of Argentina; the lower Lufeng beds of China; the Maleri Formation of India; the Red Beds and Cave Sandstone of southern Africa; the Keuper beds of Europe; and in North America the Popo Agie Formation of Wyoming, Newark Group in the East, and Dockum Group and Chinle Formation of the American Southwest.

For many years the fauna dominated by thecodont reptiles of the Chinle Formation was thought to contain only one dinosaur, the rare coelurosaur originally named *Coelurus* by Edward Drinker Cope from the Chinle beds of New Mexico in 1887. Two years later Cope renamed the small collection of coelurosaur fragments *Coelophysis.* For the next five decades little more was learned of the coelurosaurs from New Mexico, but considerable advances were made in studies of the abundant remains of the reptilian phytosaurs and aetosaurs and giant amphibian metoposaurs. Collections were amassed from widely scattered areas of Arizona, New Mexico, and Texas, and there gradually emerged a fundamental understanding of the thecodont-dominated fauna of the late Triassic in North America.

During this same interval, between 1890 and 1940, paleobotanists came to appreciate the wealth of fossil plants in the Chinle Formation, particularly in the vicinity of today's Petrified Forest National Park. The petrified logs in this region of

Figure 6. Watercolor interpretation of the Chinle flora by artist Vernon Demars, produced in 1934. The charred trunks and the burned forest in the background were probably interpreted directly from similar features to be found on logs in the national monument. These features suggest seasonality and open landscape that differs from what was presented in the contemporary diorama by Paul J. Fair.

northern Arizona are among the most spectacular in the world. In addition, the abundant fossil leaves preserved in several members of the Chinle Formation provided fertile grounds for study. An astute paleontologist can find interspersed among the petrified logs in the Petrified Forest numerous bones of reptiles and amphibians that occupied the forest floor when the Chinle sediments were being deposited by rivers and lakes. In the 1920s Charles Camp, a distinguished paleontologist from the University of California, Berkeley, was the first vertebrate specialist to scour the mudstones and siltstones amongst the petrified logs of the Chinle Formation in Arizona and New Mexico for the skeletons of phytosaurs and metoposaurs. Camp concentrated on exposures now largely contained within the boundaries of the Petrified Forest in Arizona and in the badlands of northwestern New Mexico where Cope had discovered the little dinosaur bones forty years earlier.

The Triassic world of Camp thus included an abundance of aetosaurs, metoposaurs, and phytosaurs; the dicynodont mammallike reptile, *Placerias,* which had been excavated in abundance from a quarry near St. Johns, Arizona; the rare and poorly known coelurosaurian dinosaur *Coelophysis;* forests of giant conifers dominated by *Araucarioxylon* and smaller trees and shrubs including horsetails, cycads, tree ferns, and ferns. With the establishment of the Petrified Forest National Monument in 1906, an act that protected the fossil logs (and incidentally the fossil bones) of northern Arizona, scientific investigations could be organized and perpetuated without competition from commercial interests and avid amateurs bent on amassing personal collections of fossil wood and souvenirs.

Dinosaurs were such minor characters in this conception of the Chinle biota that they were ignored in restorations of the Chinle Formation. The age of transition had scarcely been recognized. Artists working under the supervision of Lyman H. Daugherty, Myril V. Walker, and Camp at Berkeley during the depression years of the 1930s constructed a diorama for the Petrified Forest National Monument that is still on display at the Painted Desert Inn in the park. This diorama includes sculpted plants and animals produced by Paul J. Fair (Fig. 1) and a masterfully executed background painting (Fig. 2).

Dominant in the vegetation is the giant conifer *Araucarioxylon* (Fig. 2a), which is depicted with bulbous crowns that formed an open-forest canopy on the margins of stream courses. Cycads and ferns dominate the understory.

The only animals in the diorama setting are phytosaurs, including two sculpted individuals in a snout-to-snout struggle in the muds of the foreground. The landscape seems to represent a tropical river system that traverses an open-canopy forest. The river has cut through the banks of sediment it had deposited in its earlier meanderings. The river banks, only a few feet above stream level, are the highest ground in the diorama; distant uplands, which supplied the sediments borne and deposited by the river, are not to be seen in this interpretation.

The hazy, misty quality of the diorama (Fig. 2b) readily imparts a steamy tropical setting. Details in the diorama admit of little diversity in the flora and fauna, but the depiction of the landscape strikingly communicates the existing belief that the Chinle beds were all lowland, tropical, quiet-water stream deposits.

The diorama provides an excellent glimpse into the conception of the Chinle biota as perceived by Camp, Daugherty, and Walker and their associates, but working drawings that were prepared for the production of the diorama are even more revealing. Studies of the fauna by Carl P. Russell (Fig. 3) include phytosaurs from several angles, each with peculiar proportions and what now seems an awkward posture. The metoposaur drawing (Fig. 3b) differs considerably from the restoration prepared by artist Palik (full name and initials unrecorded in the Petrified Forest National Park archives) for supplementary exhibit materials at the monument in 1936 (Fig. 4). Palik's metoposaur and dicynodont are caricatures rather than realistic restorations. In the landscapes depicted in Russell's working drawings and Palik's displays are distant uplands and vast expanses of open ground between stands of giant conifers, interpretations that anticipate modern restorations of the Chinle topography.

Other depression-era drawings for the Na-

Figure 7. Close-up of the middle portion of Figure 5. The phytosaur *Rutiodon*, which has captured the lungfish *Ceratodus*, and giant amphibian *Metoposaurus* are in the water in the foreground. The stagonolepid thecodonts *Desmatosuchus* in the left midground and *Calyptosuchus* in the background were the common armored herbivores. The dicynodont reptile *Placerias* is on the right.

GILLETTE

Figure 8. A herd of *Coelophysis*, an early coelurosaurian dinosaur. The broken vegetation on the right suggests a past feeding episode by the dicynodonts, which could crush and tear at plants with their tusks.

Figure 9. The predatory thecodont *Hesperosuchus* was an ecological precursor of the coelurosaurian dinosaurs during the Age of Transition, when these two groups coexisted.

tional Monument by artist Vernon Demars (Fig. 6) reveal similar interpretations and anticipate modern concepts of the Chinle landscape while simultaneously verifying the prevailing concept of a simple fauna. Dinosaurs are not to be found in these archives; perhaps the record of dinosaurs in New Mexico, albeit in the same Chinle Formation, was too far away to include in the restoration of the Chinle biota known from the monument. These notions were to change after World War II with the discovery of a remarkable accumulation of *Coelophysis* skeletons.

In 1947 the American Museum of Natural History, New York, organized a modest expedition to the American Southwest, led by paleontologist Edwin H. Colbert. The team's destination was the Petrified Forest National Monument to work in the Chinle Formation where Camp had excavated numerous phytosaurs. En route to the monument Colbert and crew stopped for a few days in the vicinity of Abiquiu, New Mexico, near the site where Cope's type specimen of *Coelophysis* had been collected. Camp's field crews had excavated an abundance of phytosaur material at Ghost Ranch fifteen years earlier. Within a few days the Colbert team discovered the *Coelophysis* quarry site on a steep hillside east of Camp's excavations. Colbert's field crew never arrived at the Petrified Forest, spending instead the remainder of that field season at Ghost Ranch. The crew returned for another field season and closed the quarry. These excavations yielded dozens of complete skeletons of this little dinosaur. No longer would artists' restorations of the Chinle fauna be devoid of dinosaurs; the age of transition was being defined.

In addition to the abundance of *Coelophysis* skeletons at Ghost Ranch, there were also new and better specimens of phytosaurs. These and other reptiles were collected intermittently by infrequent visitors to the ranch and quarry over the next three decades. Similar interest in the Petrified Forest area by a variety of field parties resulted in expansion of the faunal list for the Chinle Formation and continued refinement in understanding of the Chinle flora.

The Petrified Forest was accorded National Park status in 1958 and officially became the Petrified Forest National Park in 1962. A decade later the park revamped the exhibits at the Rainbow Forest Museum and Visitor Center at the southern end of the park. A central feature in the new display plan was a large mural painting by artist Margaret Colbert of Flagstaff, Arizona, to show the Chinle landscape and its biota. For many years she had collaborated with her husband, "Ned," and she had a keen understanding of the flora and fauna. Her experience in book illustrations and technical reconstructions for a variety of media included many dinosaur restorations. With an experienced hand and ready supply of advice from her husband and others at the Museum of Northern Arizona, Flagstaff, Colbert produced the first mural representation of the Chinle fauna and flora.

The Colbert mural (Figs. 5, 7–9) is currently displayed at the Rainbow Forest Museum. Completed in 1978, the painting measures 4.9 by 1.2 meters. The thirty-one-year interval since the discovery of the *Coelophysis* quarry at Ghost Ranch was a time of maturation in the understanding of the paleontology of the Chinle Formation, a growth reflected in this mural. In addition to the dinosaurs, the cast of characters is now expanded and complex: phytosaurs (*Rutiodon*), metoposaurs (*Metoposaurus*), and the dinosaur *Coelophysis* are among the central figures, but also present are two varieties of stagonolepid armored thecodonts (*Desmatosuchus* and *Calyptosuchus*), the predatory thecodont *Hesperosuchus*, the dicynodont reptile *Placerias*, the lungfish *Ceratodus*, a variety of insects, and unionid clams.

The floral list is also expanded, with the giant conifer *Araucarioxylon* dominant, but also clearly depicted are cycads, the scouring rush *Neocalamites* (extinct horsetails), *Itopsidema* (tree ferns), ferns, and lycopods. The early dinosaurs are thus placed in a complicated setting, a more complex habitat than was presented in the Fair diorama in the 1930s.

The landscape ranges from open water to dry uplands, with an overall open character in the vegetation. The misty swampland of the earlier interpretation has been replaced with a drier habitat. The substrate is entirely sedimentary, consisting of red and buff muds and silts presumably deposited by prior wanderings of the river. A few rocks are evident along the shoreline, suggesting lag deposits let down from older Paleozoic formations or episodes of higher-stream velocity when larger sediments could be carried in the stream load.

Where roots of the giant conifers have stabilized the soils, river erosion has cut resistant banks with vertical slopes along the shore, but elsewhere the slopes are gentle, grading from quiet backwater to isolated pools, muddy swirls with mud cracks and dry, higher slopes. Much of the landscape is barren and open, reminiscent of semi-arid tropics. The red soils embellish the idea of arid, oxidizing conditions (the origin of red beds had been the subject of intense arguments in earlier decades).

Four habitats dominate: (1) The aquatic habitat, occupied by the lungfish as the only known obligatory member of the river water and by two semiaquatic metoposaurs (amphibians) and a phytosaur (a reptile). Clams on the mudbank are exposed, suggesting higher water level sometime in the recent past. (2) The wet lowland habitat, dominated by the emergent lycopods in the quiet water on the opposite shoreline and the scouring rush *Neocalamites*. Several of the scouring rushes have been broken, perhaps by the giant herbivorous dicynodont. (3) The shaded dry lowlands and dry uplands beneath the giant conifers are dominated by ferns and cycads and a conifer sapling; the open ground between stands of conifers is barren. (4) The uplands are capped by conifer forests. *Araucarioxylon* is the most commonly applied name for petrified wood in the Chinle Formation, and its anatomy is conjectural; the open-canopy structure in these *Araucarioxylon* forests is a reasonable departure from the interpretation in the Fair diorama.

The habitat represented in this mural is complex and diverse. Because of the compositional differences in each habitat, the plant succession that led to the *Araucarioxylon* climax forest is evident, although not strongly developed. The habitat that was home to the earliest dinosaurs is less mysterious, and the age of transition is suddenly easier to comprehend.

The fauna includes both invertebrates (in-sects and clams) and vertebrates (fish, amphibians, and reptiles). The clam shells on the river bank suggest a clam-bank community, an interpretation in keeping with the occasional high-density deposits of unionid clam shells in the Chinle Formation in the park. The insects are represented by fragmentary wing impressions, peculiar tracks and trails in the Chinle sediments, and traces of burrowing activity in much of the fossil wood.

Vertebrates are dominated by the reptiles. The only fish is *Ceratodus* (being eaten by the phytosaur), the Triassic lungfish that produced the protective burrows found in profusion in the Chinle sediments along with occasional lungfish tooth plates. The protective burrows may indicate periodic drought, a concept implied in this composition.

Metoposaurs are the only amphibians. These monsters of the Chinle grew to prodigious size by amphibian standards, to 3.05 meters and longer, and their weights approached a half meter ton or more. Bones of these labyrinthodont amphibians are among the most common fossils in the Chinle Formation. They are the last of a highly successful group of amphibians that originated in the Paleozoic. Their presence here amidst the newly originated dinosaurs signals the truly transitional nature of the Chinle fauna, for the metoposaurs (as the last of the highly successful labyrinthodonts) became extinct at the end of the Triassic Period.

The largest herbivorus reptile is the dicynodont *Placerias*, a bulky mammallike reptile with a beak for feeding and a pair of prominent tusks that might have been used to tear apart vegetation in the search for succulent edible parts. Compare this reconstruction (Figs. 7, 9) with the Palik exhibit from 1936 (Fig. 4b), in which the tusks are incorrectly restored. *Placerias* remains are now known in abundance from a quarry near St. Johns and from a few specimens from the Petrified Forest National Park.

The remainder of the reptilian herbivores are the stagonolepid thecodonts (the aetosaurs): *Desmatosuchus* and *Calyptosuchus*, shown here as upland animals. Two thecodont carnivores lurk in the foreground: the phytosaur *Rutiodon* and the agile predator *Hesperosuchus*. The small but nim-

a   b   c   d

Figure 10. The eight panels of the second Colbert mural, at the New Mexico Museum of Natural History, completed in 1985. The assembled mural is 2.1 meters high and 7.3 meters long (7 by 24 feet), almost three times the surface area of her first mural. The Chinle landscape is more varied, and the flora is more complex and lusher than in the 1978 mural. a. The thecodont reptile *Hesperosuchus* (left), a small, agile predator that competed with the early coelurosaurian dinosaurs, and the stagonolepid thecodont *Calyptosuchus* (right), an armored herbivore. b. The dicynodont *Placerias*, an herbivorous mammallike reptile; an *Araucarioxylon* forest is in the background, with the tree ferns *Itopsidema* beneath. c. The coelurosaurian dinosaur *Coelophysis* (foreground), the most completely known of the Triassic dinosaurs, and two *Placerias* individuals. d. The giant labyrinthodont amphibian *Metoposaurus* and unionid clams are shown in the foreground; both were probably food for *Coelophysis* (at rear) and other meat-eaters and scavengers. e. An undescribed rauisuchid thecodont reptile, length to 7.6 meters (25 feet) and larger, with a skull as large as that of *Tyrannosaurus;* this predator, shown amidst scouring rush *Neocalamites*, surely gave the early dinosaurs serious competition. f. In the foreground, the small, agile reptile *Trilophosaurus*, an archaic predator, and the horseshoe crab *Limulus*, evidently a freshwater-tolerant species, and its tracks; at the rear, the stagonolepid thecodont *Desmatosuchus*, an armored herbivore. g. The giant predatory thecodont reptile *Rutiodon*, one of several varieties of phytosaurs in the Chinle fauna. h. At the bank, the small archaic predatory reptile *Tanytrachelos*.

e   f   g   h

ble *Hesperosuchus* resembles the little dinosaur *Coelophysis*, with which it surely competed as a dominant predator. Like the metoposaurs, the reign of these reptiles was about to close, giving way to dinosaurs and other advanced reptiles of the Jurassic Period.

The newcomers in this mural interpretation of the age of transition are the little dinosaurs from Ghost Ranch, *Coelophysis* (Fig. 8), the only advanced reptilian group shown in this fauna. These herding reptiles, with their stiff tails held well off the ground for counterbalance, were common only locally. Their sparse remains occur in but a few localities, and the one place they are abundant is in the Ghost Ranch quarry.

In the earlier restorations animal behavior was simple and limited largely to predator-prey encounters. With the Colbert mural we now see *Coelophysis* and the phytosaurs as gregarious animals. Evidence for herding in *Coelophysis* had come from the Ghost Ranch quarry, where these nimble predators are represented by growth series, ranging from hatchlings the size of a chicken to adults the size of a turkey or somewhat larger. The parental care suggested by the phytosaur with its cluster of babies, perhaps hatchlings (Fig. 5, right foreground), was based not on fossils but on observations of living crocodiles exhibiting this behavior. Not only did the artist capture the essence of the age of transition, she also developed a theme of increasing behavioral complexity among the dinosaurs and their contemporaries, a subject that has received considerable attention during the past two decades.

In 1984 Margaret Colbert was again commissioned to prepare a mural restoration of the Chinle biota and landscape, this time for the newly established New Mexico Museum of Natural History. In 1981 and 1982 the Carnegie Museum of Natural History, Pittsburgh, organized two field seasons to excavate the Ghost Ranch *Coelophysis* quarry and remove a series of large blocks containing a wealth of fossils. These blocks were distributed to other museums, and their contents are currently being extricated from the encasing matrix. The most recent quarry operation was conducted in 1985 by the

New Mexico Museum of Natural History, which removed an eight-metric-ton block from the quarry for a working exhibit in the new Ruth Hall Museum of Paleontology on the ranch property.

In the 1970s and 1980s studies of Triassic geology and paleontology intensified throughout the Southwest, to the extent that now there are several Triassic specialists who reside in the area and others who return regularly for research in the Chinle Formation. In addition, there has been a similar worldwide concentration of studies of the Triassic, prompted largely by the biogeographic implications of plate tectonics. Colbert's second mural reflects much of the change in understanding of Triassic faunas during the past ten years.

The second Colbert mural (Fig. 10) was completed in 1985 and first displayed at the opening of the New Mexico Museum of Natural History in January 1986. It consists of a series of eight adjoining panels that can be displayed individually or together. In its production Colbert was assisted by artist Louise Waller of Flagstaff and received advice from many paleontologists and geologists, but especially from her husband.

The landscape is changed, with little barren ground and several considerably more complex habitats. *Araucarioxylon* forests dominate both lowland and upland habitats. Tree ferns and scouring rushes are abundant, set in habitats quite apart from the giant conifers. Open spaces are occupied by cycads and ferns. Uplands, the source areas for the bountiful supply of mud and silt that collected in the Chinle lowlands, are clearly visible in the distance. The meandering river has deposited a litter of clam shells and piles of water-soaked logs on its shore. In one bend the river has eroded into a steep bank where its channel has been incised into its older sediments.

The steamy tropical setting conveyed in the Fair diorama made fifty years earlier has been replaced. Now the clear blue sky and mixed habitat suggest drier conditions, perhaps subtropical with limited seasonality.

The faunal list is again expanded to include the North American Triassic *Coelophysis* fauna in the broad sense. Now included are *Calyptosuchus* (Fig. 11), *Ceratodus*, *Coelophysis*, *Desmatosuchus*,

Hesperosuchus, Metoposaurus, Placerias, Rutiodon (Fig. 12), insects, dragonflies, unionid clams, and a suite of newcomers: the gliding eosuchian reptile *Icarosaurus,* the semiaquatic eosuchian reptile *Tanytrachelos* (Fig. 13), a giant rauisuchid thecodont reptile, the lizardlike euryapsid reptile *Trilophosaurus,* the archaic fish *Chinlea* (Fig. 12), a mammal (as a fur-tipped tail; Fig. 14), the horseshoe crab *Limulus,* and crayfish.

Coelophysis is now shown in the age of transition with some advanced reptiles and a mammal in a composition that reflects a greater balance between the old and new, or the archaic and advanced. Gliding as a locomotor adaptation was a short-lived experiment; the long slender bodies of quadrupedal herbivorous reptiles such as *Tanytrachelos* and *Trilophosaurus* exemplify a different experiment in locomotion. The mammal signals advances yet to come, from a group with modest beginnings and a long history of obscurity among the dinosaurs. In this composition the new animals are principally advanced forms, although ones not long in existence.

In this mural *Coelophysis* is thus one of the experiments in the age of transition. Its lineage would inherit the landscape and eventually dominate in the Jurassic and Cretaceous periods. The others (such as aetosaurs, dicynodonts, metoposaurs, and phytosaurs) became extinct or survived through the Mesozoic with limited success (mammals, invertebrates, and fish). Other dinosaurs, presently unstudied, were here too, but restorations are not yet feasible.

This mural demonstrates our understanding of the Chinle fauna and flora as of the early 1980s. (For lists of common fossil plants (Ash 1972, 1974, 1985) and animals (Breed 1972; Colbert 1985; Long and Bellew 1985) of the Chinle Formation in the Petrified Forest National Park and vicinity, see Gillette, Long, and Ash 1986.) The story continues, however, for interest in the paleontology of *Coelophysis* fauna has intensified and promises to be a fruitful subject in dinosaur studies. The age-old questions will continue to apply to the age-old bones: Who was *Coelophysis*? Who were its neighbors? Where did they live? How did they make their living? What did they eat? What was their ecological position in this setting? Why did some survive and others go extinct? Other paleontologists are carrying on the tradition, and new artists are bringing the new ideas into visual form. The next interpretation is sure to be as different from Colbert's second mural as it was in comparison with earlier works.

Figure 11. The stagonolepid thecodont *Calyptosuchus*, another armored herbivore; detail of Fig. 10a.

Figure 12. The small archaic predatory reptile *Tanytrachelos;* detail of Fig. 10b.

Figure 13. *Rutiodon* at work, capturing the contemporary fish *Chinlea;* detail of Fig. 10h.

Figure 14. The tip of a mammal's furred tail; detail of Fig. 10f. Mammals were newcomers to the fauna, and survived the Triassic as insignificant components of the Chinle landscape.

Acknowledgments

I am indebted to personnel at the Petrified Forest National Park for permission to reproduce artwork and assistance in gathering information from archives in their charge, especially Park Superintendent E. Gastellum, Chief Ranger C. Andress, and photographer-historian P. Andress who prepared the photographs for Figs. 1–4, and 6. D. Schicketanz photographed the Colbert mural at the park as shown in overall view in Figure 5 and J. Kida photographed the details (Figs. 7–9). For the Colbert mural at the New Mexico Museum of Natural History, R. Behrman photographed the individual panels (Fig. 10) and R. Reck photographed the close-ups (Figs. 11–14). In addition, I have had the extraordinary pleasure of working closely with E. H. and M. Colbert for the past three years, and to them I extend my deepest appreciation.

Works Cited

Ash, S. R. 1972. Plant megafossils of the Chinle Formation. In: Investigations in the Triassic Chinle Formation, eds. C. S. Breed and W. J. Breed. *Museum of Northern Arizona Bulletin* 47: 23–43.

———. 1974. Guidebook to Devonian, Permian, and Triassic plant localities, east-central Arizona. Paleobotanical Section of the Botanical Society of America.

———. 1985. A short thick cycad stem from the Upper Triassic of Petrified Forest National Park, Arizona, and vicinity. *Museum of Northern Arizona Bulletin* 54: 17–32.

Breed, W. J. 1972. Invertebrates of the Chinle Formation. In: Investigations in the Triassic Chinle Formation, eds. C. S. Breed and W. J. Breed. *Museum of Northern Arizona Bulletin* 47: 19–22.

Colbert, E. C. 1985. The Petrified Forest and its vertebrate fauna in Triassic Pangaea. *Museum of Northern Arizona Bulletin* 54: 33–43.

Gillette, D. D., R. A. Long, and S. R. Ash. 1986. Paleontology of the Petrified Forest National Park, Arizona. In: Geology of Central and Northern Arizona, Field Trip Guidebook. Joint Annual Meeting of the Rocky Mountain Sections of the Paleontological Society and the Geological Society of America, eds. J. D Nations, C. M. Conway, and G. A. Swann, pp. 59–69.

Long, R. A., and K. L. Bellew. 1985. Aetosaur dermal armor from the Late Triassic of Southwestern North America, with special reference to material from the Chinle Formation of Petrified Forest National Park. *Museum of Northern Arizona Bulletin* 54: 45–66.

CONTENTS OF VOLUME II

INDEX

Compiled by Roberta Goodwin
Boldface numerals indicate illustrations.

Chasmosaurus belli, by Robert Bakker.
Detail of Checklist 91.

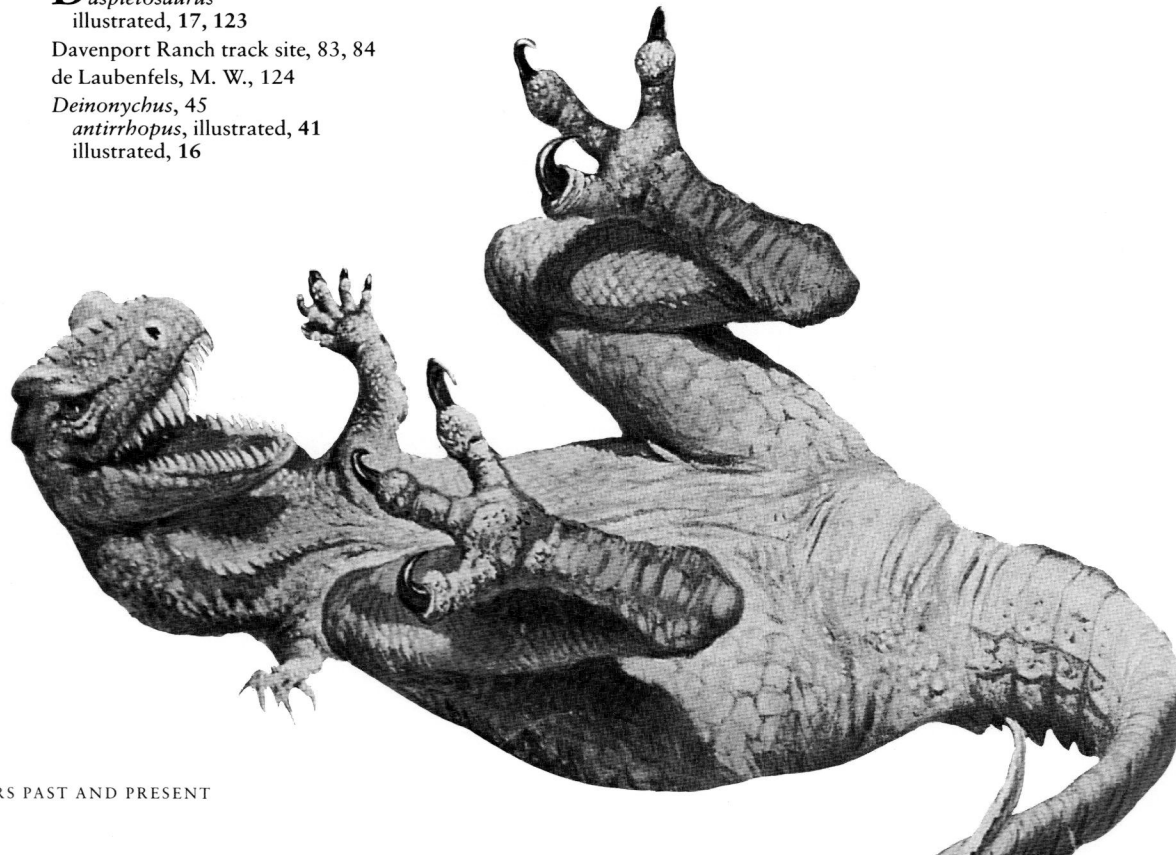

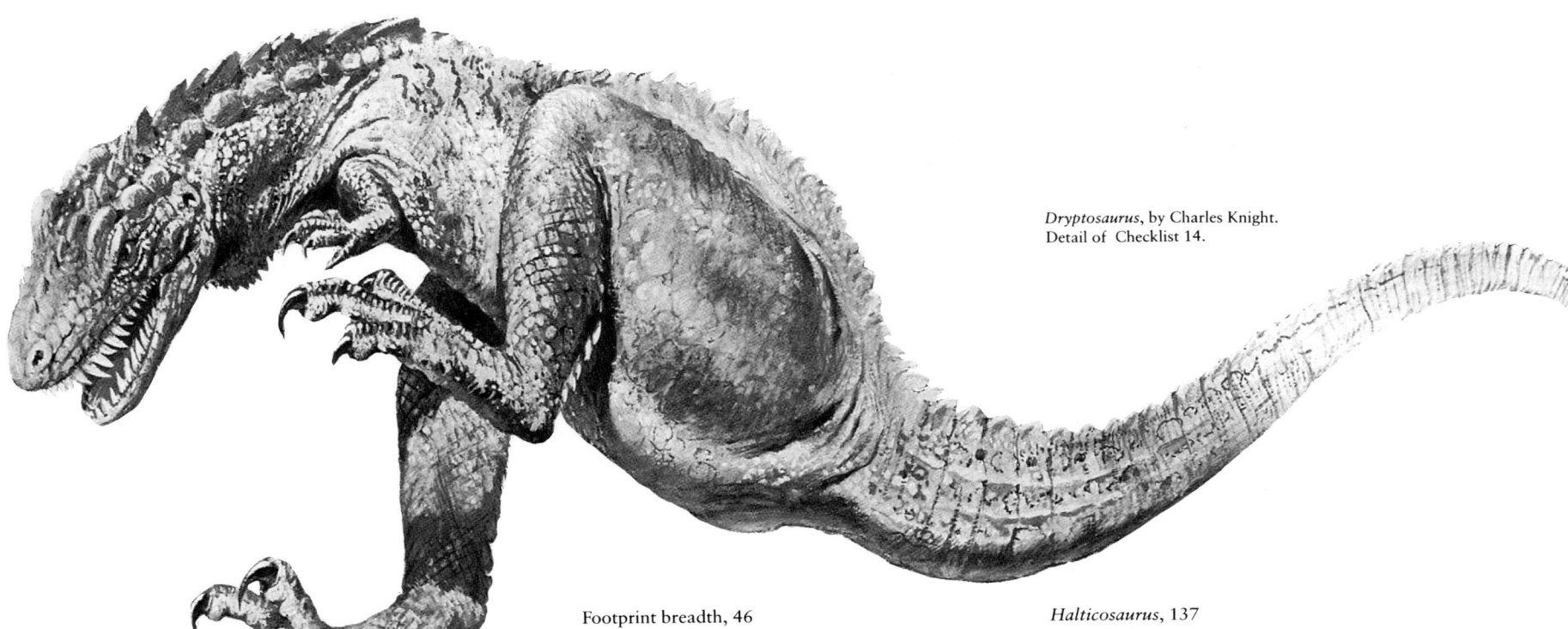

Dryptosaurus, by Charles Knight.
Detail of Checklist 14.

Tyrannosaurus rex, by Sylvia Czerkas. Checklist 56.

Deinonychus, by John Gurche.
Detail of Checklist 39.

Mamenchisaurus, by William Stout.
Detail of Checklist 115.

PHOTOGRAPHERS

Lenders to the exhibition and the following individuals and organizations
supplied photographs for reproduction in this volume.

American Museum of Natural History, Department of Library
Services: pages 10 (top, Transparency No. 2418), 30–31
(Transparency No. 1775).
Paula Andress: pages 132, 134, 135, 136, 137, 140.
Ron Berhman: pages 146, 147.
Marsha Conrad, Visual Media Corporation: 104 (bottom), 112–113.
G. R. Fitzgerald: 114, 125.
Joseph Garlington, Art and Technology, Inc.: 19.
Jeff Kida: 142, 143.
Natural History Museum of Los Angeles County, Photography
Division: i–iii, vi–viii, x–xi, xiv (right), 2, 8, 16, 17, 18 (bottom), 22–23, 24, 26–27, 28, 32, 40.
Robert Reck: 150, 151.
Robin Robin: 20.
Dale Schicketanz: 138–139.
Smithsonian Institution: page 11 (Photo No. 80-1820).
Veronica Tagland: cover, 96, 98–99, 100–101, 104 (top), 105, 106–107, 108, 109, 110, 111.

Project management by Robin A. Simpson
Copyediting by Kathleen Preciado
Designed by Dana Levy, Perpetua Press, Los Angeles
Production Coordination by Letitia Burns O'Connor
Typeset in Sabon and Gills Sans by Wilsted & Taylor, Oakland
Printed by Jardine Printing, Hong Kong